Please Pass the Torts

—A Legal Farce

iBooks
Habent Sua Fata Libelli

iBooks
Manhanset House
Shelter Island Hts., New York 11965-0342

bricktower@aol.com • www.ibooksinc.com

Library of Congress Cataloging-in-Publication Data
Morrison, T. C.
Please Pass the Torts, A Legal Farce
p. cm.

1. Humor—Topic—Business and Professional. 2. Fiction—Legal.
3. Fiction—Humorous—Black Humor. 4. United States—Fiction
Fiction, I. Title.
ISBN: 978-1-59687-883-9, Hardcover 978-1-59687-882-2, Trade Paper

November 2021

Please Pass the Torts

—A Legal Farce

T. C. Morrison

Acknowledgments

I wish to thank my publisher, John Colby, for believing in this book and its predecessor, TORTS "R" US, A Legal Farce. I also wish to thank Jacqueline Plunkett, who very skillfully created the website for both books and assumed responsibility for all things related to Social Media. Thanks also to Paul DePaola for his help on computer-related issues and to the talented folks at K Global who helped publicize TORTS "R" US. Finally, I wish to thank my many friends and colleagues who suggested I write a sequel to TORTS "R" US - without realizing I would be foolish enough to take them seriously.

Dedication

To Andy, Barbara, Blair, Bob, Cecelia, Chris, Ellen, Erik, Gene, Nirav, Paul, Steve and the scores of other talented and tireless colleagues with whom I was honored to go into battle—all of whom, after I was out of the way, went on to thrive and prosper.

"Never in the history of human endeavor have so many paid so much to so few."

     —Winston S. Churchill

"I regret that I have but one life to give for my lawyer."

     —Nathan Hale

"Old lawyers never die, they just raise their fee."

     —Gen. Douglas MacArthur

"Let them eat tortes."

     —Marie Antoinette

Critics Lavish Praise on PLEASE PASS THE TORTS

"Coming on the heels of the hilarious, laugh-out-loud farce TORTS "R" US, its sequel PLEASE PASS THE TORTS firmly establishes Morrison as the finest writer of humorous fiction since Chaucer. I haven't laughed so hard since that lady on my show said she thought it was General Lee who was buried in Grant's Tomb."
— Graucho Marx

"Having laughed my way though PLEASE PASS THE TORTS, I can only ask: Where was Peters and Peters when I needed them during the Cold War? Their solution to Russian spying and dirty tricks is truly awe inspiring. The CIA could have saved tons of money and endless lives if we had just called on the Peters Brothers to solve our problem with the Russkies.
—Allen Dulles

"PLEASE PASS THE TORTS is a worthy successor to Morrison's earlier work, TORTS "R" US. That book had me laughing hysterically from the first page to the last. It is by far the wittiest work in the English language since I wrote The Importance of Being Earnest."
— Oscar Wilde

"Having laughed my way through TORTS "R" US and now PLEASE PASS THE TORTS, I can only say that Morrison's outrageous humor shines through on every page. I especially enjoyed the sexual escapades of his characters. It made me nostalgic for my days in the White House."
—Warren G. Harding

Table of Contents

1	Red Carpet	1
2	Groundhog Day	9
3	Pass the Tortes	15
4	Congressman Earmacher	21
5	Honey Trap	29
6	Counter Espionage	35
7	Dr. Doolittle	42
8	The Playmate	50
9	All Hands On Deck	57
10	French Toast	65
11	Press Conference	72
12	Detente	81
13	Urban Renewal	88
14	Chimps Ahoy	95
15	Justice Neva Wright	102
16	Ladies Day	111
17	Chimp Speak	123
18	Torts "R" Tourism	133
19	The Tort State	143
20	Meet the Press	152
21	Wright and Wrong	160
22	Hazel Nutt	168
23	Berry Good Corny Flakes	178
24	The Big Heist	190
25	Wall of Fame	205
26	Brainstorming	210
27	Strip Clubbed	217
28	Victor Little's Secret	230
29	Bunny Hop	242
30	Money Hop	253
31	Bunny Talk	266
32	Happy Cows	282

Chapter 1

RED CARPET

Patrick Aldrich Peters, III - "Pap" to his family and friends – was having a good day. It was a Saturday and the weather was unusually mild for early March. It was just after six-thirty in the evening when a dark gray Mercedes slowed to a halt halfway up Pap's driveway. Hamilton A. Lott ("Ham" to his family and friends) emerged from the driver's side sporting an ill-fitting tuxedo left over from his college days.

Crossing around to the passenger side, he opened the door for his sixty-year-old wife Mona. Dressed in a bright green floor-length gown with a plunging neckline, Mona stepped from the car and flashed her best impression of a movie-star smile.

Ham and Mona were immediately met by Pup's nine-year-old twin daughters, Tiffany Ann Peters ("Tap") and Bethany Ann Peters ("Bap"). Like their father, Prescott Underwood Peters ("Pup"), and their mother Priscilla, Tap and Bap were serious and proper at all times, the embodiment of good manners and behavior.

"Missus Lott" said Bap, "please follow us to the red carpet." Turning to Mona's husband, she added "Mister Lott, you can park your car over there, next to the other cars on the grass."

The twins then walked Mona up the driveway to the foot of the red carpet. As they stepped onto the carpet, two cars parked in the upper portion of the driveway – where it widened onto a sweeping area paved with Belgian Blocks – suddenly turned on their headlights.

The cars had been placed on opposite sides of the driveway and were angled so that their headlights fell directly on Mona and the girls.

1

As it was only March, twilight was quickly fading and the sky was dark enough that the lights served as a sort of spotlight. When the twins stepped aside, Mona was left alone in the spotlight.

Mona had always dreamed of this: walking up a long red carpet dressed like a movie star in a slinky, revealing gown, while a spotlight caught her every step. A dream come true!

As she proceeded up the red carpet, Mona saw her closest friends standing alongside the carpet and applauding. There on the left was the effervescent Stacy Spacey and his wife Daisy. Just beyond them were Pup and his wife Priscilla, dressed in impeccable formal attire.

Standing next to Pup and his wife were Laurel Ann Hardy and her boyfriend Milo Nulow. Laurel's husband, Harry, had died tragically two years ago when he fell off a horse on a merry-go-round in Martha's Vineyard. The operator had gotten high on marijuana and lost control of the carousel so that it accelerated wildly. When Harry reached out to steady his grandson, who was on the horse just opposite, he fell off his horse – he was on the big white one he had always wanted to ride – and broke his neck.

On the right side of the carpet Mona saw their wealthy new neighbors, William and Hillary Fund. Will ran an extremely successful hedge fund down in Greenwich and had just bought an enormous house on the water side of Greens Farms Road overlooking Long Island Sound.

Actually, the Funds had also bought the property next to the house they lived in; they had proceeded to tear down the second house - which was less than ten years old - leaving only the land itself, so that they now had a huge swath of land with a panoramic view of the Sound.

Just beyond the Funds were Mona and Ham's oldest friends, Ray and Bunny Rabbitz. Ray had somehow located one of those old-fashioned flashbulb cameras and was taking photo after photo so that the flash bulbs were constantly popping. This is heaven, thought Mona, who's ambition in life was to always be the center of attention.

Standing at the top of the red carpet, looking like a glamorous couple in a Town and Country photo shoot, were Pap and his beautiful wife Piper.

Pap had fallen head over heels in love with Piper the first time he saw her. It was at a party in New York City and Pap was with his then girlfriend Naomi Norcross, an assistant curator with the Metropolitan Museum of Art where she was in charge of the Museum's collection of fourteenth century religious art from Newfoundland. While Pap had heroically bedded Naomi that night, it was their last date. The following weekend, on their first sleepover, Pap asked Piper to marry him.

Pap and Piper's twin boys – Patrick Aldrich Peters, IV ("Little Pap") and Henry Alden Peters ("Hap") - were hovering near the bushes in front of the house trying to look inconspicuous. They hated having to dress up in blazers and ties, and couldn't imagine why all the men had come dressed in those funny tuxedos. Pap had threatened to rent tuxedos for them if they did not agree to dress up in blazers and ties.

As Mona reached the top of the carpet, she was warmly greeted by Pap and Piper, each of them air-kissing her on both cheeks, French style Mona was pleased to note. Pap then raised his hand and asked for everyone's attention.

"Mona, on behalf of your lawyers – Pup and myself, of course – and your friends and neighbors, Piper and I would like to welcome you to this celebration of the release of your documentary *Mugged By Mugshots*. Pup and I were greatly pleased to represent you in your groundbreaking lawsuit against the mugshots company – despite the fact that we were only modestly rewarded for our efforts.

"And we are thrilled that the lawsuit brought you not only financial recompense for the pain and suffering you endured as a result of the widespread circulation of that awful mugshot, but also the opportunity to add to your credits as a documentary producer.

"None of us believed you could ever top the artistic success of your first documentary – *Transgender Practices Among The Iroquois*, I believe it was called – but *Mugged By Mugshots* does just that. After we've all gone to the house and picked up our drinks, we will have the opportunity to view this marvelous documentary which was recently premiered on – can you help me on this Mona?"

"Crime and Investigation" Mona replied. "Channel fourteen-forty-five if you have the Digital Preferred Super Triple Play Package. If you don't have that package, you're out of luck. I don't know why PBS didn't pick it up, it would have been perfect for them."

"Right" said Pap. "Now why don't we move to the veranda and grab some drinks. You may need them while watching the documentary."

"Where did you ever get that beautiful red carpet?" Mona asked Piper as they moved toward the house.

"Oh, I went to that wonderful carpet store in Norwalk and asked if they had any red carpet remnants. Someone went down to the basement and came back with this runner. They sold it to me for practically nothing. Of course I would have gladly paid full price for it. After all, how could we ever have a proper celebration of your new documentary if we didn't have a nice red carpet for you to walk on?"

* * * *

Everyone seemed to be enjoying having drinks on the veranda. No one showed the slightest inclination to move toward the living room to watch the documentary. So Pap had to gently coax everyone toward the living room, explaining that they needed to finish the viewing by the time dinner was ready. He then stepped in front of the seventy-inch TV screen and began speaking.

"I am going to ask Mona to say a few words about her documentary, and encourage her to offer occasional comments as we view it together."

Pap knew full well that Mona would offer more than an occasional comment. Mona loved to talk to a captive audience.

During the court hearing, she had totally exasperated the judge, the Honorable Patricia ("Patty") Kake of the U.S. District Court for the District of Connecticut, Bridgeport Division.

Judge Kake constantly admonished Mona to just answer the question she was asked and not elaborate. Her instructions were simply ignored; Mona was intent on saying everything she wanted to say, never mind what Judge Kake wanted to hear. And Judge Kake was not amused when Mona asked if she would sit for an interview for the documentary Mona planned to make about the case.

But this was Mona's night and Pap decided he should give her free reign to do whatever she wanted.

"Before I turn this over to Mona, I want to call your attention to the little surprise we have over there in the corner." Pointing to a large easel covered with a velvet cloth, he continued: "We will unveil this little surprise after we've all seen the documentary. Mona, I'm turning it over to you."

"Thank you Pap darling" she began. "And thank all of you for coming. I promised Pap I would keep my remarks to a minimum, and just let the documentary speak for itself. So to speak. As all of you know, I really hate speaking in front of an audience. And having everyone's eyes on me."

Mona hesitated while everyone chuckled. Then she continued. "So why don't we just start the film – Pap, I don't know why you gave me the remote, I don't know how to use these high-tech things. That's why I married Ham, he's good at all this tech stuff. He even knows how to set the kitchen oven."

Handing Pap the remote, she said "Pap, can you just start the film? I won't say very much. As you will see, the film isn't really about me, it's about the court case."

As Pap hit the start button, the screen was filled with a close-up of the bronze plaque at the foot of the Lott's driveway announcing the name of the estate: HAMALOTT.

"That's the sign Ham and I put up so that people would know the proper name of our estate" explained Mona. "And that's our house" she added, as if none of the neighbors recognized the Lott's rambling colonial. "And there's our pond, where it all started."

"Those look like geese on the pond" said Ray Rabbitz as he pointed toward the screen. "But they don't look like they're moving."

"I think Mona shot them" said Stacy Spacey. "With her assault weapon. That's why they're not moving. And that's why Mona was arrested. She shot the geese with an assault weapon."

"But if she shot them, why are they still sitting there on the pond?" demanded Ray.

"Those aren't real geese" said Mona, anxious to regain control of the narrative. "Those are wooden decoys. I got them at an outdoor store, to use in the documentary. For heaven's sake, I couldn't use real geese."

"That would've started everything all over again" said Stacy excitedly. "Mona would have had to get out her assault weapon, shoot the geese, and then she would have been arrested all over again. And then had her mugshot taken down at the police station in Bridgeport."

"And then Pap and Pup could have represented her in a new lawsuit" added Ray. "Maybe another class action."

"And then Mona could have made another documentary and we could celebrate it with another party" said Stacy.

"Will you two please stop" said Mona sternly. "Everyone's trying to focus on the documentary. And by the way, I didn't shoot the geese with an assault weapon. That bitch Nina, who reported it to the police, just made it up. I only used a BB gun. My boy Tommy had it when he was little."

Just then Mona emerged on the screen. Walking from her house to the pond, she was carrying a BB gun. And she was wearing a hot pink tank top and red capri pants. Her hair was a mess and she had a scowl on her face.

"Why Mona" said Stacy's wife Daisy, "isn't that the outfit you were wearing when you were arrested? When they took you to the police station in Bridgeport? And when they took your mugshot?"

"Yes, I . . . ."

"And isn't that how you looked on that mugshot that appeared on posters all over town? And on the Internet?" added Bunny Rabbitz. "And isn't that why you sued in the first place? Why would you ever wear that hideous outfit again?"

"You dopes" said Mona. "This is a documentary. It's based on what happened. It has to be true – or at least kinda' true. So I had to wear the same clothes, I couldn't get all dolled up.

"And as I've told you all a hundred times, those are my gardening clothes. I was heading out to work in the garden when I saw the geese. I wasn't expecting to have Nina, you know, that slutty bitch Nina

Nosenyorbus, come by and accuse me of shooting geese with an assault weapon.

"And I wasn't expecting to be arrested. Or to have my picture taken at a police station. Or to have the picture appear on the Internet for the whole world to see. But the documentary had to depict all that. For heaven's sake, don't you all understand the integrity we artists must bring to making a documentary?"

And so it went throughout the fifty-minute documentary. Mona in every scene. Mona on the film narrating every scene. And Mona now, in Pap and Piper's living room, narrating her narration of every scene. The film ended with Pap, in an interview with Mona, explaining the settlement reached with the defendant and why that settlement would soon become a landmark in the Internet world.

Pap turned off the TV. Stepping back in front of the screen, he announced that dinner was almost ready and so any questions about the documentary would have to be addressed one-on-one with Mona later in the evening. He was sure she would be happy to answer any such questions. But before that, there was the surprise gift. He moved over to the corner and stood in front of the shrouded easel.

"Piper and I thought that Mona should have something to commemorate her ground-breaking lawsuit. Something more than the very generous amount of money she received as a result of the settlement – and of course the very modest amount of money the lawsuit allowed Peters and Peters to receive. As Mona knows, Pup and I and our firm's associates all put an enormous amount of time and effort into the case. I . . . . ."

"Ha!" piped up Ray Rabbitz. "We all know that Pup and your associates do all the work. All you do is stand up in court and take all the credit. And present your firm's fee application."

"Well, there is some truth to that" admitted Pap. "I've always said that Pup is the brains behind the operation. Now, I'm the one who thinks up most of the cases we bring, but Pup's the one who finds a way to fit them into the law. After all, he went to law school at Yale; he knows lots of stuff I never learned at Fordham. But look, we're getting off-track here. Let's get back to our gift for Mona.

"I'm sure you all know the famous Fairfield County painter Arthur Artz. 'Just call me Arty' he tells everyone. Well, Arty is best known for his landscape paintings – in fact, Piper and I have one of them hanging in our dining room. What's less well known is that Arty Artz is also an excellent portrait painter. And so Piper and I commissioned him to paint Mona's portrait."

"How could he have painted my portrait?" asked Mona. "I've never met him and I certainly didn't pose for him."

"Mona dear" said Pap patiently, "as someone so well versed in the arts, you surely know that portraits can be painted without the subject posing in person. For example, working from even a small photo, a good painter can create a wonderful portrait. And that is what Arthur, just call me Arty, has done."

And with that Pap pulled off the velvet cover to reveal Mona's portrait. Exactly as it appeared in her mugshot. Hot pink tank top. Bright red capri pants. Hair a mess and a scowl on her face.

The unveiling was met with stunned silence. Surely this was not how Mona would want to be remembered. What on earth was Pap thinking? Pup always complained that Pap thought up too many crazy cases and then had to be persuaded to drop the idea.

The silence continued. No one could think of anything to say.

Suddenly, Mona burst out excitedly "Why that's me! That's just how I looked that day in Bridgeport when you came down and got me out of jail. Pap darling, you are wonderful. I always knew you were a good lawyer, but I never knew you had such an artistic sensibility. Ham, dear, where do you think we should hang it?"

As the laughter and banter began to subside, Piper stepped up and announced "Dinner's ready. Please serve yourselves from the buffet and then find a seat at either the dining room table or the table in the den. We can all convey our congratulations to Mona while we dine."

Chapter 2

GROUNDHOG DAY

Mona was sitting at the large table in the dining room, which seated eight. She had quickly rushed there after lifting up a generous helping of baked salmon, rice pilaf and green beans – "*haricot verts*" she insisted on calling them. She wanted to sit with the largest group of guests, the table in the den only seated six.

Pup and Hillary Fund were seated to her left. Laurel Ann Hardy was on her right. Stacy Spacey was across from Mona while his wife Daisy was at the far end of the table next to Laurel Ann's boyfriend Milo Nulow. In the seat to Stacy's right was Mona's husband Ham; she wished Ham had sat at the other table, she saw him every day.

Pup's girls, Tap and Bap, had been consigned to the kitchen table along with Hap and Little Pap.

"So, Mona" asked Hillary, "what are you going to do now that the lawsuit is over and your documentary is completed?"

"Well, to tell you the honest truth, I'd like to file another lawsuit. Maybe even a class action."

"A lawsuit for what?" asked Hillary.

Pup grimaced and began to squirm. A new lawsuit with Mona as the plaintiff was not what he and Pap needed.

"Hillary dear, can I call you 'Hil'? I'm so glad you asked." Mona immediately had the attention of the entire table.

"You see, last month we had Groundhog Day. Tuesday February second. Groundhog Day is always important to me. If the groundhog sees his shadow, we've got six more weeks of winter. So it's a good time to go to Florida or out west to do some skiing.

"But if the groundhog doesn't see his shadow, it means an early Spring. And that means I need to start preparing my gardens. And that's exactly what happened last month. Charlie, the groundhog from the Staten Island Zoo, came out of his hole and . . . ."

"I thought the Staten Island groundhog was named Charlotte" said Daisy.

"She had a sex change operation and was renamed Charlie" said Stacy. "You know, transgender is all the rage these days."

"Say, that could be your next documentary" said Daisy. "When Charlotte became Charlie, Transgender Practices Among the Groundhogs."

"No, no" said Milo, who always seemed to know about everything. "That's not what happened. Charlotte died a couple of years ago. The Mayor, who was holding her during a live press conference celebrating Groundhog Day, dropped her. Cracked her skull. So they had to find a replacement. The replacement was Charlie."

"That's right" said Laurel Ann Hardy. "I remember that. I felt really bad for Charlotte. But what's all this got to do with a lawsuit?"

"Charlotte's heirs could file a lawsuit" suggested Stacy. Against the Mayor. A suit for wrongful death I think it's called – am I right Pup?"

Pup was scarcely known for his wit, but he was getting caught up in the banter. "Well, people can sue for wrongful death, but I'm not sure about groundhogs. I could have one of our associates look into it."

"I don't think Pap would be interested in such a lawsuit" said Daisy. "He only wants to do class actions. I don't think the Mayor dropped enough groundhogs to warrant a class action."

Mona was exasperated, she was supposed to be leading this conversation. "Wouldn't you all like to hear about the new lawsuit I want to bring? Isn't that what dear Hil wanted to know?"

"Sure, Mona" said Laurel. "Tell us abut the lawsuit you want to bring regarding Groundhog Day. But it better be good. We kind of liked the wrongful death thing."

"Well, here's the thing" Mona began. "The Mayor was holding Charlie – he was careful not to drop him, he didn't want two dead groundhogs on his hands. And while he was holding Charlie, he announced that Charlie had *not* seen his shadow, so that meant Spring was right around the corner. That's exactly what the Mayor said. So I immediately got out all my garden tools and began working in the gardens."

"But Mona" interrupted Daisy. "We had that huge snowstorm in the middle of February. I think we got almost a foot of snow."

"My dear" replied Mona, "that's precisely the problem. Instead of an early Spring, we got a snowstorm. Now my gardens are a complete mess."

Stacy was beside himself. "You're blaming Charlie for that? Any groundhog can make a mistake now and then. You can't go around suing groundhogs every time they get their predictions wrong. Am I right about this Pup?"

"Peters and Peters is not in business to sue groundhogs" said Pup. "We only sue defendants with deep pockets. Groundhogs don't have deep pockets. In fact, they don't even have pockets."

Mona was getting irritated. How could she be the center of attention if everyone else kept talking?

"If you folks would quit interrupting me all the time" she said irritably, "I could explain this. It's not the groundhog I want to sue, its the Mayor."

"Did he drop Charlie this time around?" asked Stacy. "Maybe Charlie was so concussed he couldn't remember whether or not he had seen his shadow. In fact, two dropped groundhogs is beginning to sound like animal cruelty to me. What do you think Pup?"

Pup wanted no part of suing the Mayor of New York City for dropping groundhogs. But before he could respond, Mona said:

"That's not what I want to sue him for. The Mayor and the zoo really screwed up. You see, they had pre-taped the event on the first, the day before Groundhog Day. It was quite cloudy that day, so of course the groundhog couldn't see his shadow. As a result, they announced that Spring would be early.

"But if they had waited until the actual Groundhog Day, it would have been different. *Très* different, as they say in France. You see, it was sunny on the second, the real Groundhog Day. Had they done it on the proper day, they would have proclaimed six more weeks of winter. So I would have known winter is going to hang around. And I would not have gone out and started working in my garden.

"Now here's what Pap and Pup taught me" Mona continued. "I'm certainly not the only one who was misled. Everyone in New York City – in fact, everyone in the tri-state region who relies on the Staten Island groundhog for a forecast - was misled. That's what class actions are for. We could have another class action."

"Pup, what do you think about this?" asked Daisy. "Can Mona bring another class action? Maybe some of us could be part of the class if we started in on our gardens after Groundhog Day."

"Look" said Pup, "this is all quite fun. But even Peters and Peters wouldn't bring a lawsuit for this. And even if some other law firm would – you wouldn't believe some of the crazy lawsuits these class action firms dream up – Mona couldn't be the plaintiff."

"Why not?" demanded Mona. "Wasn't I a good witness in the mugshots case? I think that judge – Judge Kake – liked me."

"Mona, I don't want to spoil your evening by talking about whether or not Judge Kake liked you. Because, like you or not, that's not the reason you couldn't be the plaintiff.

"The real reason is that the same person can't keep bringing class action lawsuits, they would never have any credibility after the first one. And no judge would ever certify a class action where the lead plaintiff had just been a lead plaintiff in a previous class action. That's why we have to keep finding new plaintiffs for our cases."

"You mean it's one and done?" asked Mona. "I was so looking forward to doing another one with you and Pap."

Laurel Ann Hardy was convinced. "Mona, perhaps a new lawsuit isn't such a great idea. But what about a new documentary? Now that you've done two of them, and with the second one being shown on that Crime and Investigation station - channel fourteen hundred and something I think you said, my cable package only goes up to fifteen channels – you should have no difficulty getting funding for a third one."

"But what would the subject be?" asked Daisy. *Transgender Practices Among The Iroquois* and *Mugged By Mugshots* – those were blockbuster topics. Mona needs another blockbuster topic if she's gonna make a new documentary."

"Say, Mona" said Milo, "I know what your subject could be. There was an article in the papers a few months ago about a minister at that large cathedral in New York near the Hudson River. It was a woman minister. She and two associate ministers were in Minneapolis for some sort of church conference. During a break in the conference, she took them to a sex shop and bought them all a collection of sex toys. Vibrators and other sex gadgets."

"You're kidding" said Hillary. "No minister would ever do that."

"I'm afraid you're wrong" said Milo. "There was a lengthy article about it in the New York *Post*. There was an investigation and the minister was fired."

"You never told me you read the New York *Post*" said Laurel Ann Hardy indignantly. "I don't particularly want to go around with someone who reads tabloids all the time."

"But I read it for their sports coverage" said Milo. "They have the best sports coverage of all the New York papers."

"Don't believe him" said Stacy. "We guys all buy the *Post* for its girly pictures. They have them every day. And extra ones on Sundays."

"I don't think this is worthy of a serious documentary" said Laurel. "As Daisy just explained, Mona does serious documentaries about important social issues. Besides, why would you want to humiliate this poor minister further?"

"Defrocked minister" said Stacy. "She's now defrocked, or at least she should be. People need to know what our ministers are up to — especially women ministers."

Daisy had an idea. "Mona, couldn't you do this documentary but not use the minister's real name?"

"Right" said Stacy. "She could just make up a name. Maybe something like Reverend Joy Lord."

"Or maybe Angel Zinger" suggested Daisy.

"What about Bella Ringer?" said Milo.

"I like Joy Lord best" said Hillary, "I think we should stick with that."

"Okay, but now we need a name for the documentary" said Stacy. "How about 'Bringing Joy to the Lord's Work'?"

"Or how about 'Vibrators in the Vestry'" said Daisy. "That could be good."

"What about 'Sex in the Sarcistry'?" suggested Milo.

"No" insisted Hillary, "if the minister's name is going to be Joy Lord, the title's got to be 'Bringing Joy to the Lord's Work.'"

"Now that we've got that settled" said Daisy, "what about the Minneapolis sex shop where she got the stuff? Did the newspaper give the name of the shop?"

"It was called 'The Smitten Kitten'" said Milo. "Right in downtown Minneapolis."

"You know the name of a sex shop in Minneapolis?" asked Laurel petulantly. "Milo, I never knew this side of you. My late husband Harry never would have known about a sex shop in Minneapolis."

"The reason I asked" broke in Daisy, "is that Mona could go to Minneapolis and interview the owner of the shop. Find out what other kinds of customers they have. Maybe there are other ministers or priests who buy stuff there. Or politicians and businessmen."

"Maybe even hedge fund guys" said Stacy as he shot a glance at Hillary.

"And then it could be turned into an *exposé* of the sex shop industry" said Laurel. "That would make it a serious documentary, like all Mona's other ones."

And so, for the next fifteen minutes everyone around the table threw out ideas for Mona's new documentary. Character names, scenes, even marketing strategy. If Mona couldn't file a new lawsuit, at least they could help her with a new documentary project.

Chapter 3

PASS THE TORTES

At the dining table in the den, Pap had deliberately chosen a seat across from Will Fund, the hedge fund guy.

"Will" said Pap, "I know you've been operating your fund, the Fund Fund, for years. But didn't I read that the fund has started to invest in lawsuits? That seems to be a lucrative business. I know a lot of litigation funding firms have been set up in recent years."

"That's true" said Will. "The name we're known by – the Fund Fund - is just the name of the overall entity. That entity oversees several different funds, each of which has its own investment purpose and strategy."

"So then you have a separate fund that invests in litigation?"

"Correct. That would be our newest fund, the Lien On Me Fund. That's Lien – L-I-E-N – On Me. We invest in a lawsuit and, in exchange, we get a percentage of the recovery. We secure that investment by taking a lien on the eventual recovery."

"What sorts of lawsuits do you invest in? I assume they're big commercial cases with a potential for large damages?"

"You bet. Our investors expect large returns on their investment. And that means we look for cases where the damages will be huge. Like a patent case, where the invention is in widespread use. In a case like that you could be looking at a verdict worth tens, maybe even hundreds, of millions.

"Please understand, we're not interested in your everyday commercial case where the damages are only a million or two. A million dollar recovery might be good for the plaintiff, but that level of recovery would be of no interest to a fund investing in litigation."

"What about class actions?" said Pap, getting quickly to the point.

"Depends. A huge case involving hundreds of thousands of class members suing a large national corporation, that's the kind of case we could get interested in."

"What about . . . ."

But Will quickly cut Pap off. "I know you want to talk to me about your firm's cases. That's why you invited Hillary and me, even though we've barely moved in and you barely know us.

"Judging from what I've seen and read, your cases all sound clever, and you're probably having fun with them. But seriously, Pap, why would we invest in a case for a bunch of strippers suing a handful of small-time strip joints? Even if you managed to recoup a fee for your firm, there's no real money in a case like that.

"Same with Mona's case" Fund continued. "You sued a start-up that had no established revenue stream. You got your injunction and some attorneys fees and Mona got her documentary. But you didn't get much in the way of money except some promises and IOUs. Pap, you're never going to interest a litigation funding firm with cases like that. Come up with something big and I'll be happy to talk with you."

Pap thought a minute and then asked, "What about a case against Colonel Mills over one of its cereals?"

"Which cereal?"

"Corny Flakes. It's been one of the leading cereals on the market for years.

"Yeah, I know that. Everybody's eaten Corny Flakes at some point in their life. But what's the claim?"

"They've got a new line extension that just came out. 'Berry Good' it's called. 'Berry Good Corny Flakes.'"

"Okay, but what's the beef?"

"It's not the beef, it's the berries. Or, I should say, the absence thereof. There are no berries in 'Berry Good Corny Flakes.'"

"Well, does the package say it contains berries?"

"Yes. Well, indirectly. The front of the package shows a bowl of Corny Flakes with blueberries on top."

"Maybe they're just showing that Corny Flakes are good with blueberries on top."

"That's not what our client thought. She thought she was getting Corny Flakes with blueberries added. She was so disappointed she had to go out and buy some blueberries to make the cereal look like it does on the front of the package."

"Who's this client?"

"A lady from Scarsdale. Name's Hazel Nutt. Nice lady, maybe a bit intense."

"Sounds like she's a bit of a nut."

"But Will, look at how many people across the country have purchased a box of Berry Good Corny Flakes, probably millions."

"You better look at how many of those millions bought a second box. After knowing there were no blueberries."

Pap was exasperated. "You sound like my brother. He's always finding some flaw in our cases, drives me crazy. It got so bad I had to create a separate room for him to go to when he wants to worry about a case. We call it 'The Worry Room.'"

"Look Pap, the Fund Fund has made an awful lot of money by making good investments. We owe it to our investors to worry about each investment. But I must admit, we don't have a separate room where we go to worry. We just worry in place, so to speak. Anyway, this Corny Flakes thing does not sound like a good investment to me."

Will could see that Pap was not happy with the turn this conversation had taken. As he was a guest, he needed to let Pap down gently.

"Look Pap, your firm is still in its infancy. Your future is in front of you. In fact, it's in the future. I'm sure you'll have lots more cases down the road. Let me know if you come up with something that might be worthwhile for the Lien On Me Fund. If we can make a boatload of money on one of your cases, we'd be happy to help."

Pap was disappointed. Corny Flakes was about to be their first major case against a big corporation. Everyone ate Corny Flakes, so the class should be huge, even if only half of regular Corny Flakes eaters tried the new line extension. And Colonel Mills was certainly a deep-pocket defendant, so there was plenty of money there if they settled or won. He thought Fund was underestimating the money to be had from the case.

Maybe he could re-approach Fund after the case was certified as a class action. That would be a signal that the judge thought the case had merit.

Or maybe they could find another food case. Lots of large companies were in the packaged foods business, and everyone today was fussy about what was in the food they ate. The field was rife with opportunity. On Monday he would ask Melissa or Brandon to get busy and find them a second food case. One that would be big enough to interest his new friend and neighbor Will Fund.

* * * *

After everyone had finished their main course, Piper came into the dining room with a plate stacked with dessert goodies and announced: "We have some lovely tortes for desert. Three flavors: chocolate, lemon and apricot. I hope you like them."

"Ham," she said as she handed him the tray, "would you please pass the tortes."

"Oh, they look yummy" said Laurel Ann Hardy.

"Can we have more than one?" asked Milo.

"Piper" announced Stacy after she had taken a bite of an apricot torte, "you are the Queen of Torts. Just like Pap is the King of Torts. That makes you two the King and Queen of Torts."

"Well" said Piper, "I think you're improperly mixing your torts. Pap's torts are different from my tortes. Pap's torts are spelled T-O-R-T-S. They are not edible, although they do help put food on the table. My tortes are edible and they're spelled T-O-R-T-E-S. They have an E in them."

"But that would make them 'tortees' " said Stacy. Stacy was not the sharpest tool in the box. His friends liked to say that's why his parents chose Spacey as his last name.

"Stacy" said Piper patiently, "the E in my tortes – the edible kind – is silent. So the word is still pronounced 'torts.' It's like the silent E in the name of that farmer – Olde McDonald – where we got Pup and Pap."

"You got Pap from a farmer in New Jersey?" said Stacy. "I thought you got him at a party in New York. And I thought Priscilla got Pup at the country club in Greenwich."

"I'm talking about the dogs" said Piper. "Pap and Pup got them down in New Jersey from a farmer named Olde McDonald. Spelled his name O-L-D-E. It had an E on the end but it was silent. So his name was pronounced the same as the Old McDonald in the children's song."

Hillary, who was meeting most everyone for the first time, was confused. "Piper, let me get this straight. Your husbands are named Pap and Pup?"

"That's correct" said Piper.

"But the dogs are also named Pap and Pup?"

"Sure" said Piper. "Our dog is named Pup and Pup's dog is named Pap."

"How can you tell the difference between your husbands and your dogs?"

"Sometimes they can't" said Stacy. "One night after a party Piper came home with Pup and Pup's dog Pap. And Priscilla brought home Pap and his dog Pup. They didn't sort things out until the next morning."

"Hillary, don't listen to anything he says" said Piper. "He's always making things up, he should have been a lawyer."

"Yes, I can see that" said Hillary. "But seriously, why were the dogs named Pap and Pup?"

"The kids came up with those names in the car on the way home from Olde McDonald's farm" said Piper.

"Well, that's not one hundred percent true" said Pup. "It was Pap who suggested the boys name their dog Pup. I thought it was a terrible idea and I said so at the time. But Pap wouldn't listen. He kept saying I should view it as an honor that his boys wanted to name their dog after me. But it was never the boys' idea, it was Pap's idea."

"So then why did you name your dog Pap?" asked Hillary.

"The girls and I decided that" said Pup. "If Pap insisted on naming his dog after me, we thought we should name our dog after him. Sauce for the goose, sauce for the gander."

"What's a gander?" asked Stacy.

"A male goose" said Hillary, "everybody knows that."

"Then what's a female goose?"

"A goose. What else would it be called?"

Stacy thought about that for a moment, then looked at Mona and asked: "So Mona, when you went after those geese with your assault weapon, were they geese or ganders?"

"How would I know, they all look alike" Mona responded irritably. "And as I've told you a hundred times, I didn't use an assault weapon . . . ."

"You should have clarified that in your documentary" insisted Stacy. "Viewers will want to know whether you were shooting at geese or ganders. That's important. You can't go around killing all the females of a species."

"But I . . . ."

"Let's get back to the dogs" said Daisy. Directing her question to Pup, she asked: "Their having the same names as you and Pap must be confusing. For instance, when Pap says 'Come here, Pup', how do you know whether he's calling you or his dog?"

"I don't. And neither does the dog. And that's the problem. I tried to tell him that but he just wouldn't listen. When Pap makes up his mind about something, no amount of reason will dissuade him. He's been like that ever since we were kids."

"Yes, Pap can sometimes be strong-willed about things" said Piper. "But that's one of the things I like about him. He insisted on our first date that we should get married. No dilly dallying, like most guys. I found it quite charming.

"Now, could someone please finish passing the tortes, I need to take them to the guests in the other room."

Chapter 4

CONGRESSMAN EARMACHER

On Wednesday morning, immediately after Pap arrived at the firm's Fifth Avenue offices, his secretary Vera Pesky followed him into his office. Vera was strictly no-nonsense; she was the only person in the office Pap was afraid of.

"A lot of stuff came up yesterday while you were away. I hope you had a good meeting. By the way, who were you meeting with, I need to enter it into our billing records."

After hesitating a few seconds to decide whether he really wanted to answer her question, Pap finally said "It was three guys. Len Bogan, Alan Allen and Harley Farley."

"I don't recognize those names" said Miss Pesky. "What case are they involved in?"

"Well, you've probably never heard of them. But don't worry about it. Now, tell me what happened yesterday . . . ."

"We'll get to that" said Miss Pesky. "But first I need to know who those guys are. We need to account for your time yesterday."

"Okay" said Pap, "they're members of the country club. I played golf with them. The weather was really great and we thought it would be a good way to kick off the season at Stanwich."

"You said you needed to be at your boys' basketball game in the afternoon, and so after your morning meeting in Greenwich you were going straight to Westport to watch the game."

"That's totally true" said Pap. "After my meeting with Len Bogan, Alan Allen and Harley Farley I drove up to Westport and watched the boys' basketball game."

"I thought you always played golf with your brother. He was in the office all day yesterday. Working," Miss Pesky added as she gave Pap a stern stare.

"Well, somebody had to be here to run the office. Who would run it if Pup and I were both out playing golf?"

There was nothing worse than being on the wrong side of Vera Pesky. Pap regretted having brought her with him when he left his partnership at Rogers and Autry to start up Peters and Peters. "Pesky acts like she runs the Goddamn place" he constantly complained to Pup.

Miss Pesky finally changed the subject and went through the list of calls he had to return, pleadings and briefs he needed to review and expert witnesses who had called to offer their services.

"Oh, and Congressman Earmacher called. He wants you to call him back. Said it's extremely urgent."

"Did he say what it's about? Or why it's so urgent?"

"No. Just said you should call him when you got back from your meeting. I told him the meeting might last all day. I didn't want him to know that your boys' basketball game was more important than speaking with him."

"That was smart, Miss Pesky. Good thinking. So let's call him now, better not keep him waiting."

* * * *

Earnest Earmacher was a liberal Republican who had represented Connecticut's Fourth Congressional District – the "Gold Coast" district – for more than ten years. He was best known for his work in getting billions of dollars in federal money earmarked for Connecticut's thriving defense industry. Earmacher could do this because of his position as the senior-most Republican on the powerful Defense Appropriations Committee.

Pap had known Earmacher for years, and had long been a significant contributor to his re-election campaigns. Pap occasionally contacted the Congressman about an issue, and was even now working on a scheme for which he hoped to enlist Earmacher's support. But Earmacher had never contacted him. Pap was anxious to see what Earmacher wanted to speak with him about.

"The Congressman is on the line" Miss Pesky said when she buzzed Pap.

"Hello Congressman. This is Patrick Peters. I understand you called yesterday while I was out at an all-day meeting. What can I do for you?"

"Actually, I'm not the Congressman. I'm Kate Kisme, Congressman Earmacher's assistant. If you will hold, I'll try to get him on the line. He's in a staff meeting but maybe he'll take your call."

Damn that Miss Pesky, said Pap under his breath. She said Earmacher was on the line. Ha! Now I, not her, have to wait while Earmacher's assistant tries to see if he will take the call. As soon as I'm off the call, I'll give Vera Pesky a piece of my mind.

After two minutes of waiting while "Beautiful Ohio" played on the phone, Earmacher picked up.

"Hello Patrick. Thanks so much for getting back to me. How are you? How's your firm doing? I read about that case you had down in Bridgeport. It was before Patty Kake, wasn't it? She's getting up there in age, maybe she'll retire and I can get a Republican appointed to that seat. I've got a mile-long list of donors who'd like to be a judge."

"Yes, that was our case, but Judge Kake was not particularly amused by it. We need judges with a sense of humor. I hope you'll keep that in mind when she retires."

"By the way" asked Earmacher, "how's your golf game? We should try to get in a round this summer."

"Well, I haven't had a chance to play yet this year. Our firm's pretty busy. Lots of people want to sue these days. We try to help 'em if we can. I hope you don't have to sue anyone, Congressman."

"Ha! No I don't need to sue anyone. The last thing a Congressman needs is to have his constituents think of him as a plaintiff in a lawsuit."

"Well, that's better than being a defendant in a lawsuit. That could be a career killer."

"Agreed. But look, I need to meet with you. Not about a lawsuit but about a very delicate matter. It requires the utmost tact and secrecy. You might even say it involves a matter of national security."

"Congressman, you know I'll do anything I can to help you. But I'm not a national security guy. I'm a litigator. Peters and Peters, we sue people. As we say on our website, Peters and Peters blows into a case like a . . . ."

"You're a lawyer" interrupted Earmacher. "With a good head on your shoulders. You've got common sense, not like all those smarty-pants intellectuals who went to Harvard and Yale."

Now Earmacher really had his attention. There was nothing Pap liked better than to be viewed as superior to the conceited snobs who had gone to Harvard and Yale. He would seize this opportunity, whatever it was. Besides, working with Connecticut's longest-serving Congressman could turn out to be very good for the firm.

Pap knew that, like all Congressmen and Senators, Earmacher only spent three days, three-and-a-half at most, in D.C. Earmacher always flew back to Connecticut on Thursday night and was in his Norwalk office every Friday. So Pap made a suggestion.

"I could meet you on Friday at your Norwalk office. Just name the time and I'll be there."

"We can't do this in Norwalk. We need to meet in person, right here in my office. There's someone else involved. Can you come down and meet with us tomorrow?"

"Okay" said Pap as he tried unsuccessfully to think of what he was supposed to be doing tomorrow. "I can get the nine o'clock shuttle and be in your office by ten-thirty. Would that work?"

"Perfect" said Earmacher. "I'm in the Rayburn office building. Room four-fifty-two. I'll arrange for Miz Kisme to meet you downstairs. You'll like her, she's quite attractive. And a damn good secretary too" he added, lest Pap get the wrong impression.

"Great. See you tomorrow Congressman."

After hanging up, Pap called in Ms. Pesky. "Get me a ticket on the D.C. Shuttle for tomorrow. Nine o'clock. Open return. Also get me some cash, I'll need it for cabs.

"And by the way, don't you ever again tell me to pick up a call for Congressman Earmacher when he isn't on the line. I had to wait several minutes listening to 'Beautiful Ohio' while I waited for him to pick up, when all that time I could have been working."

"Seems to me you wasted several hours – not minutes – on the golf course yesterday when you could have been here working. Like your brother and all the associates."

"That'll be all Miss Pesky. Just get me the damn tickets and the cash. And ask Chip to come in, I need to talk with him."

* * * *

Charles Powell Pierpont, III, had long been known as "Chip." While Chip hadn't set the world on fire as a lawyer, he had great connections, which was why Pap had brought him along from Rogers and Autry when he and Pup started up the firm. It was Chip, for example, who arranged all the firm's press conferences. He had connections at all the city newspapers and all the New York-based media.

Tall, fit and handsome, Chip had played quarterback at Dartmouth and was immensely popular with the ladies. Women seemed to fall into his lap like leaves falling from a tree. It was this attribute that caused him to be summoned to Pap's office that day.

"Chip" Pap began, "this has gotta stop."

"What's gotta stop?" asked Chip.

"Your having sex with Candy in the Worry Room. You know it's against firm policy."

"Sure, I know about the policy . . . ."

"Yeah, you should know about it. We sent around a firm memo about it. Because you and Candy were using the Worry Room as a place to have sex."

"Candy" was what all the guys called Candice Ann Topper, the beautiful paralegal with a body to die for. She had worked with Pup at

25

his old firm, Oliver and Cromwell, and Pap had suggested Pup get her to join them at their new firm. Pup had been surprised when Candy said she would love to join the new firm.

Pap continued his lecture to Chip. "As we pointed out in the firm memorandum, we set up the Worry Room as a place where Pup and the other lawyers could go to worry about a case. Not as a place to fornicate. That's why we did not name it the Fornication Room."

"Sure, I know all that" said Chip. "But I haven't used it for fornication since you sent around that memo. I don't even use it for worrying. In fact, I don't have any worries. So I don't need to use the Worry Room."

"Chip, I'd like to believe you but I know you're lying. We can't have a successful firm if the associates are always lying to Pup and me."

"Why would I lie to you? You brought me into the firm and its been a great ride."

"Well, I know you've had some great rides with Candy. And you can keep having them as far as I'm concerned, you just gotta stop having your rides in the Worry Room."

"But I told you, I haven't taken her to the Worry Room since you sent around that memo."

"Well, if it wasn't you, who else would have been having a ride with Candy in the Worry Room last Thursday night? You suddenly have some competition?"

"I don't know what you're talking about" said Chip defiantly. This was getting aggravating.

"I'm talking about finding these on the sofa in the Worry Room" said Pap as he reached into his desk drawer and pulled out a pair of skimpy black-laced panties.

"Where did those come from?" Chip asked. He was starting to worry.

"I found them under the pillow on the sofa when I went in to take a nap last Friday. As you know, the partners are allowed to use the Worry Room for naps, although I've never known Pup to take a nap, he's always too busy worrying about our cases."

"Well . . . ." Chip stammered.

"Obviously these are Candy's panties. Melissa would never wear skimpy, lacy panties like these. And I doubt that any of the secretaries would either. Certainly not Miss Pesky, she probably wears wool underwear.

"So, if these are Candy's underpants, she took them off for someone in the Worry Room. And I doubt she took them off for Pup or Brandon. That leaves you."

"Okay" said Chip with a sigh. "I might as well come clean. Especially since you're the one wearing the pants. I mean, have the pants."

"I'm glad to hear you're finally gonna come clean. But please tell me, why are you deliberately disobeying firm policy? Our policy is that there is to be absolutely no fornication in the fucking Worry Room. The policy couldn't be more clear."

"Well, the memo also said that, if it was an emergency, fornication *in situ* – '*in situ*', that's how you referred to it - was permitted. And this was an emergency."

"Thursday night after everyone had gone home was an emergency? Why didn't you just take her to your apartment?"

"I couldn't take her there, what would Francoise say?"

"Who's Francoise?"

"My new girl friend. She's a translator at the UN. Moved in with me last week."

"Okay, I see that taking Candy to your apartment might not have been a great idea. But what about Candy's apartment? Why didn't you just go there?"

"Candy lives down in Soho. A block or so away from Lydia. Lydia moved there after she made all that money from being *Playboy's* Playmate of the Month and then started doing that modeling work."

The gorgeous Lydia Lowlace had been the firm's first major client. A lap dancer at a series of gentleman's clubs in Manhattan, Chip had brought her to the firm to meet Pap and Pup after she told him how she and her fellow dancers were being cheated out of wages and tips by the clubs' owner. The resulting lawsuit brought the firm considerable publicity, albeit only meager attorney's fees.

"What's Lydia got to do with you and Candy?" asked Pap.

"Well, I still see Lydia from time to time. Lydia wouldn't care about Candy. But Candy would care about Lydia, she thinks my fling with her was over after the case was over. Women can be funny about things like that."

"Jesus, Chip" said a flabbergasted Pap. "You're walking quite a tightrope here, I can see that. But look, you gotta stop fucking Candy in the Worry Room. You need to find some other place to fuck her."

"Can you suggest somewhere?"asked Chip hopefully.

"I'll think about it. But that's it for the Worry Room, okay? I don't want to have this conversation again."

"Okay, Pap. But you should give Candy back her underpants. She's probably wondering what happened to them" he added as he walked out of Pap's office leaving Pap holding the pants.

Chapter 5

HONEY TRAP

On Thursday, when Pap walked into the Rayburn Office Building just across Independence Avenue from the Capitol, a gorgeous young blonde in a tight-fitting gray suit approached him.

"Mister Peters? Hi. I'm Kate Kisme, Congressman Earmacher's assistant."

"Pleased to meet you Miz . . . Kisme was it?"

"If you want to kiss me you can call me Kisme. Otherwise, just plain old Kate is fine."

"I think I'd better stick with Kate" Pap said as he looked her up and down. Damn, he said to himself, how did Ernie Earmacher get his hands on an assistant like this? While he was stuck with that old battleaxe Vera Pesky. Life wasn't fair.

Looking her in the eye to see if she might be flirting, Pap said: "But just because I call you Kate doesn't mean I think you're old and plain. You are neither."

"Congressman Earmacher told me I'd like you. Said you were a cool guy but also a gentleman."

"I'd rather be known as a cool guy. I can take or leave the gentleman part." Pap tried hard not to stare at her.

After he had shown his photo ID and signed in, Kate directed them to the elevator. "We're on the fourth floor. Great view. We look directly into the Cannon Office Building, just opposite us on the east."

"Well I suppose that keeps you all focused on your work. No looking out the window and wishing you were outdoors."

"On no. We love looking into the offices in Cannon. There's always something going on. Staffers doing silly yoga exercises. Politicians looking in the mirror all the time. Lobbyists making passes at the secretaries. Stuff like that."

"That's good to know" said Pap. "I've always wondered what it would be like working on Capitol Hill."

"By the way" he said as they entered the elevator. "How did you know who I was when I came in? I'm sure Congressman Earmacher doesn't keep a picture of me in his office."

"Oh, that's easy. He told me you looked just like you brother. Pup, I think his name is. Said you two were twins."

"Yes, but how did you know what Pup looks like?"

"Well, now that I've seen you, I know just what Pup looks like."

Pap wondered if everyone in D.C. talked in circles like this.

* * * *

When Kate ushered Pap into her boss's office, Congressman Earmacher rose and greeted him enthusiastically.

"Patrick, good to see you. Thanks for coming down on such short notice."

As they shook hands Pap saw a man of medium height with dark hair and wire-rimmed glasses rise from a chair facing Earmacher's desk. The man was nice looking and well-dressed but looked to be extremely uncomfortable.

"Patrick, I'd like you to meet my friend and colleague Biggs Splendor. Biggs is from California, represents the State's Fifteenth District – it covers the East Bay area near Oakland. Biggs is a Democrat but we're good friends. We've served together for several years on the Intelligence Committee. Technically, it's the House Permanent Select Committee on Intelligence. Because of the nature of the Committee's work, we're pretty bipartisan."

"Nice to meet you" said Pap as he extended his hand. "Any friend of Congressman Earmacher is a friend of mine. Even if he is a Democrat."

Splendor gave a tight smile but continued to look like he wanted to be somewhere else. Well, thought Pap, he wanted to be somewhere else too, like having lunch at the Hay Adams with Kate Kisme.

Earmacher ushered them into a group of overstuffed chairs in the corner of the office. "Let me explain why I asked you here. But first, you need to understand that everything we tell you is not only confidential, it is highly secret. In fact, it's classified national intelligence information."

Pap had no idea what was going on or why he was here. He needed to stop daydreaming about Kate Kisme and focus on what Earmacher was about to say.

"As I said, Congressman Splendor and I serve on the House Intelligence Committee. In that capacity, we are given access to everything going on at the various intelligence agencies. CIA, DIA, Homeland Security, et cetera. Anything involving intelligence eventually gets reported to our committee.

"Last week, we saw a preliminary CIA report. They've been conducting an investigation, 'Operation Honey Pot' they call it. It seems they stumbled onto a Russian operation that's been going on for some time. It's a traditional honey trap. Beautiful Russian agent wanders around the corridors of D.C. luring businessmen, politicians, Defense Department officials - even UN personnel - into a honey trap. I'm afraid Congressman Splendor is one of the victims."

"Jesus" said Pap. "I've read about this kind of stuff in books but never thought I would be dealing with it first-hand."

Pap looked at Splendor. He felt sorry for him, so he resisted the urge to ask if he had experienced splendor in the grass. Instead, Pap asked: "How did you fall into this trap anyway?"

"I didn't fall into the trap. I jumped into it feet first."

"So who was this lady anyway?"

"Ah . . . she was beautiful. Flaming red hair. Slender as a reed. Always wore an elegant black dress. I knew her as Tanya. Tanya Bertina Zhivago. She told me her great grandfather was the famous Doctor Zhivago."

"Doctor Zhivago? Wasn't that a . . . ."

"That was the hook she used with me. Told me she had always admired this country because we helped get her great grandfather's manuscript published when it had been banned in Russia."

"We were involved in getting Doctor Zhivago published?" asked Pap.

"Yes" said Splendor. "Tanya's great grandfather had been sent to the Gulag for publishing anti-Soviet materials. So there was no way they were ever going to let him publish his masterwork. Remember, this was during the height of the Cold War.

"Now, the CIA really wanted the book published, so it mounted a clandestine operation. First it smuggled the manuscript out of Russia. It got the book printed and then smuggled it back into Russia and other countries behind the Iron Curtain. Tanya told me that ever since learning about this, she has loved the United States."

"So you thought she was related to Doctor Zhivago? Who you thought was the writer, not just a character in the book? And fell right into her trap?"

"Yeah, I'm afraid so. But so did a lot of other guys. Turns out she was sleeping with officials in the Defense Department and the intelligence agencies. And also CEOs in the defense industry, such as Bernie Byrne; he's the CEO of a Lockheed subsidiary, boy did he ever get burned. She had quite a sting of conquests."

"You saw her a lot?"

"Yeah. We first met at a bar in the Ritz Carlton over in Arlington. She seemed like a classy lady. Beautiful black dress. Nice strand of pearls. Quietly sipping white wine at the bar."

"How many times did you see her?"

"Probably a couple dozen. My family stays back in California, so I'm by myself all week."

"Okay" said Pap, "but you didn't pass her any secrets did you?"

"Well" Splendor began slowly. "She said she knew the Russkies were trying to disrupt our electronic networks. She thought that was horrible and we should be doing something about it.

"She would tell me things she had learned from her uncle back in Russia. Vanya was his name. Uncle Vanya. He would tell her what he thought the Russkies were up to. And then she would ask me what we were doing to counter what they were doing. She wanted to make sure we were acting on the information she was giving us."

"Where did you spend your time with her? Pap asked.

"Well, after I met her at the Ritz Carlton bar, she took me to her apartment. On future dates, we generally had dinner in some out-of-the-way restaurant in D.C. and then went back to her apartment."

"You never took her to your place?"

"Are you kidding? I live with three other legislators – one's a Senator, the other two are in the House, like me. We live in a cramped apartment near the Capitol. It feels like a college dormitory."

Splendor paused, then continued. "One of our roommates – he's actually the party's Majority Leader in the Senate – is a Goddamn slob. Leaves his clothes all over the place. Never makes his bed. Tubes of toothpaste and hair gel everywhere. How could I take a lady like Tanya to a dump like that?"

"Yeah, I can see that" said Pap sympathetically. "So where was Tanya's apartment?"

"It's in a fairly new building in the northern part of Arlington, overlooking the Potomac River. The Winter Palace it's called. I understand it was built by a Russian oligarch. He built it in the style of the old Czarist Winter Palace in Saint Petersburg."

"So you had sex with a Russian agent in an apartment building built by a Russian oligarch. Jesus."

While Pap was a lawyer, not a spy, he knew before he asked the next question what the answer would be.

"I assume the apartment was bugged? Picked up everything you and Tanya said every time you were there?"

"I'm afraid so. But even worse, I think the apartment also had a video recording system installed. I'm sure they videotaped everything we did."

"Jesus" said Pap. "And you're a member of the House Select Committee on Intelligence? No wonder the Russkies are eating our lunch."

Splendor looked sheepish but said nothing. He knew he had been foolish. But damn, those romps in the hay with Tanya had been sensational, he'd never had it so good. He didn't think he should tell that to this lawyer.

"Have you seen the videos?" asked Pap.

"No. Thank goodness the CIA doesn't seem to have copies. At least not yet, but I'm sure they'll get them soon. What they have at the moment are recordings of the audio recordings, which they picked up from listening in on the Russkies."

"So the Russkies were recording you and the CIA was recording the Russkies listening to the recordings?"

"You got it" Earmacher broke in. "This is Espionage one-o-one. The Russkies were recording everything said and done in the honey trap. And we recorded them listening to and watching the recordings. It doesn't get more simple than that.

"Now, let me tell you what we know about Tanya" Earmacher continued. "Her real name is Olga Vogelinski. She's a graduate of the Andropov Institute – the place where the Russians train their spies. Her controller is Vladimir Gorelikov, a member of the SVR – that's the new name the Russkies gave to the old KGB. Gorelikov works right here in the Russian embassy as a so-called cultural attache."

"Jesus" said Pap. "This is getting worse by the minute. But I still don't see what I can do for you. It appears that your problem goes far beyond the legal realm."

"Before we talk about that" said Earmacher as he stood up, "I'll have Kate bring us some coffee. We need you to be wide awake while we discuss what we wanna do."

Pap was not only wide awake, he was on the edge of his seat. But he kept wondering what all this spy stuff had to do with him, he was a lawyer.

Nevertheless, thinking about the beautiful Kate Kisme walking in with a tray of coffee and smiling discretely at him as she placed a cup in his hands brought a tingle of excitement to his loins. This would be a welcome intermission.

Chapter 6

COUNTER ESPIONAGE

After Kate had served them coffee, Earmacher resumed the discussion.

"Patrick, I'm sure you're wondering why we're bringing you into all this. But I think you can help us.

"Right now this story is, as I said earlier, top secret. It's buried in preliminary intelligence reports. But it won't stay buried for long. You know how Washington works. Someone will leak this to the press. And then the media will run with the story for weeks. And because Biggs is on the Intelligence Committee, the media will have a field day at his expense.

"Of course it's not just Biggs who will get caught up in this. Scores of other prominent people will be dragged in. Politicians, defense contractors, even U.N. diplomats. And we know we can't do anything to stop it.

"So, when the story breaks, we need to be ready to pounce. And for that we need you. We need you to be prepared to file a lawsuit. For libel and defamation. In the lawsuit, and in a press conference or two, you can deny that Biggs passed on anything resembling a state secret to Tanya Zhivago. And you can say that the allegation that he did so is false and defamatory.

"We figure that once you've sued a couple of the big media companies, everyone will become more careful about what they report. For example, maybe they'll start publishing Biggs' denials whenever they mention the accusations against him. Or maybe they'll focus on other victims rather than Biggs."

As a slight frown crossed Pap's face, Earmacher added: "I've told Biggs this is probably the most we can hope to accomplish. It's not a great solution, but it's the only solution I can see."

"I think that would simply make matters worse" said Pap. "You don't want Congressman Splendor publicly denying the charge when he's also suing for defamation. He'll eventually have to answer for his denial in court – at a point when everything in the CIA report will have come out. A false denial will destroy his credibility."

"But politicians always deny allegations against them" said Earmacher. "We never admit that an allegation's true, that would look terrible."

Pap was silent. This whole plan seemed off. It was like locking the barn door after the horse was gone. They needed a different strategy for this mess. They couldn't allow the story to emerge via a leak, they had to do something before the report was leaked.

"Here's what I think" he began slowly. "First of all, a defamation lawsuit would put Congressman Splendor at great risk, both politically and legally. The political risk is obvious. But the legal risk is worse - you would be setting him up for a perjury charge.

"But more important, your plan is purely defensive. The report will come out first and then you will be on defense the entire time. You won't be able to control anything once the report is leaked. We need to get the story out first, in our own way. We need to take the offense, that's our only hope."

"Take the offense? Precisely how?" asked Earmacher. "We can't just lob some grenades into the Men's Room at the Kremlin, as Goldwater used to say. Actually, I always thought that was a good idea.

"On the other hand" Earmacher continued, "I suppose we could get Tanya, or Olga or whatever her real name is, thrown out of the country. But what would that accomplish? I'm afraid I don't see any offensive strategy here."

"I'm talking legal strategy" said Pap. "You suggested a lawsuit after the news gets out. I'm saying just the opposite: we sue them before the news is out. Before the story breaks. The first person out with a story controls the narrative."

"You want Congressman Splendor to start a lawsuit?" said Earmacher incredulously. "That's crazy, he'd be putting himself directly in the media's cross hairs. That would just make everything worse. Patrick, you're a lawyer, lawyers are supposed to make everything better, not worse."

"But it *will* make everything better" said Pap. Addressing Congressman Splendor, he asked: "Didn't you say that Tanya entrapped dozens of men in this scheme?"

"Yeah, maybe twenty or thirty, although I don't think the CIA has a final number yet."

"Twenty or thirty is more than enough" said Pap. "With that many victims, we can file a class action. As defendants we can name Olga Vogelinski as well as the Russian government. Maybe even the Russian intelligence service – what did you say it was called now?"

"SVR" said Earmacher.

"Right. We can sue Olga Vogelinski, the Russian government and the SVR. We can file the case as a class action on behalf of all the men who were entrapped. They don't have class actions in Russia, I'm sure Putin would never allow 'em. So, they won't know what hit 'em."

"But even in a class action you need a plaintiff, don't you?" asked Earmacher. "Surely you're not suggesting that Congressman Splendor be your plaintiff?"

"Of course you need someone to be the lead plaintiff. The one who's name is in the complaint. But it doesn't have to be Congressman Splendor. It could be any one of the other guys who were entrapped. We just need to pick out one of them as our guy. Now, wouldn't that CIA report you keep talking about have all the names? If you can let me have a copy, I'll bet we can identify someone we could use as our plaintiff."

"It's classified" said Earmacher. "We can't just hand over classified information. Like Biggs and all the other guys who fell for the honey trap did."

"Ernie, for God's sake" said Splendor.

Ignoring this exchange, Pap asked Earmacher: "Why can't I get the report? Are you afraid I'll pass it on to the Russkies or something?

I wouldn't do that. Even if they caught me in a honey trap, which they won't because I don't do honey traps. The report will be safe with me."

"I still gotta get approval before I hand you that report. It's classified, Patrick, for God's sake."

"Okay" said Pap. "Get an approval. But look, I've got a scenario figured out. You get me the CIA report. My firm will go through it and identify a likely plaintiff. Someone to be our patsy. You or your Committee, or someone in the Government, puts pressure on him to cooperate with us. He signs a complaint on behalf of himself and John Does one through thirty. Then we file the lawsuit."

"You mean I'm just a John Doe?" asked Splendor. "My name doesn't have to be in the complaint?"

"Exactly" said Pap. "And the next thing we do is we call a press conference and announce the filing of the lawsuit. Against the SVR and the Russian government. Our firm is good at press conferences, we do them for all the cases we file.

"And then" Pap said excitedly, "Bingo! The lawsuit will be the news! And the news is not Congressman Splendor but rather the Russians' odious honey trap. Honey trap means sex! The public loves to read about sex! So now that will be the story. You see, now we are not on defense. We are on offense. You always want to be on offense. Especially against the Russkies."

"What's the basis for the lawsuit?" asked Earmacher. "I went to law school, you know. What's the claim, the 'cause of action' as they call it?"

"There are probably lots of claims we can come up with. Most likely blackmail. Maybe extortion. Entrapment. I'll get my brother and Melissa to look into it – that's Melissa Muffett, our smartest associate, we call her Little Miss Muffett; she could find a way to sue a ham sandwich."

Congressman Splendor was still not looking particularly splendid. "You sure this is a good idea?" he asked as he looked from Pap to Earmacher.

"Look" said Pap. "You're already in a huge mess. Trapped in the honey pot, so to speak. If you just sit and wait, news of your involvement is going to come out for sure, likely in the very first report of the scandal. At that point you're toast, if you don't mind my saying so. Its no longer Splendor in the grass. Now its Splendor in the toaster.

"Now, on the other hand, if we take the offense and sue, we have a chance of controlling events. For starters, we might be able to protect the names of you and the other John Does. But even if all the names eventually come out, the impact won't be nearly as bad as it would be if it comes out now, via a leak."

"Okay, I think that might actually be a good plan" said Earmacher. "It will certainly surprise the hell out of the Russkies, they're not accustomed to solving their disputes in court. But I can't authorize you to file a lawsuit of this nature. We'll need to get lots of approvals."

"Won't that just increase the possibility of a leak?" asked Pap. "Based on what I know about Washington, the more people who know about this, the more chance there will be of a leak."

"I think we can control that" said Earmacher. "Remember, this is an intelligence operation where everything is secret . . . ."

"Yeah, but isn't that why I'm here in the first place?" protested Pap. "You're worried you can't contain this thing. That there will be a leak."

"Well, leak or not, I can't just go off on my own and tell you to file a lawsuit against Russia. Jeepers, Patrick, surely you can see that."

"Okay, so who do you need to get approvals from."

"Well, the first approval I need is from Big Apple."

"Who's Big Apple?"

"Alfred E. Appleby. He's a Congressman from New York City, upper west side. He's a rather large guy, so everyone calls him the Big Apple."

"Why does he have to be involved?"

"He's the majority leader on the House Intelligence Committee. He's a Dem like Biggs, so I'm sure he'll want to do whatever he can to protect Biggs from a scandal.

"I'll also have to run this by the State Department. I can't just go off and sue the Russian government without telling the State Department."

"You think they'll pose a problem?" asked Pap. "Aren't they one of the worst bureaucracies in D.C.?"

"It's only the Department's Russia Desk I have to speak with, it'll be their call. But I know the guy who heads that desk. Roy Rogerstrumm. They call him Mister Rogers."

"Why's he called Mister Rogers?"

"He's a very nice, quiet guy, sort of a milk-toast. Wants to make everyone happy, never picks a fight with anyone."

"Jesus" said Pap. "Why is a guy like that in charge of the State Department's Russia Desk? That's crazy."

"It's part of the President's effort to reset relations with Russia. Remember the famous Reset button? Well, the President wants someone on the Russia desk who will make nice with the Russkies. There's no one better suited to make nice with the Russkies than Mister Rogers.

"Anyway, I think I can get both Big Apple and Mister Rogers to approve this thing. But it may take a few days. And when I speak with Big Apple, I'll ask him about getting you a copy of the CIA report."

"You need to get us the tapes as well" said Pap. "Both the audiotapes and the videotapes."

"Why do you need them?" asked Splendor. "Particularly the videotapes? They're probably a bit pornographic. Tanya was very, shall we say, sexually creative. I hate to think of those tapes floating around lawyer's offices in New York City."

"We can't represent you effectively unless we know all the facts" Pap replied in his most lawyer-like voice. "The good facts and the bad facts, that's our job. Besides, I've never had an opportunity to see a female Russian agent in action."

Earmacher didn't mind if Pap got hold of the videotapes. In fact, he wanted to watch them himself.

"Let's get back to the authorizations" he said. "Once I get authorization to show you the report, I'll have to send it down to New York via diplomatic pouch. And you'll have to sign a document acknowledging that you have possession of classified information."

"That's no problem, I'm happy to sign . . . ."

"And that you acknowledge that any disclosure of classified information – deliberate or inadvertent – will subject you to prosecution under the National Security Laws. For which you could face ten years to life in prison."

"I've always wanted to sign something like that" said Pap. "So just get it down to me as soon as possible. Locating the right plaintiff will be the hardest part of our work and we need to get started on that right away."

Earmacher stood and began walking toward the door. "Patrick, I appreciate your coming down here today. I hope your plan works out as you think it will."

"Congressman Earmacher" said Pap, "I can assure you that all the attorneys at my firm will be working hard on this case. And like we say on our website, 'Peters and Peters blows into a case like a hurricane.'"

"Well, I just hope your hurricane blows away the Russkies and not us."

"Kate" shouted Earmacher as they left his office. "Could you show Mister Peters to the elevator?"

"Maybe she could ride down to the lobby with me" asked Pap. "I don't wanna get lost."

Chapter 7

DR. DOOLITTLE

On Thursday morning, while Pap was on his way to D.C., Melissa walked into Pup's office to talk about their upcoming meeting.

"Doctor Doolittle is coming in at nine-thirty" she said. "I thought we should talk about how we're going to approach this thing. We've never dealt with an expert who talks to animals before."

"Good idea" said Pup. "But first, I need to ask you to do something with these."

And with that Pup opened the top drawer of his desk and pulled out a pair of black lace panties.

"Pup, what on earth are you doing with those?" Melissa said. "I've never known you to be a skirt chaser."

"I'm not."

"Then why do you have a pair of black lace panties in your desk? They didn't just get there on their own."

"I think Pap put them there."

"Why would Pap have a pair of black lace panties in the office?"

"I think he probably found them in the Worry Room. You know he likes to take afternoon naps there."

"But doesn't he nap by himself? Surely he wouldn't take a nap with one of the secretaries. Especially Miss Pesky, he hates her."

"You're right. I think he just found them there. And I think they belong to Candy."

Melissa was starting to get suspicious. "Why do you think they belong to Candy? And how do you know she wears black lace panties?"

Pup was still holding the panties in his left hand. This discussion wasn't going well.

"Look" he said. "We know Chip and Candy are still hooking up in the Worry Room. In the evening, after everyone's gone home."

"But that would violate the firm's Fornication Policy" said Melissa. "You and Pap made that clear in the memo you sent around. No more fornicating in the Worry Room. The Worry Room's for worrying, not fornicating. That's what you said in the memo."

"Well, that may be our policy but that's where Chip and Candy seem determined to do their . . . ah . . . fornicating. And Candy probably got careless and left them there. And Pap found them."

"So why wouldn't Pap just give them back to Candy?"

"Melissa, you're not looking at this from the partners' standpoint. Pap can't just walk down the hall with a pair of black lace panties in his hands and go into Candy's office with them. What would everyone think?"

"Everyone would think that Chip suddenly had some competition. It would be exciting to see how it played out."

"I don't think Pap wants to compete with Chip for Candy's affection. He just wants to get her panties back to her. Without having to deliver them himself."

"So how else are you guys going to get them back to her?"

"I think that's why Pap put them in my desk. He wants me to figure out how to get them back to Candy so that he's not involved."

"Look, Pup, we need to talk abut our meeting with Doctor Doolittle, he'll be here any minute."

"Not until we figure out how to get these panties back to Candy."

Pup continued standing there holding up the panties. "I was hoping you could help me. Take them and give them to Candy. Tell her one of the partners found them in the Worry Room."

"Pup, now you want me to walk out of your office holding a pair of black lace panties? For heaven's sake, what would people think?"

"Okay, Melissa, you don't have to openly carry them around. All you need to do is put them in one of our interoffice envelopes. Here, I'll even give you one. Write Candy's name as the recipient and then, when you see she's away from her office, just drop it off on her desk. That'll be the end of it."

"All right" said Melissa reluctantly. "But I don't see why you couldn't have just done that yourself."

"I can't address the envelope to Candy, she'd recognize the handwriting. And I can't give it to Miss Dropo to address, she'd see that it contained panties. And it would suddenly be all over the office that I was sending panties to Candy. Jeepers, Melissa, can't you see we need you to do this? It's the only way."

"Well, okay. Now can we talk about Doctor . . . ."

At that moment Pup's secretary Eva Dropo buzzed him. "Doctor Doolittle is here to see you and Miss Muffett. Shall I send him in?"

* * * *

After introducing himself and Melissa, Pup ushered the three of them into the firm's conference room. Once they had helped themselves to coffee, Pup began the interview.

"Doctor Doolittle, I must confess we don't really know much about you. Melissa saw your name in an article about that case out in California. The one involving a monkey who claimed copyright ownership of a selfie he took. Since . . . ."

"We shoulda' won that case" interrupted Doolittle. "Nabuto – that's the name of the monkey – he's the one that took the selfie. Actually, it was a series of selfies he took with a camera some wildlife photographer had left on the ground. The photographer had no right to publish the pictures, let alone take out a copyright on them. Nabuto took the pictures, he should own the copyright."

"Okay, you could be right" said Pup diplomatically. "But that's not what we want to talk with you about. We're looking at a case involving chimpanzees. You see . . . ."

"Chimpanzees are right up my alley. I can certainly help you on that."

Pup wished Doolittle would stop interrupting. This guy could be difficult to control; sort of like Mona Lott as an expert witness, he said to himself with a feeling of despair.

"Look" he said, "before we talk about the case my brother wants to bring, we need . . . ."

"Your brother? Is he a lawyer too?"

"Yes. My brother is Patrick Peters. He's a lawyer, we're partners. That's why the firm's called Peters and Peters. He thinks up crazy cases and then tells Melissa and me to figure out how to win them.

"So now you know about us. But we don't know much about you. So please tell us about your background and how you came to be a doctor who talks to animals."

Doolittle liked nothing better than to talk about himself. And his credentials. He talked about himself every chance he got, even when there was nobody else around.

"Okay, here goes" he began. "I grew up on a farm in Vermont. Dogs, horses, cows, pigs, goats, chickens – the whole nine yards. I meant that – the whole nine yards – literally. We had nine separate yards. One for cows, one for horses, one for goats, et cetera. Nine in all. I think that's where the saying originated.

"Anyway, I loved all the animals. Talked to 'em all the time. Wanted to make sure they were happy and getting enough to eat.

"After college, I got my Masters in Anthropology. Then a PhD in Primatology. My thesis was based on my experience talking with the animals on our farm. It was called 'Communicating With Farm Animals: It's No Manure.' Here, I've got a copy of it for you.

"After getting my PhD . . . ."

"Doctor Doolittle" said Melissa as she looked at the first page of the thesis. "This says it was written by someone named Klint Kwak. Who's he?"

"Oh, that's me. I only started using the Doolittle name when I started up my practice as an animal communicator. All my materials make it clear I'm Klint Kwak, doing business as Doctor Doolittle. Most people ignore my real name and just call me Doctor Doolittle. And that's fine with me, that way everyone knows right off what I do."

Pup was frowning. He couldn't quite put his finger on it, but something was off with this guy. He decided to just listen and let Melissa steer the interview.

"So tell us about your practice" she said. "What exactly do you do? Who are your clients? That kind of thing."

"I like to think of the animals as my clients. I've had over five thousand animal clients."

Pup couldn't restrain himself. "So all those animals called you up and hired you? And then paid your bill after the engagement was over? Did they pay you in cash or by check?"

"Ha!" said Kwak/Doolittle. "That's good. Of course, the animals are only my clients figuratively speaking. It's their owners who hire me and pay the bills. But only after the animals have looked at the bills and approved them.

"Now, I get hired for a wide range of things. For example, and this is actually a big part of my business: couples who are getting divorced always argue about who gets the dog. Each spouse claims the dog is really theirs and wants to be with them. The judges in divorce court have figured out the fairest way to resolve the dispute is to ask the dog. Let's say the dog's name's Fido. They hire me to talk with Fido and find out which spouse he wants to go with."

"You're kidding" said Pup.

"Why would I kid about that? It's my profession. I talk with Fido and then tell the judge what Fido wants to do. The winning spouse is ecstatic. The losing spouse is disappointed, but what can they do? It's Fido's decision."

"Who else hires you?" asked Melissa.

"Horse owners. Particularly owners of race horses. As you probably know, race horses are hard-wired. And temperamental. The owner is always trying to keep the horse happy and eager to compete. And frequently they can't figure out why the horse runs so well in trial heats but fades in a real race when money is on the line."

"So I suppose you talk with the horse and ask it why it doesn't do better in real races?" Pup's question dripped with sarcasm.

"You're a fast learner" said Kwak/Doolittle. "That's exactly what I do. Sometimes the horse tells me he's not getting enough to eat. Or his diet is out of whack – maybe too much hay, not enough oats. Sometimes they tell me the jockey is doing it wrong, maybe pushing too hard out of the gate so that it has nothing left down the stretch.

"And, sometimes they tell me the other horse was just faster. That happens a lot, I hate to have to convey that to the owner. They always think their horse is the next Seabiscuit."

"So what about chimps?" asked Melissa. "That's what the case we're thinking about involves."

"Oh, I can really help you there. I've been talking to chimps ever since I set up shop. You see, chimpanzees are very much human. Did you know that humans and chimpanzees share 99 per cent of the same genes?"

"No, I didn't . . . ."

"Chimpanzees are intelligent, autonomous beings. They have remarkably sophisticated social, cognitive and communicative capabilities. And just like humans, they have the capacity to suffer. They deserve to be treated with respect and dignity."

"My brother wants to bring a class action on behalf of chimps" explained Pup. "Not sure who, I mean which chimps, should be in the class. But I believe he's thinking all the chimps in the Bronx Zoo and perhaps other zoos in the state."

"You need to include all the chimps in the country. They don't deserve to be kept in cages. And by the way the Bronx Zoo looks like a country club compared to some of the zoos in the south and midwest. You need to get 'em all moved to Florida."

"Legally" said Pup, "if we sue under New York law we can only represent chimps residing in New York State. Besides, I don't think we'd be able to contact all the chimps in the country, they probably wouldn't respond to our phone calls and emails."

"Okay" said Kwak/Doolittle. "First you guys free all the chimps in New York State. Then someone else can help with the out-of-state ones."

"So what exactly could you do for us in such a case?" asked Melissa.

"Well, I'd do what I always do. Go and introduce myself to the chimps and talk with 'em. Find out if they're happy or unhappy. See if they're allowed to visit with their friends. See if they have sexual companionship. You know, that's especially important for chimps."

"It's the same for lawyers" said Melissa, "especially the ones around here."

"Right. As I said, ninety-nine per cent of their genes are the same as yours. Also, I might ask whether it bothers them to have humans watching them all the time. I bet none of us would want to be in a cage with a bunch of chimpanzees coming by and watching everything we do."

"I never thought about that" said Pup.

"And now here's the big one" said Kwak/Doolittle. "I'd ask if they wouldn't prefer to retire and move away to a nice big nature preserve in Florida. Where it's always sunny and warm. And where they're free to roam far and wide all day; or, if they prefer, just hang out with their friends. And also a place where they can eat all they want, anytime they want.

"I'm sure the overwhelming majority will want to leave. A handful might prefer to stay put, maybe they're too lazy to forage for their own food. But that's their decision. I always want to do what my clients feel is best for them. But the vast majority will want to leave, I'm sure of that. In fact, you can take that to the bank."

"That's the object of all the cases we do" said Melissa. "Getting stuff to take to the bank."

"So, you'll be willing to testify in court about all this?" asked Pup. "Testify under oath, in front of a judge who might be a bit dubious about this stuff?"

"Of course. I testify all the time. I'm sure I can convince your judge to let 'em go to Florida. By the way, who's the judge in your case?"

"We're getting a little ahead of ourselves" said Pup. "We're only in the early stages of this. We haven't decided whether we will file a lawsuit. Or where we will file it. Or who, if we do file it, will be members of the class."

For God's sake, Pup said to himself, I can't believe I'm even having this conversation.

"Well, if you decide to file the lawsuit – and I sure hope you will – I'm your guy."

"I'm sure you are" said Pup as he stood up and gestured toward the door. "Thank you for coming in. We'll be in touch."

"Right" said Kwak/Doolittle. "By the way, I've authored several articles about chimpanzees, they're all published in scholarly journals. Should I send them along to you?"

Pup had no interest in reading scholarly articles about communicating with chimpanzees. "No, I don't think . . . ."

"Sure" interrupted Melissa. "Send them to me."

Melissa knew that, after hearing about this interview, Pap would insist on going forward with the lawsuit. With Kwak/Doolittle as an expert witness. She might as well start getting familiar with the literature about communicating with chimpanzees, Pap and Pup certainly weren't going to do that.

Chapter 8

THE PLAYMATE

Later that morning, as Pap was meeting with Congressman Earmacher in Washington D.C., Lydia Lowlace walked into the offices of Peters and Peters at 555 Fifth Avenue and asked for Chip.

Chip had first met Lydia at a gentleman's club in midtown Manhattan where she was working as a lap dancer. The following morning, when the two of them woke up exhausted, Lydia told Chip about how she and the other dancers at the three clubs – Bottoms Up, Tops Down and Below the Belt – were being cheated by the club's owner. They were not being paid the minimum wage and their tips were being stolen.

That led to a visit to the office at 555 Fifth Avenue where Lydia quickly became a client of Peters and Peters. In a class action widely publicized in the New York City tabloids and on the local TV stations, the firm succeeded in forging a settlement on behalf of a class of 250 "dancers" who worked at clubs owned by a variety of corporate defendants. The case made Lydia an instant celebrity and brought fame, but only a modest fee, to Peters and Peters.

When the receptionist called Chip to inform him that Lydia had arrived, Melissa and Brandon - as well as Candy, the paralegal who had also worked on the case - rushed into the reception area to greet her. Lydia was their most famous client. Actually, she was their only famous client.

As the three of them shook Lydia's hand and gushed their hellos, Chip strode into the reception area, hugged Lydia and kissed her on both cheeks.

"Chip" Lydia said, "I'm thrilled you'se invited me to lunch. It's been two whole weeks since I seen you."

Candy looked at Chip and scowled. Chip told her he had stopped seeing Lydia after the case was over.

"I saw your spread in *Playboy*" said Brandon. "You looked sensational."

"*Playboy*?" said Melissa. "I didn't know you were in *Playboy*."

"Yes siree" said Lydia. "Playmate of the Month. November I think it wuz. But the magazine came out in October so maybe I wuz the October playmate. It wuz one of them Fall months, they had all them red and yellow leaves fallin' on me in the photos."

"You looked great with red and yellow leaves all over you" said Brandon. "But you looked even better without the leaves."

"So what have you been up to since the *Playboy* spread?" asked Melissa. "Between the lawsuit and *Playboy*, you must really be famous now."

"Oh, yes, I's sort of a celerybrety now. I get marriage proposals from guys I's never met. All the time. Over eighty so far, I can't keep track of 'em."

"What about fan mail? I'll bet you get lots of it" said Brandon.

"Well, to tell you the honest to goodness truth, some of it ain't so nice. Guys send me pictures of themselves. Without their clothes on. Same with emails, they attach photos of themselves with their privates exposed. It's creepy. 'Cept for Chip, most guys don't look so hot with their clothes off."

Candy shot Chip a withering look.

"Have you met any really famous men?" asked Melissa.

"Well, I met that big shot money guy. Harvey Jepstein. See, he came to the party at *Playboy* when I was Playmate of the Month. Either October or November, one of them Fall months."

"Did he make a pass at you?" asked Melissa.

"Well, I do'no if it wuz a pass or not. He invited me to join him and his friends for a weekend on some island. In the Bahamas I think he says. Says he owns it. Can someone own an island?"

"Someone has to own it" said Brandon. "And if an individual is wealthy enough he can own the whole island. And I think Harvey Jepstein is wealthy enough to own an island. Do you think you'll go?"

"Well, I do'no. I never been to the Bahamas before. Don't they have snakes and stuff down there? And maybe even alligators? Or crocodiles? I can't never see the difference, ain't they really the same?"

"I wouldn't go" advised Chip. "That guy Jepstein has girls all over the place. You wouldn't mean anything to him. And you'd have to give him a message all the time, I hear he gets them four or five times a day."

"I don't wanna give nobody no message five times a day" said Lydia. "Especially if they's snakes all around."

"So maybe" said Melissa "being famous isn't all it's cracked up to be."

"Yeah, that's watt I come here to talk with Chip about."

"To talk about with Chip" said Candy to herself, you dumb slut.

"I think I been taken a'vantage of" Lydia continued. "And I think I should maybe do somethin' 'bout it. I need Chip to help me figure this here thing out."

"That's exactly what we're gonna do" said Chip as he took Lydia's arm and led her toward the door. "We're having lunch at Twenty One. I'll see you all later this afternoon."

But they did not see Chip later that afternoon. By five o'clock Candy realized Chip would not be back that afternoon. "The dirty bastard" she said to herself. "He's never taken me to Twenty One."

* * * *

"I ain't never been to this place before" said Lydia as they were seated in the famous 21 Club dining room. "Looks like lots of important folks is here. Is it famous?"

"Sure is" said Chip. It's been famous since Prohibition Days, when it was a speakeasy."

"What's a speakeasy? And watt wuz they prohibitin'?"

"Prohibition started in about 1920" said Chip. He was glad he had gone to Dartmouth, he might never have known that. "The

Constitution was amended to prohibit the sale of liquor. Prohibition lasted until the early 1930's. Speakeasies were places where you could get liquor despite the law. This was one of the most famous ones."

"Well ain't that somethin'. I never heard 'bout that. Do you think they had this pro-bition thing back in McKeesport PA, my home town?"

"It was everywhere. Although some cities and states enforced it more than others."

"Well, they's probably enforced it in McKeesport. We's all very law abidin' in McKeesport. But I remember one time I heard my grandfolks talkin' 'bout havin' some sort of still in their back yard they didn't want nobody to see. That woulda' been okay, wouldn't it?"

"Probably not" said Chip. "Your grandfather was probably bootlegging it across the state and maybe even over into Ohio."

"You mean my granddaddy was a crook?"

"Look, everyone was breaking the Prohibition laws. They were very unpopular, your granddaddy would have been doing something hundreds of others in McKeesport were doing. But look, let's talk about you. Tell me what you've been up to lately."

"Well, when I last seen you I told you 'bout my new modelin' career. Modelin' underwear – watt's that fancy name for women's underwear?"

"Lingerie."

"Yep, that's it. I model longjuree for that brand called Barely Enough. They put pictures of me wearin' their longjuree in a catalog. Sometimes even in newspapers.

"But here's the thing, Chip. Last week I gits a call from some guy. Says his name's Victor. Victor Little. He's got a new line of . . . what's it called?"

"Lingerie."

"Yep, longjuree. Calls it 'Victor's Little Secret' longjuree. Wants me to model stuff for him. He says they got a hot new catalog comin' out. None of that plus-size or full-bodied stuff. Who wants to see fat ladies in their underwear anyway? But, says Mr. Victor, this here new catalog will have real sexy longjuree for real sexy ladies. That's watt guys all wanna see. Do you think I should model for him too?"

"Depends on your contract with Barely Enough. Do they have exclusive rights to you?"

"How would I knows? You'se the lawyer, not me."

"You're right Lydia. Send me the contract and I'll take a look at it."

"Why do I needs to send it to you? I can give it to you when we's at my apartment after lunch."

"That's a good idea."

After they had ordered, Lydia remembered all the things she needed to ask Chip. "Listen, Chip, here's where I really needs your help.

"You know I don't work at them three clubs no more. Ever since I wuz in *Playboy* and then started modelin' underwear. But last week I wuz havin' lunch with Honey Combe – you remember her, she worked with me at them there clubs.

"Well, Chip, you can't imagine what she shows me. She had some newspaper ads for other clubs. Not the ones I used to work at, but other ones, none of 'em classy like Tops Down and Bottoms Up. And these clubs - which I ain't even heard of before – is usin' my pi-ture in their ads. My pi-ture from *Playboy*. And I don't even work for 'em."

"They can't do that. Not unless they pay you to use your picture."

"They ain't paid me a cent. Now here's them there ads."

Lydia reached into her purse and pulled out three neatly folded newspaper ads and handed them to Chip. The first was for a club in Manhattan called "Sins of the City." The second was for a club in Long Island City called "Sugardaddy's Place." The third was for "Empty Laces" in Jersey City. All the ads featured Lydia displaying her marvelous charms, looking just as she looked in the *Playboy* spread.

"They can't do this" said Chip. "There are laws against this. Right of privacy laws. And right of publicity, now that you're a celebrity."

"I's definitely a celerybrety" said Lydia. "If you'se been a Playmate of the Month – don't matter watt month – you'se a celerybrety."

"We can sue them for this" said Chip excitedly. "Do you think they're using photos of any other girls without permission? We could make it a class action, just like the last one. If we can make it a class action, I'm sure I can get Pap to let us represent you again."

"Well, Chip, I do'no if they's usin' any other girls' pi-tures. I didn't even know they wuz usin' mine."

"We can do some investigating . . . ."

Lydia quickly interrupted. "But listen, Chip, that's not the worstest. You see, Honey also tells me her little brother sees me in some Internet game. Said I wuz some sort of aviator."

"Aviator? You mean they showed you flying a plane?"

"No, I ain't flyin' no plane. Accordin' to Honey, her little brother says I wuz workin' at a truck stop and just movin' all around talkin to them there truck drivers and such. Like a real person. An aviator."

"Oh, you mean avatar. That's what they call a character in a video game. A-V-A-T-A-R. Have you seen the game?"

"No, I ain't never played no video game."

"What was the name of the game? I can go and buy it."

"Honey said it wuz . . . . Here, I wrote it down, I thought you wuz gonna ask me that." Looking at a small piece of paper, she read: "'Grand Theft Trucker.' That's a funny name. Does people play that game a lot?"

"Kids not only play that game a lot, they buy the game a lot in order to play it! This is terrific!"

"It don't seem so terrific to me, see-en's how they's usin' me as an aviator. I don't want to be no aviator at a truck stop in some kids game."

"Lydia, this is wonderful! It has the makings of a big new lawsuit. Not just against those three clubs you mentioned, they probably don't have a lot of money behind them. But a lawsuit against the video game company, now we're talking turkey."

"Honey didn't say nothin' 'bout turkeys bein' in the video game."

Chip thought of trying to explain that "talking turkey" was just a figure of speech, but decided it wouldn't be worth the effort.

Instead, he said "Lydia, video games are big business. They sell these games to kids all over the country. They make millions from them. And now they are getting rich by using your likeness as an avatar without your permission. We can sue their pants off."

"Speaking of pants off" said Lydia. "Let's finish our lunch and git down to my apartment. We can git some pants off there."

It sure was wonderful being a lawyer thought Chip, as he called for the check.

Chapter 9

ALL HANDS ON DECK

After Pap had left Congressman Earmacher's office on Thursday, he called Pup and asked him to call an "all hands on deck" meeting for Friday morning. Everyone needed to drop whatever they were doing and prepare to focus on an exciting new matter.

And so, at ten on Friday morning, all the lawyers at Peters and Peters filed into Pap's office. Pup and Melissa were the first to arrive. Melissa, known behind her back as Little Miss Muffet, was the smartest and hardest-working lawyer in the firm; as usual, she had been at her desk since 8:00, she was always the first person in the office.

Brandon Muffinsky came in next; he had come with Pap from Rogers and Autry when Pap started up Peters and Peters. The last to arrive was Chip. He rushed into the room at three minutes past ten with wet hair and an anxious look on his face; he looked as if he had just gotten out of the shower.

"Looks like you and Francoise had a late night" said Pap cheerfully.

"All of our nights are late" said Chip. "Sometimes I can't get out of here until ten or so."

"Who's Francoise?" asked Melissa.

"Chip's latest" said Pap. "Maybe he'll bring her in and introduce her to all of us."

"But what about Candy?" Melissa asked as she shot a disdainful look at Chip.

"Oh, I think Candy's still in the picture" said Pap. "That's why Chip's always here until ten at night."

"He's here with Candy until ten and then home with Francoise?" Melissa was having hard time figuring this thing out. "And what about Lydia? She came in on Wednesday and Chip took her out to lunch; we never saw him the rest of the day."

"Well" said Pap, "Chip has a 'top ten' list. Sort of like a weekly hit parade. The same ten stay on the list, but the order changes from week to week."

"I've never dated ten girls at the same time" protested Chip. "Maybe three or four but never ten."

"The final four" said Brandon. "He has a final four. What we want to know is who is going to come out on top this week?"

Pup was getting irritated. Meetings with Pap always got sidetracked with endless banter. "Pap, you asked for an 'all hands on deck' meeting. You said it was urgent. So why don't we get down to business. For once."

Pap needed to keep Pup happy. He knew that, without Pup's legal skills, the new firm wouldn't work out. "Okay" he said, "we'll get down to business."

Pap proceeded to relate the details of his meeting with Earmacher and Splendor, the Russians' honey trap, and Earmacher's concern that the matter would soon be leaked to the press. He told them of Earmacher's reason for wanting to get the firm involved, the preparation of a libel suit for after the story broke.

Pap then explained how he had convinced the Congressmen that an after-the-fact libel suit was a losing strategy. And then he explained the strategy he had sold to them: a class action lawsuit against the Russkies. All the Russkies – Tanya, her controller Gorelikov, the SVR, maybe even the Russian Government itself.

"Pap, this is insane" said Pup. "Why are we getting involved in this spy stuff? You want to take on the Russians, you could join the CIA. Or get a job in the Pentagon. We're a law firm, this isn't a matter for us."

Pap had known that Pup wouldn't be happy about this. Pup was a perpetual pessimist. He had not really believed in any of the cases they had filed. And even though he had played a significant role in each of them, he worried from the day Pap thought up the case until the day it ended. Which was why Pap had set up the Worry Room.

"Pup" Pap began calmly. "We're not gonna be spies. We're just gonna do what we always do: sue people! In a class action! It's just that this time the defendant is a country, not a company."

"But that's the problem" said Pup. "We probably can't sue Russia. I'm pretty sure a foreign country can't be sued, it would have sovereign immunity."

"To hell with sovereign immunity. We'll have Melissa find a way to get around it. I'll bet she can find an exception that fits our case. Like crimes against humanity. I think you can always sue a foreign government for crimes against humanity."

"I don't think spying is a crime against humanity" said Pup. "Every country engages in it all the time."

"Pup, it's not just the spying part. It's the honey trap part. And making audio and visual recordings of U.S. citizens exercising their Constitutional right to . . . ah . . . their right to freedom of association. We're a free country. People should have the right to freely associate with members of the opposite sex, even engage in sexual activities with them, without someone taping their every sound and grunt. I'm sure interference with that right is a crime against humanity."

"I don't . . . ."

"Besides, we've got other defendants even if we can't sue the Russian government. We've got Tanya, or Olga, or whatever her real name is. And her controller, that Gorelikov guy. And also the SVR, we can sue them too."

"Jeepers, Pap," Pup was really worried now. "The SVR is really just the KGB in new clothes. I've read a lot about them. They may have a new name but they're still just as ruthless as the old KGB. You don't want to be on the wrong side of the KGB."

"Well, Pup, when the case is over I can ask Earmacher to have the FBI put you into its Witness Protection program. In fact, I'm sure the CIA has a similar program. For spies who defect and whose lives are in danger. They can give you and Priscilla new identities. Maybe move you to North Dakota. Some place where the KGB will never find you."

"What if they find us before the case is over? We're not hard to find."

Melissa hated it when Pap and Pup got into one of their ridiculous arguments, so she decided to break in. "I think what Pup's saying is that it's hard to see this case going anywhere. The KGB, call it the SVR if you like, is never going to hire a law firm to defend the case. They'll just ignore the lawsuit and make a statement to the press about how Americans file lawsuits at the drop of a hat."

"Right" said Pup. "And we will have spent all this time and energy – more than likely hundreds of hours – and we'll have nothing to show for it. When we could have been focusing on the other cases you've dreamed up, a few of them at least have a slight possibility of getting us some attorneys fees."

"You two aren't thinking straight about this" said Pap sternly. "First of all, the publicity alone will be great for us. Our name will be in all the newspapers and magazines and on all the cable news shows. What other class action firm has ever gone up against the Russian government? This is a huge opportunity.

"Moreover, don't worry about getting paid. We'll have a retainer agreement with the government. I'll make sure they agree to pay us at our normal billing rates, that's standard procedure when the government hires an outside firm. And by the way, I'm raising everyone's hourly rate as of today.

"Furthermore, we have a duty to protect our country's lawmakers. What happened to Congressman Splendor shouldn't happen to any red-blooded American male. We need to teach the Russkies a lesson. Believe me, they're going to be sorry that Peters and Peters is on the case."

Pup knew there was no use arguing. When Pap had made up his mind about something, no amount of reason or common sense could dissuade him. So they might as well go along. "Okay" he said, "where do we start?"

"That's more like it" said Pap. "I knew you'd listen to reason. Now, here's my current thinking.

"First we need Melissa to do some legal research. Figure out what claims we can allege and who we can allege them against. Pup, you can start drawing up the complaint as soon as Melissa lets you know what she's found.

"Next, we need Chip to figure out who the named plaintiff, the class representative, should be. I told Splendor it doesn't have to be him."

"How am I supposed to figure that out?" asked Chip. "Other than Splendor and that guy Byrne, we don't know who else was caught in the trap."

"Earmacher is getting us the CIA report. It should have all the names in it. Use the Internet and see if you can find a profile on each of them. Look for the biggest sucker in the group. Someone we can browbeat into being the plaintiff."

"Don't we need a smart, articulate guy who would be good in court?"

"Are you kidding?" said Pap. "A smart articulate guy will tell us to get lost. We need someone who's scared of his own shadow. Someone we can bully into helping us.

"Now Brandon, I want you to start drawing up some discovery requests. We can serve them with the complaint. Maybe we can get a court order for the discovery materials to be produced on an expedited basis."

"What do we want to ask for?" said Brandon with a helpless look on his face.

"Everything you can think of. Emails or texts or reports from Tanya to Gorelikov. The SVR's instructions to Gorelikov. Gorelikov's instructions to Tanya. Just use your imagination.

"Oh, and be sure to demand copies of all the audio and video tapes. Not just transcripts, the actual tapes."

"What are we gonna do with them when we get them?" asked Brandon. "I thought our job was to keep them from ever coming out."

"We'll watch 'em" said Pap. "I'd sure like to see what went on in Tanya's bedroom in the Winter Palace."

* * * *

The following Tuesday, the group convened again in Pap's office at ten o'clock. This time, Chip had been the first to arrive.

"Pap" he said as soon as everyone had assembled, "if you don't mind I have something to report. I think it will impact what everyone is doing."

"Sure, Chip, go right ahead." Pap had never seen Chip excited about any of their cases other than the one where Lydia fell into their lap. Actually, it was Chip's lap she fell, or perhaps jumped, into.

"So" Chip began, "there are about forty names mentioned in the report. A couple of Congressmen. Some mayors in the midwest . . . ."

"Midwest mayors?" said Pap incredulously. "Why would the KGB entrap midwestern mayors, for heavens's sake? And how could Tanya work New York, D.C. and the midwest?"

"Tanya wasn't their only Sparrow. They . . . ."

"What's a Sparrow?" asked Melissa.

"A female Russian agent trained to lay honey traps" said Chip. "They have a special school for them. I think it's called Sparrow School. Anyway, several Sparrows were involved in this operation."

"But the mayors?" asked Pap. "I don't understand why the Russkies would go after mayors."

"I think they're playing the long game" said Chip. "With guys like Splendor and Byrne, they're looking for immediate stuff. But it looks like they also target guys who have bright futures. They might be mayors today but tomorrow they could be congressmen.

"But look, here's where I'm going with this" Chip continued. "Most of these guys seem to be like Splendor. Smart, accomplished guys who made a mistake by putting their hand in the cookie jar. Well, actually that's not what they put into the cookie jar. Anyway, these kind of guys would never agree to help us in a lawsuit."

"So have you identified someone or not?" asked Pup. "That's what we're all waiting to hear."

"I have" said Chip. "As Pap said last week, a couple of the guys work at the UN. They used a New York Sparrow for this. Lara was the name she used with her victims. Sounds sort of Western. But her real name was Dominika Bloykin.

"One of the UN guys she entrapped is Raoul Castrato, from Cuba. At the moment he's president of the UN Human Rights Council. He's obviously a tough Commie, not our guy."

"A Cuban is president of the UN Human Rights Council?" asked Pap. "There weren't too many human rights in Cuba the last time I checked."

"Most of the countries on that Council are notorious human rights violators" said Melissa. "Iran, Venezuela, Zimbabwe, all the bad actors get put on the Human Rights Council, that's why it has no credibility."

"We're getting sidetracked again" said Pup. "I think we can all agree that Castrato is not a candidate to be our plaintiff. So what about the other UN guy?"

"Right" said Chip. "The other guy is Pierre Dupre. He's a member of the French delegation. He's a former professor of economics and focuses on economic and trade matters.

"But here's the poop on Pierre. Rumors about him have been circulating for a couple of years. Rumors about money. It seems he may have been misappropriating delegation funds to support his lavish life style. He has an apartment at UN Plaza. A weekend place in Sag Harbor. Drives a Jaguar. You get the picture. They're certain he's been using delegation funds for all this but they've never been able to come up with any definitive proof."

"How do you know all this" asked Pup. "I don't recall reading anything about him."

"Francoise told me."

"Remember" said Brandon, "Francoise is one of the gals in Chip's final four."

"Look, everyone" said Chip, ignoring Brandon's remark. "Francoise has worked in the French delegation to the UN for three years. She knows everything that's going on there. She's heard all the rumors about Pierre and she's told me everything she knows about him."

"I'm not sure I see how this helps us" said Brandon.

"Brandon, it's obvious" said Pap excitedly. "The French will sacrifice Pierre Dupre in a nanosecond. They'll be only too happy to help us out on this. Am I right Chip?"

"Absolutely."

"So" said Pap decisively, we get the CIA to have a quiet talk with the head of the French delegation. Maybe show them what they've got on Dupre. And then ask the French to lean on Dupre to work with us. If he refuses, he gets sent back home in disgrace."

"Yeah" said Chip. "Francoise said they would love to find a way to bring him to heel, he's a real embarrassment to the delegation."

"Chip, you are brilliant" said Pap. "I never knew jocks from Dartmouth could be so smart."

Chapter 10

FRENCH TOAST

The following Tuesday, Pap walked into the Rayburn Office Building where he was met in the lobby by Kate Kisme, once again looking gorgeous in her beautiful gray suit.

"Kate, nice to see you again" said Pap.

As they walked toward the elevator, Pap looked at Kate and said: "It seems like we could be having more of these meetings. Congressman Earmacher appears anxious to move our little matter forward."

"Yes" said Kate, "he told me we might be seeing more of you until this matter is over. Naturally, we'd be very pleased to see more of you."

Putting on his best Pap smile, Pap said as casually as he could: "I think our meeting today will be over by noon. I don't have to be back in New York until this evening. What about having lunch with me at the Hay Adams before I head for the airport?"

"Well, I'll first have to see if my uncle needs me."

"Your uncle? What's your uncle got to do with it?"

"Congressman Earmacher. He's my uncle. On my mother's side. Ernestine Earmacher was her maiden name. They're very close. They both still live in Fairfield, where they grew up – but of course Uncle Ernie now lives in the Southport section of Fairfield. His house overlooks Long Island Sound."

"I didn't know . . . ."

"When I came to DC to take this job, mom asked Uncle Ernie to keep an eye on me. She was worried about all the lawyers and lobbyists making passes at me. So Uncle Ernie agreed he would keep an eye on me."

Damn, thought Pap, what a bummer. He couldn't have Congressman Earmacher thinking that he was making a play for his niece. Of all the rotten luck.

"Kate" he said decisively, "I just remembered. I have a meeting with two of our associates this afternoon. Three o'clock I think it is. So I need to get to the airport as soon as our meeting's over. We'll have to have lunch some other time."

* * * *

Congressman Earmacher came out of his office as Pap and Kate walked into the outer office. "Patrick, great to see you again" he said as he extended his hand.

"Kate here was just telling me that she's your niece" said Pap. "You never mentioned that."

"You never asked. You were too busy looking her up and down."

Thinking quickly, Pap replied "I've always heard that all the prettiest women in D.C. work on Capitol Hill. I was just confirming that to be true."

"You should meet Kate's mom, my sister Ernestine. Next time I have a fund raiser in Fairfield County I'll let you know. Ernestine almost always attends them. I'm sure she'd like to meet you. I think you two are about the same age."

"Yeah, that would be great" grunted Pap sheepishly.

After they entered the interior office, Earmacher gestured toward a large man standing near the desk and said: "Patrick, I'd like you to meet Congressman Alfred Appleby from New York. The City, upper west side. We all call him 'Big Apple.' As I told you when we last met, Big Apple is the majority leader on the House Select Committee on Intelligence."

Earmacher ushered them into the soft corner chairs where they had sat during the meeting with Congressman Splendor. Earmacher got down to business immediately.

"I've told Big Apple what you've learned about that Frenchman, Pierre Dupre. And about your suggestion that he be recruited – so to speak – as the plaintiff for your lawsuit. We both like the idea. Al, why don't you take it from there."

Big Apple was a large gregarious guy. Always ready with a quip or a wisecrack. A consummate politician. But when it came to his duties as head of the House Select Committee on Intelligence, he was all business.

"Let's start with the New York Sparrow" he began. "Dupre knew her as Lara. Lara Egorova. But her real name, according to the CIA, is Dominika Bloykin. She's beautiful, just like Tanya, the one that honey trapped Congressman Splendor.

"Speaking of Splendor, what a dumb bastard. He's a member of the Intelligence Committee, for God's sake. After all this is over, we'll have to find a way to ease him off the Committee. What a stupid fuck-up he turns out to be.

"Anyway, let's get back to Dominika, aka Lara. She's from St. Petersburg, so she's very cosmopolitan. Perfect for trapping a vain Frenchman like this guy Dupre. She got her training at the SVR's Sparrow School. CIA thinks this was her first assignment.

"Now, it appears that she first met Dupre at the Monkey Bar in New York . . . ."

"Monkey Bar?" said Pap. "I've worked in New York all my life but I've never heard of it."

"That's unfortunate" said Big Apple. "It's a bar and restaurant in a French hotel in midtown, east Fifty-fifth, just off Madison. Lots of French tourists stay there. And apparently a lot of monkey business goes on in the bar."

"How does the CIA know that's where they met?" asked Pap.

"From the tapes. They heard Lara and Dupre talking about it on the videotapes. Christ, you should see those tapes! The two of them are in a frenzy. Dupre is moaning in French – repeatedly saying '*mon Dieu, mon Dieu*' - and Dominika is shrieking hysterically in Russian. Extraordinary! You should watch them sometime."

Big Apple paused, then added "But don't bill us for the time you spend watching 'em."

"No, we wouldn't bill you for that" said Pap. "Well, at least not for all five of our lawyers watching 'em. But one of us will have to watch them, we'll need to get the full picture of what happened."

"I think I can guess which one of you we'll be paying to watch the videos" said Earmacher.

Ignoring Earmacher's remark, Pap continued: "I assume Dupre and Dominika spent most of their time in Dominika's apartment? And that the apartment was bugged?"

"Yep. She has a luxury apartment in LeRumpe Tower. That's the expensive tower that flamboyant builder, Ronald LeRumpe, put up on Fifth avenue, near Tiffany's. That's where she and Dupre spent their time together. He frequently didn't even bother to take her to dinner, the cheap bastard."

"I assume the recordings were then sent to her controller. Who was he?"

"He's an SVR operative named Yevgeny Zyuganov – name's a mouthful. Fucking Russians have names that're impossible to pronounce."

"What's his cover?" asked Pap. He wanted Big Apple to know that he knew SVR agents needed a cover.

"Works in Russia's UN delegation. That's where he found out about Dupre. Probably heard all the rumors and realized Dupre would be a perfect subject for a honey trap.

"Now here's the best part" Big Apple continued. "I spoke with our UN ambassador, General Barks – General Wesley Barks. I'm sure you remember him from his days heading up NATO. Of course he's not a general any more, he's retired. But he likes to be called 'General'.

"From his days with NATO, Barks is good friends with all the European big shots. So he knows the French UN Ambassador, Henri Giraud. Knows him quite well. So, Barks had a long lunch with Giraud. Told him about Operation Honey Trap. And how a member of Giraud's delegation – Dupre – had been caught in the trap with his pants down. And his dick up.

"He then told Giraud we needed Dupre to agree to be the plaintiff in a lawsuit against the Russkies. Well, it turned out this was music to Giraud's ears. He hates Dupre. Thinks he's an egotistical, useless bastard. Very lazy, he doesn't do much of anything on the commercial and trade fronts, which is the only reason he's a member of the delegation in the first place. And Giraud's long suspected Dupre of dipping into the till to support his lavish lifestyle."

"So why wouldn't they just send him back to France?" asked Pap.

"Well, according to Barks, Giraud's hands are kind of tied. It seems Dupre knows about Giraud's affair with some hot American model. Barks couldn't remember her name but she models for one of those lingerie companies.

"So, when Giraud confronted Dupre about his lifestyle and demanded to know where he gets the money to support it, Dupre threatened to expose Giraud's affair with the model to the press. Nobody in France would care, I'm told everyone there is having an affair with someone. But it would look bad in the American press, the tabloids and cable channels would have a field day with it. I can just see the headlines: 'French Kiss' or 'Squeezing the Ambassador', stuff like that."

"I hope the Ambassador's girl friend isn't part of another honey trap" said Pap.

"No, she's just a hot model willing to give a good time to a Sugar Daddy, especially if he's someone well-known. Probably enhances her reputation with her friends.

"Anyway" continued Big Apple, "this CIA report gives Giraud just what he needs. He plans to confront Dupre with the report. Demand that Dupre admit to the escapade and agree to cooperate with us in the lawsuit. If Dupre won't agree, Giraud will threaten him with exposure – exposure of being caught in a Russian honey trap. And explain that, after the exposure, the delegation will have no choice but to send him back home."

"And if Dupre agrees to cooperate?" asked Pap.

"Then you can use him for as long as you need him. But after the case is finished, so is Dupre. He's toast then. French Toast."

"This is great. When will Giraud confront him? Remember, we need to get the lawsuit filed as soon as possible. Before the report leaks out."

"Giraud will do it this week. I'm sure he'll get Dupre to say yes. Then you can file your lawsuit."

"When will I be able to meet Dupre?"

"You need to meet him?" Big Apple was astonished. "We'll be lucky if we get him to serve as your plaintiff."

"Well, he's gonna be our client" Pap began. "Lawyers usually meet with people before they take them on as clients. It's a quaint tradition. Think how bad it would make lawyers look if we started filing lawsuits without meeting our clients."

"Don't you lawyers already look pretty . . . ."

Pap interrupted quickly. "And in this case our client is also going to be the representative for an entire class of plaintiffs. For heaven's sake, Congressman, Dupre's a really important guy here."

"Come on, Patrick" said Big Apple. "You class actions guys represent thousand of plaintiffs you've never met, why is it so important to meet this plaintiff?"

"Well, there's another reason" said Pap. "We also need to hold a press conference the day we file the lawsuit. On the front steps of the courthouse. That's where we announce what the Russkies have been up to. That's where we shape this entire story. Shaping the story, that's the whole point of the lawsuit."

"Okay, but what's the press conference got to do with Dupre?"

"We need him to be at the press conference. It can't be just us lawyers. The press will want to see the plaintiff – the victim of the scheme that led to the lawsuit."

"Well, I can't promise that we can get Dupre to meet with you – or to attend your press conference, for that matter. You may have to figure out a way to proceed without him. Ernie told me you were a clever guy, I'm sure you'll figure something out."

Earmacher suddenly broke in. "Pap, you gotta be careful what you say at the press conference. You can't disclose that some of our own politicians are involved. And you cannot even hint that a member of the House Select Committee on Intelligence got honey trapped."

"Don't worry" said Pap, "I won't spill the beans. I mean the honey. And the complaint won't give any names. Now that we've got

Frenchy for our plaintiff, everyone else is anonymous. Just a bunch of John Does, as the complaint will say."

"But you're gonna get asked who all the John Does are" Earmacher insisted. "That's what the press will want to know."

"I can handle the press" Pap insisted. "We're gonna make the subject Dominika and Yevgeny and all the other Russkies, not the John Does. Trust me, we'll have a great press conference. The Russkies won't know what hit them."

Chapter 11

PRESS CONFERENCE

On the day the lawsuit was to be filed, Pap assembled all the lawyers in his office. As he started to brief them on the day's plan, Vera Pesky buzzed him on his phone. "Mister Dupre is here."

"Send him right in."

Vera opened the door and in walked a good looking, mid-thirties Frenchman wearing a suit but, rather than a tie, a paisley print cravat around his neck.

"Mister Dupre – or should I say *Monsieur* Dupre – I'm Patrick Peters. And this" pointing to Pup "is my brother Prescott."

"You two look alike" said Dupre.

"Many people have said that over the years" said Pap.

"We're twins" said Pup.

"Ah, perhaps that is why you look alike."

"And these" continued Pap "are our three brilliant and hardworking associates: Chip Pierpont, Melissa Muffet and Brandon Muffinsky."

Turning to the three of them, Pap said "I want you all to meet our client, Pierre Dupre."

Melissa stared. Finally, she turned to Pap and said "He doesn't look like Pierre Dupre."

"What are you talking about?" said Pap.

"Dupre is older. Also a little shorter and has a receding hairline."

"How do you know what Mister Dupre looks like?" said Brandon. "We're all meeting him for the first time."

"I stayed late last night and watched the videotapes."

Pup was astonished. "You watched the videotapes? They're practically x-rated. Melissa, I'm shocked."

"Just because you guys call me 'Little Miss Muffett' behind my back doesn't mean I'm not old enough to watch videotapes containing . . . uh . . . 'sexual situations' as they say in the movie warnings."

"They don't just depict 'sexual situations' as you so delicately put it, they're downright pornographic" Pup insisted. "The EEOC would have us up on charges if it knew we allowed our associates to watch stuff like that in our office."

"Okay, next time I'll take them home and watch 'em there."

"But then you'd be arrested by the CIA for having classified materials in your apartment" said Brandon.

"Let's leave all this for later" said Pap. "We've got to get Pierre ready for the press conference."

"But Melissa says this guy isn't the real McCoy. I mean the real Dupre" said Pup. "Are you sure this is the right guy?"

"Yes, I'm sure this is the right guy" said Pap.

After pausing for a moment, Pap continued. "Look, I want you all to meet Henri Bonnet. He's the chauffeur for the French UN delegation. But for today, he's Pierre Dupre, the delegation's Representative for Trade and Commercial Affairs. Right, Mister Dupre?"

"*Oui*, that ees correct" said Bonnet/Dupre.

"Why isn't the real Pierre Dupre here?" asked Melissa. "This is going to be a disaster."

"The real Pierre Dupre, as you refer to him, is at this very moment locked in his office at the UN. From which he will not be allowed out. So he cannot be here. To be more precise, he refuses to be here. He was, shall we say, persuaded, to be the plaintiff in our lawsuit. But he adamantly refused to take part in a press conference. Doesn't want his picture in the papers or on TV."

"But why are we using a stand-in?" asked Melissa. "This is really dangerous."

"We need the Russkies, when they see a clip of the press conference on TV, to see that the victim of their honey trap is willing to stand up and tell the world what happened. We need them to believe that Pierre Dupre will not be embarrassed or intimidated and is willing to stand up to them in court."

"For God's sake" said Pup, who was on the verge of hysteria. "The Russians have videos of Dupre. They'll know what he looks like. Even with his clothes on. They'll know this fellow isn't Dupre."

"We've thought of that" said Pap. "That's why Andre – I mean Pierre – will be wearing sun glasses and a fedora. And he'll be dressed just like Dupre. Especially the cravat. Dupre always wears a cravat instead of a tie."

"For heaven's sake, Pap" said Pup. "This isn't Halloween. This is serious business. The Russkies won't be fooled."

"Doesn't matter whether they're fooled or not. It won't affect their reaction to the lawsuit. As Big Apple told me – he's the majority member of the House Intelligence Committee – the Russkies might even assume we will pass off Andre as Dupre in court.

"The important thing" Pap continued, "is for the Russkies to understand that we have someone – the real Dupre or the pretend Dupre – who will stand up and admit to being caught in the honey trap. They'll probably assume everyone, including the judge, is in on it too. That's how things are done in Russia, so they won't be surprised to see it happening here.

"Now, I want everyone to forget about Andre Bonnet. You've never set eyes on anyone by that name. This gentleman is Pierre Dupre. He is our client and he is the plaintiff in our lawsuit. Any more questions?"

Everyone was too dumbfounded to respond. So Pap proceeded to brief them on the plan for the day. When they reached the courthouse, Chip, Melissa and Brandon were to go out front and mingle with the press and media. Let them know they're with the firm filing the lawsuit. He, Pup and Dupre will go in the side entrance to the courthouse and Pup will take the complaint to the Clerk's office and get it filed.

The three of them will then go upstairs and exit the main door of the courthouse and walk down the long steps to where the press and media will be waiting. Pap will give them a passionate summary of the lawsuit and make sure that Dupre is asked only a handful of questions.

And finally, Dupre's answers will be short and sweet. They will practice them in the car on the way downtown. Chip, Melissa and Brandon were to keep the press from asking too many questions. Such as by offering to answer any questions the reporters haven't been able to ask Dupre. And by stressing that the case involves matters of national security, which is why Dupre must be circumspect in what he says.

"Any questions?" asked Pap.

"Okay, we've got two cars waiting outside. Remember, this case involves the honor of our country. Now let's go kick some Russian ass."

* * * *

"Thank you all for attending" Pap began the press conference. "I'm Patrick Peters and here on my left is my brother Prescott Peters. As some of you know, last year we formed the law firm of Peters and Peters, where we specialize in cutting-edge class action lawsuits.

"On my right is our client, Pierre Dupre. Mister Dupre is a distinguished member of the French UN delegation. He's the delegation's Representative for Trade and Commercial Affairs.

"A few minutes ago we filed a lawsuit in this court – the United States District Court for the Southern District of New York. This lawsuit is one of the most serious cases to be filed in this court this year. In fact, in any federal court in the United States. And its possessions, including Puerto Rico and Guam.

"The complaint – and we will provide each of you with a copy when we're finished – exposes a venal plot by one of our country's most relentless adversaries. A plot that could seriously compromise our national security. You will be shocked to see the lengths to which the enemy has gone in an effort to learn our country's most closely guarded secrets.

"Our client Pierre Dupre is, I am afraid to say, one of more than thirty diplomats, defense contractors and elected officials across the country who have managed to get themselves entrapped by the Russian government in a widespread honey trap operation. I'm sure you all know what a honey trap is. Well, this honey trap was a honey. A honey of a honey trap.

"This trap utilized a bevy of beautiful Russian women to lure their victims – important and upstanding men - into their respective honey pots. Once caught in the honey pot - with their pants down, so to speak - the victims were persuaded, most likely during pillow talk, to divulge sensitive information that could be exploited by the Russians in their ongoing effort to undermine the free world.

"This kind of espionage cannot be tolerated. Preying on lonely, vulnerable men like our client is not right. It's extremely unfair and uncivilized. By this lawsuit we will make the defendants pay for their dastardly scheme.

"Now, as I said, our client is one of more than thirty distinguished gentlemen ensnared in this scheme. The other victims, referred to in the complaint as John Does one through thirty, all fell into the honey pot and suffered the same indignities as Mister Dupre. That's why Peters and Peters is bringing this lawsuit. We want to secure not only compensation but also formal diplomatic apologies for all of the victims. They deserve no less.

"Now, you're probably wondering who we are suing. Well, we're suing every person and organization involved in this evil operation. At the top of the pyramid is the Russian government, legally the Rossiyskaya Federatsya – in English, the Russsian Federation. Below them is their state intelligence operation, legally known as The Foreign Intelligence Service of the Russian Federation. You probably know them as the SVR. I won't try to pronounce its full name. Its a mouthful, but you can find it in the complaint if you're interested.

"Further down the line are the so-called controllers – the individual spies who controlled the ladies in question. At the moment we have named two of them: Vladimir Gorelikov, who operates out of D.C., and Yevgeny Zyhganov, who is right here in the City. Don't worry about spelling their names, they're listed in the caption of the complaint.

"And finally, we are suing the Russian honeys who furnished the honey for the honey pots. Working for defendant Gorelikov in D.C. is Olga Vogelinski, who used the name Tanya Zhivago in her work. And in New York, working for defendant Zyhganov, is Dominika Bloykin, who's working name was Lara Egorova. So those are the six defendants.

"Now, the complaint sets forth a number of claims against these defendants. They include criminal espionage in violation of 18 U.S.C. section 792 et seq; economic espionage in violation of 18 U.S.C. section 1831; criminal blackmail under 18 U.S.C. section 873; and civil entrapment under the common law of New York, the District of Columbia and the several states.

"At the earliest possible moment we will ask the court to certify this matter as a class action under Rule 23 of the Federal Rules of Civil Procedure. We will prosecute this case vigorously and aggressively, and will seek an award in favor of the members of the class to compensate them for the indignities they have suffered. That award will also send a message to the Russians and our nation's other enemies. That message is simply this: this type of spying will not be tolerated. It is unfair and uncivilized. And it hits below the belt, where none of these fine gentlemen deserved to be hit.

"Okay, I'll be happy to answer any questions you might have."

"Mister Peters, Mort Kaplonsky of the Daily News. You said that this matter is a threat to our national security and that many U.S. citizens and politicians were victimized. Yet the plaintiff is Mister Dupre. Why is a Frenchman the plaintiff?"

"That's easily answered Mister Kaplonsky. None of the U.S. victims would allow us to use their name. Think of it this way: if you found yourself in a Russian honey pot with your pants down, would you want the whole country to know?"

"Well, no, to tell you the truth. But why is it different for Mister Dupre? Why . . . ."

"He's French. As you know, the French aren't as uptight as Americans about sex. In fact, they expect their leaders to engage in stuff like this."

"Mister Peters, Pat Downes of 1010 WINS News. How did your firm get involved in this? I don't recall you guys having experience in national security law."

"We were asked by the Department of Agriculture to handle the case. So we agreed to do so."

"What's the Department of Agriculture got to do with spying?"

"Nothing."

"So why . . . ."

"They were simply asked by the CIA to find a law firm to handle the case" said Pap.

"I should probably explain how it happened. One of the Department's top officials, Lesley Lettus, is the Under Secretary of Agriculture for Soybeans. He and my brother Prescott were in law school together at Yale. So Lettus called Prescott and asked if we would do the case."

Downes was now really confused. "This guy Lettus is a lawyer who went to Yale Law School and he's now the Under Secretary of Agriculture for Soybeans? What's he know about soybeans?"

"Nothing" said Pap. "That's why they put him in charge of soybeans."

"Mister Peters, Miranda Marvello of Fox 10 News. Was the State Department involved in this? Isn't this their bailiwick?"

"Well" Pap began, "CIA doesn't trust State on this kind of thing. By that I mean matters relating to Russia. They think the Administration is soft on the Russkies. That whole 'Reset' business, for example. Also, if the State Department was involved, Mister Rogers would have final say. And that just wouldn't work."

"Why is Mister Rogers involved?" Marvello asked. "He's not in the State Department, he has a kids TV show."

"Oh he *is* in the State Department. He runs the Russia desk at State. Name's Rogerstrumm. Roy Rogerstrumm. But they call him Mister Rogers because he's so nice and never gets mad at anyone. Not even the Russkies. So you can see why the CIA wouldn't have wanted State involved in this."

Pat Downes of 1010 WINS was dumbfounded. "You mean you're bringing a lawsuit against the government of Russia and our State Department isn't even involved?"

"That's correct."

"But how can you possibly . . . ."

"Miz Downes, have you ever tried to get the State Department to do anything? It's hopeless. Anyway, this is a private lawsuit brought by private individuals who are just trying to protect their private parts. I mean protect their privacy.

"I think we have time for a couple more questions. Ah, Mister Jablonsky, I see you have your hand up. And your pants as well. That's good."

"Yes, Jeb Jablonsky of the New York *Post*. I always keep my pants up. Except when I'm taking them off. Then of course they're down. I have a question for Mister Dupre if I may."

"Sure" said Pap. "Ask away."

"Mister Dupre, my question isn't about national security stuff, it's more personal. Mister Dupre, seeing what your indiscretion has led to, don't you think you made a mistake falling for this Russian lady – I assume it was the one named Dominika, the one who works New York City? Was it worth it?"

"*Oui, certainement*" said Dupre. "Dominika – I knew her as Lara – she ees beautiful. We had a wonderful time."

"Mister Peters" shouted Miranda Marvello of Fox 10 News. The Fox 10 reporters were always shouting. "Why are the French allowing Mister Dupre to participate in your lawsuit? Surely they would rather keep this quiet?"

"You'll have to ask Mister Dupre" Pap responded.

"Okay, so Mister Dupre, why is your government allowing you to participate in this lawsuit?"

"You can't answer that" Pap said to Dupre. "It's classified."

"Who are the other victims of this operation?" asked Downes.

"That information would be classified" said Pap.

"But their names will all come out in the lawsuit, they can't be John Does forever."

"Miz Downes, unlike the Russians, we Americans believe in transparency. So, the time for disclosure will come. But not now. Now is the time to call an end to this press conference. Mister Dupre is a very important official in the French UN delegation and he needs to get back to his duties.

"So I want to thank you all for attending. My colleagues have copies of the complaint for each of you. Good day."

Chapter 12

DETENTE

One week after the press conference, Pap walked into the lobby of the Rayburn Office Building. Where he was once again met by the beautiful Kate Kisme.

"Good morning, Mister Peters" Kate began as she greeted Pap with a big smile. "I saw a clip of your press conference on the news. You did a terrific job. I could tell the press and media were enthralled."

"Well, thanks" Pap said as he flashed a big smile at Kate. This is promising, he said to himself. She sees me as a bit of a celebrity.

"I really liked the French guy" Kate continued. "He's really handsome. I'd love to meet him. Do you think you could arrange it?"

How quickly women could let the air out of a guy's balloon, Pap thought. It wasn't fair.

"His name's Dupre, Pierre Dupre. He's in the French delegation to the UN. But I don't know him all that well, we only just met the day of the press conference."

"But you're both in New York. Next time I'm there could you introduce me to him?"

As they entered the elevator, Pap decided he should put a damper on this idea.

"What about your mother?" he asked. "You said she's worried about your getting hustled by lawyers and lobbyists. She'd really be worried if she knew you were being hustled by a French guy. They're much worse than lawyers and lobbyists. They have moves we haven't even thought of."

"Oh, the fact that he's French will be a plus for Mom. She's always urging me to get more exposure to foreign cultures. Especially French. Mom loves everything French."

And so they walked into Congressman Earmacher's reception room with Pap feeling deflated. His dream of Kate Kisme had been vanquished. By his make believe client Pierre Dupre. Who was really a chauffeur named Andre Bonnet.

* * * *

Pap's spirits began to improve upon being greeted by Congressman Earmacher in his inner office.

"Patrick, I've got good news. The Russians are not coming!"

"What do you mean, not coming. Not coming where?"

"To court! They're not coming to court. They want no part of a class action lawsuit. Said they've seen how such cases can destroy an American company, they can only imagine how much worse it would be for them."

"You'd better start at the beginning" said Pap. "What exactly happened?"

"So here's the story" said Earmacher. "On Tuesday, the day after your press conference, a low-level guy in the Russian embassy contacted a State Department guy he knew. Told him he was speaking informally, and off the record, on behalf of the SVR and the Russian government. Said they knew State was behind this, they knew the Department of Agriculture had nothing to do with the lawsuit.

"By the way, Patrick, that was brilliant. Putting the finger on Agriculture for getting your firm involved. And keeping our Committee out of it.

"Anyway, the Russian guy told our guy at State that they didn't think a class action lawsuit was the best way to resolve this matter. He wanted to know what we might be looking for in order to resolve things.

"Luckily, the State Department guy is an old time hard-liner. While he was duty-bound to pass the inquiry up to Mister Rogers, he didn't trust that milk-toast to deal with it properly. So he also reported the contact to CIA, which jumped right on it."

Pap was spellbound. He'd never seen a defendant in a lawsuit capitulate the day after the lawsuit was filed.

But then he began to have second thoughts. His firm had just started working on the case. They had not yet racked up a huge number of billable hours that they could bill to the client. And the case wasn't yet a class action, how could they get a fee based on a recovery by the class?

Earmacher continued his narrative. "CIA managed to convince Mister Rogers to let the agency's general counsel, Grant Little, talk directly with the SVR lawyers. Nobody knows if the SVR lawyers are real lawyers, probably not, but that didn't matter to us. So long as we could negotiate spook to spook, and keep the State Department out of it, we figured we could get what we needed."

"And did we get what we needed?" asked Pap. "I've never had the CIA negotiate a settlement for me, if this turns out well I'll have to try it more often."

"We did just fine. First of all, it was agreed that both sides would destroy all copies of the audio and video tapes in their possession."

"What about the tapes our firm has? The associates have been watching them, they want to see first-hand what spies do."

"Tell them if there's anything they haven't seen or listened to, they'd better do it fast. You're going to have to destroy that stuff in a few days. Personally, I think they shouldn't bother with the Splendor and Tanya videos, it's just straight-up sex. I'd focus on the videos of Dupre and Dominika. They're really something, those French guys are certainly creative."

"How do we know the Russkies will actually destroy their copies?" asked Pap. "Maybe we should get them to sign a certificate of compliance. That's what we do when a case is over and each side has to destroy all the discovery materials in its possession."

"A certificate of compliance?" said an astonished Earmacher. "From the Russian SVR? Are you crazy? They're not about to put any of this in writing. And you think they'd let a piece of paper control what they do if they wanted to keep copies of everything?"

"Then how do we know they'll keep their promise?"

"Pap, we've got two intelligence agencies dealing with each other. On matters like this, they just have to trust each other to do what they say they're gonna do. Otherwise, they both realize they could never do a deal again."

"Okay, so what else does the deal involve?"

"Lots more. CIA insisted the Russkies put Olga and Dominika out of action, recall them. The Russkies agreed. Said they'd reassign them to another country, probably Italy. They think Italian businessmen and government officials – especially the businessmen, the government officials seem to change every few months - will really fall for the two of them."

"What about money?" asked Pap. "Shouldn't they be required to pay damages? Not to mention attorneys fees. We put a lot of time into this matter."

"Pap, you worry too much. I thought your brother was the only one in your family who worries."

"Well, that's generally true. But when it comes to our fee, I sometimes worry myself."

"Well, you needn't worry here. When Little said they had to cough up some money, they asked what number we had in mind. So Little threw out the first number he could think of: one million.

"The Russkies agreed, said we could use it any way we want. Big Apple and I talked about it and here's what we decided. Your firm gets half, five hundred thousand. Not bad for a week's work. We're giving your plaintiff one hundred thousand. And we'll keep the other four hundred thousand."

"You're giving Dupre one hundred thousand? He didn't do anything, he wouldn't even show up for the press conference."

"Not Dupre. We're giving it to Bonnet, he earned it. He was almost as good as you at the press conference."

"I wouldn't go that far . . . ."

"We've already had General Barks clear it with the French. They're happy to have the money go to Bonnet. Oh, and by the way, they're pulling Dupre out of the UN. They're reassigning him to one of their embassies in North Africa, Sudan I believe. His carefree playboy days are over."

"You said you were keeping the other four hundred thousand. Who exactly is keeping it?"

"The House Select Committee on Intelligence. We've had a hard time getting enough funding to do our work. This four hundred thousand will help a lot. But please don't tell anyone. If the Appropriations Committee hears about it they'll cut our budget by that amount."

"So what's the procedure for our firm getting our share? What do we need to do to make it happen."

"Nothing. The SVR is not about to send out a check payable to Peters and Peters. That's not how it's done. The spooks will work out some arrangement so that the money can't be traced. They'll probably set up some secret bank account in Switzerland, that's how they do it in the movies."

"What will happen to Congressman Splendor?"

"Every piece of evidence in the possession of the Committee or the CIA, whether paper or electronic, is being destroyed. Of course, CIA is telling us it will all be destroyed but we don't really believe them. Those guys get paid to lie. But we think they'll be really careful to keep anything they retain under lock and key. So, unless there's a leak at State, Splendor should be safe."

"So he comes out of this okay" said Pap. "I kinda liked him, he just made a mistake any guy could make."

"Well, of course we can't let him stay on the Intelligence Committee, he's proven himself untrustworthy. So Big Apple has already met with the Speaker and Splendor's being reassigned to CODAFTY."

"What's CODAFTY?"

"Committee on Drugs, Alcohol, Firearms, Tobacco and Yogurt. He can't do the country any harm there."

"Congress has a committee that deals with Yogurt? Jesus, no wonder my taxes are so high."

Ignoring Pap's remark, Earmacher decided it was time to wrap things up. "So, as you can see, everyone comes out of this a winner.

Splendor gets off the hook. You guys get half a million. Our Committee gets four hundred thousand. And Andre Bonnet, a chauffeur at the UN, is suddenly rich."

"Speaking of Bonnet" said Pap, "Kate told me in the elevator she thinks he's really handsome. Even asked if I could introduce her to him. I told her that wasn't such a good . . . ."

"Kate and Bonnet!" said Earmacher excitedly. "What a great idea. Do you think you could arrange for her to meet him? I'm sure they'd hit it off."

"I don't think that's a very good idea. I think Kate's mother would be worried – a French guy who's suddenly flush with money. You should worry too."

"Nonsense. She can develop a relationship with him. He'll fall head over heels for her. And then she'll be in a position to pump him for information. We're always trying to figure out what the French are up to. You can't always trust what they tell you."

Pap was flabbergasted. "You mean you're going to set up a honey trap for the French using your own niece?"

"Why not? It worked for the Russkies. Amazing what you can learn during pillow talk."

"But I . . . ."

"Of course, I'll have to find her another position on Capitol Hill. If the French know she works for the minority leader of the House Intelligence Committee, they might get suspicious."

"I'd hate to see her lose her job."

"She won't lose her job. I'll get her an identical job with another Congressman. In fact, I think I can get Farmer Dell to take her on, his office is just down the hall. I could still keep an eye on her, just like her mother asked me to do."

"Farmer Dell?" Pap said. "Is he a Congressman?"

"Mel Dell is his name. Democrat from Iowa. He's been chair of the House Agriculture Committee for at least twenty years. Always trying to get more money for farmers. So everyone calls him Farmer Dell."

Pap couldn't think of anything more to say. He couldn't quite get his hands around how things worked in D.C. He needed to get back to practicing law in New York. As he started to stand up, he remembered what he had been wanting to talk with Earmacher about before all this spy stuff came up.

"Congressman, the next time you're in Norwalk and have an hour free, I'd like to come over to your office and talk with you about an idea I've had to regenerate the State's economy."

"No time like the present" said Earmacher as he looked at his watch. "It's noon, why don't we have lunch over at the Hay Adams? I know you've been wanting to have lunch there."

"Sure. Maybe we could bring Kate and . . . ."

"No, not Kate. It's B-2 we need. He works on all matters involving Connecticut business."

"B-2?" said Pap. "That's a name?"

"Sort of. Bernard Barnaby. Irish guy. We all call him B-2. He jokes around a lot and drinks too much, but he sometimes has good ideas."

"Kate" Earmacher called as he opened the door to the reception area. "Call the Hay Adams and have them hold a table for three. And then tell B-2 to join us, we're leaving now."

Pap shot a final wistful look at Kate Kisme and then left for lunch at the Hay Adams. Without the gorgeous Kate Kisme. Who, as it turned out, was not in love with Pap but with a Frenchman she thought was the diplomat Pierre Dupre but was really a chauffeur named Andre Bonnet.

Chapter 13

URBAN RENEWAL

Pap, Earmacher and Bernard Barnaby – a short, wiry, red headed forty-year-old with a blunt manner of speaking - walked into the dining room of the Hay Adams. They were quickly seated at a spacious table in the corner. After exchanging pleasantries and ordering, Earmacher got quickly down to business.

"So tell us Patrick, what's this idea you have for rejuvenating our state's economy?"

"What economy?" said Barnaby. "Connecticut doesn't have one anymore. All the old manufacturing companies have moved south or gone out of business. And almost all the big corporations who moved their headquarters here in the seventies and eighties have left for lower-tax states. You got an idea for reversing all that?" Barnaby said as he gave Pap a dubious look.

"Yes I do, Bernard, I . . . ."

"Just call him B-2" said Earmacher, "everyone else does. It's easier to say than Bernard."

"All right, sure. Let me start by asking both of you some questions."

"Fire away" said B-2.

"Okay. First of all, what do Bridgeport, New Haven and Hartford all have in common?"

"That's easy" said B-2. "They're our three largest cities. And they're all depressed as hell. No business. No industry. Poor schools. Middle class folks all moving out."

"Right on target" said Pap. "But you left out one important thing."

"They're all run by Dems" said Earmacher. "The Dems have long controlled all three cities and all three have gone to hell under their rule."

"Let's keep politics out of this" said Pap. "My plan's going to require a bipartisan approach. It will need the support of both parties.

"So" Pap resumed, "let me ask you again. Besides their poverty and mismanagement, what do these cities have in common?"

"Why don't you just tell us instead of turning this into twenty questions" said B-2.

Pap realized he needed B-2's support, he couldn't risk him killing the idea when he was alone with Earmacher. So he said: "Okay, I'll tell you what else they have in common. They all house a federal court. They're all part of the District of Connecticut, but each of them is a separate division within the District."

"What's a federal court got to do with improving the state's economy?" asked B-2.

"Federal courts mean lawyers. From all over the state. And sometimes from around the country. But here's the problem. Right now, we don't have enough of 'em – lawyers I mean – coming to the courts in these cities. These courts mostly handle criminal cases and a handful of civil cases, many of them appeals from social security determinations. Really small potatoes stuff."

"I've never heard anyone complain that we don't have enough lawyers in Connecticut" Earmacher said.

"And I don't see what this has to do with invigorating the state's economy" said B-2.

"Look" said Pap. "What do out-of-town lawyers do when they come to federal court in Bridgeport, New Haven or Hartford?"

"Now we're back to that twenty questions stuff" said B-2. "How should we know what out-of-town lawyers do when they go to federal court in Bridgeport? Or New Haven or Hartford for that matter?"

"I'll tell you what they do" said Pap. "If the case lasts more than a day, they stay overnight in a motel. They eat breakfast, lunch and dinner at the motel or a restaurant – if they can even find a decent one near their motel. And if they've come from another state, they've likely come via plane or train and have to use taxis to get around."

Pap was getting on a roll. "Now, what if the case they're on is a big case? Involving big corporations and a huge damages claim? In that case it's not just one lawyer coming to town for each side, it's a whole team. One or two partners. Two or three associates. A couple of paralegals. Probably a secretary, the young secretaries love to do out-of-town trials, they can rack up lots of overtime. And nowadays, most firms also bring an IT person to prepare visual stuff for court. So, we're talking a whole team of people. All of whom need a place to stay and places to eat."

Earmacher finally spoke up. "Patrick, I'm not aware we have those kinds of cases – big million-dollar cases - in the Connecticut courts. If we do, I certainly haven't read about it."

"You're right, Congressman. We don't have many of those kinds of cases. And that's exactly the problem."

"So how would we get more of 'em?" asked B-2. "You must have an idea here, why don't you just tell us instead of beating around the bush."

Pap was a lawyer. He liked asking questions better than he liked answering them. So he asked: "How many class action lawsuits do you think have been filed around the country in the past five months in which the complaint alleges some sort of false advertising or consumer deception?"

"Probably twenty or thirty" said B-2. This was good, thought Pap, B-2 was starting to play along.

"One hundred" said Pap. "And where do you think most of them have been filed?"

"I don't know but I think you're about to tell us" said Earmacher.

"California. Fifty-eight percent of those cases have been filed in the California courts, some in California state court but the majority in California federal court. And do you know why all those cases have been filed in California?"

"Probably because California has great weather" said B-2. "And nice hotels and restaurants."

"We'll get to the hotels and restaurants in a minute. But there's a reason all those cases have been filed in California. It's because of a state law: section seventeen two hundred of California's Business and Professional Code. Lawyers all over the country know about it, they simply refer to it as 'seventeen two hundred.' It's the broadest consumer protection law in the country. Any kind of consumer deception you can think of is almost certainly covered by seventeen two hundred.

"That statute applies to every category of consumer product you can think of. Food and beverage products. Cosmetics. Pharmaceuticals. Dietary supplements. Vitamins. Paper products. Computers and electronic products. Cars. Trucks. Tires. And all of these are products sold by large national companies and used or consumed by millions of people every day.

"To give you an idea of what Connecticut has been missing out on, let me mention just a couple recent cases in this field. There's a pending class action involving Junior Mints. A lady claims the package is only filled to fifty-seven percent capacity, yet comparable candies such as Milk Duds and Good n Plenty are filled to seventy-five or eighty-five percent capacity. You know how many people there are who've purchased Junior Mints and are now part of that class action?

"Or how about this: there's a case that claims Rocker and Handle's 'Flushable Wipes' aren't really flushable, although God knows what you're supposed to do with them if they aren't flushable. So, everyone who has purchased some flushable wipes in the past few years is part of the plaintiff's class in that case.

"So you see, we've been missing out on the opportunity to provide a venue for important, ground-breaking cases like these. Cases where consumers have been duped and deceived by greedy corporations."

"I certainly agree consumers have been tricked if they buy what they think are flushable wipes that turn out not to be flushable" said Earmacher. "Someone should put a stop to that."

"Congressman, you are entirely right. And that's where we lawyers come in. Only lawyers can stop a huge company like Rocker and Handle from selling flushable wipes that aren't flushable.

"Now" Pap continued, "what do you think happens when a case like this is filed against Rocker and Handle or some other large corporation?"

"So we're back to twenty questions again?" said B-2.

"No, that was a rhetorical question and I'll answer it. What happens is that the plaintiff, because it's a class action, hires a big class action firm with lots of lawyers to represent him. And the . . . ."

"I thought it was just the opposite" said Earmacher as he smiled at Pap. "The plaintiff doesn't go looking for a lawyer. You lawyers identify the case and then go look for someone to be your plaintiff."

"We would never do that" said Pap.

"Anyway" Pap continued, "the defendant, because it fears a large damages award and a possible injunction shutting down a major marketing claim, hires the best law firm it can find. And then both sides descend on the city where the case has been filed and participate in an endless series of events. Conferences with the judge. Motions. Depositions. Hearings. Maybe even a trial."

"I think I see where you're going with all this" said Earmacher. "All those lawyers are bringing their wallets and credit cards to wherever the trial is."

"Actually, they're bringing their client's wallet and credit cards to the city where the trial is" said B-2. "Lawyers don't spend a dime of their own money when they're out of town."

"Bingo" said Pap. "Gotcha" he added as he pointed his forefinger and thumb, like a gun, at B-2. "Because it's their client's wallet and credit cards they're using, they – the lawyers – are uninhibited in their spending. Everyone enjoys spending someone else's money.

"Now, have either of you ever heard of Marshall, Texas?" Pap asked.

Getting no response, he explained. "Marshall is a one-horse town in eastern Texas. About ten years ago the town's business community began looking around for a way to boost the town's economy. One of the things they noticed was that the country was in the midst of an explosion of patent cases. Looking into it further, they discovered that, under the patent laws, a patent infringement case can be filed pretty much anywhere the defendant has sold the infringing product.

"So, the town's managers and business community decided to make Marshall a friendly venue for patent cases. They managed to get a former patent litigator appointed to the federal bench there. Then they got in touch with the leading patent lawyer in the state and urged him to file a couple of his cases in Marshall. And they took out ads in the town's newspaper touting Marshall as a patent-friendly town, pointing out that patents are the key to the success of American industry and that companies that infringe patents are the scum of the earth.

"With the state's best patent lawyer representing the plaintiffs and a patent-friendly judge presiding over the cases, patent owners started winning huge verdicts. And the more big verdicts that came in, the more new patent cases were filed. In 2006 alone, two-hundred and thirty-six patent lawsuits were filed in tiny Marshall, Texas. The plaintiffs won eighty-eight percent of them."

"And the town itself?" asked Earmacher. He was starting to get excited.

"The town had phenomenal growth. New hotels. New restaurants. New bars, barber shops and hair salons. And message therapists came there in droves. Marshall became a boom town."

"You think we could duplicate that in Bridgeport?" asked Earmacher. "Or Hartford?"

"Sure. Look at these cities now. They have nothing in the way of decent hotels or restaurants. Look at that motel on the outskirts of Bridgeport just off the Merritt Parkway. The 'Heigh Ho' it's called. Good, I suppose, for quickies. Just drive in off the Parkway and you can be done and back on the road in half an hour. I'm pretty sure the motel's target audience isn't patent lawyers from Chicago or Philadelphia."

"Some new hotels would be a great idea" said Earmacher. "And new restaurants as well. Good jobs for builders and good jobs for the people who work in 'em. And nice places for all those lawyers, paralegals and young secretaries to stay." Looking at Pap, he added "You guys must have a lot of fun when you're in anther city for a trial."

"Wait a minute" interrupted B-2, "I think we're putting the cart before the horse. What is it you propose to do to get all those lawyers and their entourages to come to Bridgeport?"

"You're right to zero in on that, B-2. And here's the answer. My firm has drafted a proposed new consumer protection law. We modeled it after the California law. It's as broad as it can possibly be. It will allow for class action lawsuits on behalf of injured consumers and will permit recovery of both compensatory and punitive damages.

"I'll be meeting in the next week or so with my friend Sam Snake, he's a Democratic Assemblyman from Bridgeport. He chairs the General Assembly's Committee on Economic Development. I'd like to convince him to have his committee consider the bill."

"So where do I come in?" asked Earmacher.

"As I said earlier, Congressman, this issue shouldn't be political. Rebuilding our state's economy should be bipartisan. You're the most prominent Republican in the state. Your support would be huge; it could influence Republicans in the state legislature to support the bill."

"Well, you've got my support" said Earmacher. "Anything to get big shot lawyers to come to Connecticut. And spend their client's money at our hotels, bars and restaurants. Why should California get all their money?"

"See" said Pap. "It's a perfect opportunity for politicians. Rebuild the state's economy and get lawyers from across the country to pay for it. What's not to like about the idea?"

Just then the check arrived and the waiter placed it in the center of the table. Handing it to Pap, Earmacher smiled and said:

"I know you've been wanting to bring Kate here for lunch. And maybe more. Well, you got her uncle instead. Kate's certainly better looking than me, but it's me you need to help you with this crazy idea."

Rising from his seat, Earmacher added "Please make sure you include a generous tip, Patrick, I have a good reputation here.

"Come on B-2, we need to get back to the office. And Patrick, thanks for lunch. I'll tell Kate we had a good time."

Chapter 14

CHIMPS AHOY

One morning in May, Pap rang his secretary, Vera Pesky, on his telephone intercom. "Miss Pesky, please get Mister Fund on the phone."

"Who's Mister Fund?" she asked.

"William Fund. He runs a hedge fund. The Fund."

"But what's the name of the fund?" she demanded.

"I just told you. The Fund. Actually it's The Fund Fund."

"That would be redundant. Can't you just tell me the name of the fund, then maybe I can locate him."

"Miss Pesky, why are you having so much trouble with this? His last name is Fund. He runs a fund. So he named his fund the Fund Fund."

"What's his phone number? He's not on my Rolodex or my computer contacts list."

Miss Pesky had a way of getting under Pap's skin. Why the hell didn't he just leave her at Rogers and Autry when he and Pup started up the firm? Dumbest thing he had ever done.

"Look it up" he said as forcefully as he could. "For heaven's sake, that's your job."

"If you kept me better informed about all your contacts, I could have his number at my fingertips. Then, when . . . ."

"Just look it up, Miss Pesky. And after you've looked it up put it in your Rolodex. And on your computer contacts list. Or both. But for now, just get him on the phone."

"I'm just trying to make things run more smoothly" she said firmly. Miss Pesky always liked to get in the last word, especially with her boss.

* * * *

When Miss Pesky finally managed to get William Fund on the phone, Pap cheerfully greeted him: "Hello Bill, this is Patrick Peters. How are you? And how many millions has your fund made this morning?"

"Patrick, we don't look at things on an hourly basis. We have much more of a long-term outlook. I'm much more interested in how much our funds have made by the end of each day."

Pap thought about responding to this, but decided he shouldn't be surprised by the answer. What else would hedge fund guys do except worry about having more money today than they had yesterday?

"Bill, I know you're busy, so I'll get right to the point. Did you happen to see any of the news clips about our press conference the other day?"

"You sure do a lot of press conferences. When do you find time to be in court?"

"Well, in our line of litigation, we . . . ."

"I assume you're referring to the press conference about the new case you guys filed in New York. Your plaintiff's name was Katy Kong, as I recall."

"Yes, that's the one."

"You usually have your client with you at these conferences. But you didn't this time. Why not?"

"Ha! That's a good one Bill. As you well know, Katy Kong is being held in the Bronx Zoo. The zoo has her under lock and key. They wouldn't let her out for the press conference. Even after I promised I would bring her right back."

"I thought that might be the case" said Fund.

"Look, Bill. We think this is going to be a groundbreaking case. It will establish civil rights for people like Katy. Zoos shouldn't be able to keep them locked up. They need to be allowed to go out for a jog, talk with their friends, run an errand, just like other people."

"Isn't that your problem?" said Fund. "What court is ever going to rule that Katy Kong – she's King Kong's girl friend, as I understand it – is a people? I mean, a human being with civil rights like you and me?"

"That's where you're wrong, Bill. She does have civil rights like you and me. And we intend to prove it. We have an expert witness, Doctor Doolittle. He's one of the country's leading primatologists. He'll be able to convince the court that Miz Kong, as well as her boyfriend King and all the other apes who are members of the class – this is a class action, by the way – deserve to be released from the custody they're in.

"We plan to get them all released and then moved to an animal sanctuary in Florida. We might even ask for damages, although we haven't figured out what they could do with the money if we got it for them."

"Well Patrick, all I can say is good luck. Your case looks pretty shaky to me."

"Bill, trust me, the case is not shaky. It's rock solid. But it's going to be expensive. This Doolittle guy charges by the hour, he's as bad as a lawyer. And once he starts meeting with Miz Kong and the other members of the class, the time he spends on the case is going to go through the roof. Look, I don't need a ton of money. Just enough to pay for Doctor Doolittle's fee and expenses. We'd be happy to give you double your investment once we get a recovery. The zoo . . . ."

"We take a much higher multiple of our investment when we put money into a case. Usually four or five times the amount of our investment plus a percentage of the recovery."

"You're kidding" said Pap.

"No, I'm quite serious. How do you think our Lien On Me Fund has such a great track record? Getting our money back, or even getting back double our money, is of no interest to us.

"All of our funds are in business to make money, lots of money. And I have to answer to our investors for the use of the money they've entrusted to us. I can't risk their money on some lawsuit based on a crackpot theory about chimpanzees having civil rights. Call me when you've got a real case. With a real plaintiff. Not some ape who won't even show up for a press conference."

"Well, if that's how you feel" said Pap.

"Yes, that's about it. Look, I've gotta run. The manager of one of our funds is coming in for an update. I need to see how that fund has done this morning. Take care, Patrick, and thanks for calling the Fund Fund."

* * * *

A week later, all the lawyers filed into Pap's office for a meeting on the case.

"We have some news on the Katy Kong case" said Pup. "Some good, some bad."

"Let's have the bad news first" said Pap. "That way the good news will seem even better."

"Well, the zoo – I'm sorry, they've renamed themselves the Wildlife Conservation Society, I don't think they like being called a zoo anymore. Anyway, they've filed a motion to dismiss. Basically arguing that chimpanzees aren't people and therefore cannot be parties to a lawsuit."

"We expected that" said Pap. "Is that the bad news?"

"No. You remember we thought the zoo would use its regular counsel – Bell, Booke and Kandle? They're a decent firm but hardly a firm that's going to ring your bell."

"So who . . . ."

"They've hired Melissa's and my old firm, Oliver and Cromwell. As you know, its probably the best firm in the city. I don't know why I ever let you talk me into leaving it.

"And by the way, they were really annoyed when I left. No partner ever leaves Oliver and Cromwell for greener pastures. In fact, there are no greener pastures as far as they're concerned. Anyway, they would love to see me lose this case."

"Who's the attorney handling the case?" asked Pap. "Who signed the motion?"

"Horvath" said Pup. "Hortescue Horvath the Fourth. He's viewed as one of their best litigators."

"Hortescue?" said Melissa with a smirk. "One of their top litigators? I don't think so."

"Tell us more about him" said Pap. "Judging by his name I'd say he's probably a stuffed shirt."

"You can say that again" said Melissa.

"Judging by his name I'd say he's probably a stuffed shirt."

"He's a typical Oliver and Cromwell dilettante" said Melissa. Prep school, Columbia College, Harvard Law. But a very boring guy. The associates refer to him as 'Hortis will bore us'."

"What's he look like?" asked Pap.

"I'd say he's average height. Average weight. Average hair. In fact, he's average in everything except humor. He has absolutely no sense of humor. On a scale of one to ten, his sense of humor is minus ten. The associates always said the only time they ever saw him smile was when he was talking about making law review at Harvard, like it was the highlight of his life."

"This is great" said Pap. "He won't stand a chance against me and Pup and the other apes. I mean, me and Pup and the apes.

"So, if that's the bad news" Pap continued, "the good news must really be good."

"It is" said Pup. "Now that they filed a motion to dismiss, a judge has been assigned to the case."

"Justice" said Chip, speaking up for the first time. Looking at Pup he continued: "You're the one who explained it to Lydia that first day we were in court. In New York, judges on the lower court are called justices, not judges. Remember, she even corrected that attorney when he referred to Justice Leghetti as Judge Leghetti."

"Thanks, Chip" said Pup. "Maybe you can remind Lydia of that episode when you see her tonight at her apartment. After you've had sex with Candy in the Worry Room. But before you go home to be with Francoise."

"We're getting a little bit off the subject here" said Pap. "We can't spend every meeting marveling at Chip's love life. Marvelous though it may be. So now, who's our judge?"

"You mean our justice" said Pup. "It's Wright. Justice Wright."

"Moose Wright?" said Pap. "That big burly guy from the Bronx who's always letting criminals go free? 'Turn 'em loose Moose' they called him. When I was in the DA's office we crossed our fingers our case wouldn't be assigned to him. But I thought he died a couple years ago."

"He did" said Pup. "This is is niece, Neva Wright. She's a fairly new judge, got appointed after her uncle died. Like him, she's extremely liberal. Always ruling for the person who's the underdog, doesn't matter whether it's a criminal or civil case. And always makes her decision based on emotion and sympathy. I think she could be an excellent judge for this case."

"Maybe she'll want to turn loose the chimps just like her uncle turned loose all the crooks" said Pap.

Brandon spoke up for the first time. "The problem is she gets reversed a lot. Lawyers say she's never right. They say that's why her parents named her Neva. They knew she would neva be right."

"We can't worry abut her getting reversed now" said Pap. "We need to start by getting her to see this case our way. But I'd say the stars are coming into alignment here. The zoo has a stuffed shirt defending it. And we have a judge who has lots of sympathy for underdogs. Who can be more of an underdog than an ape imprisoned in a zoo?"

"Do you want me to start on the brief in opposition to the motion to dismiss?" asked Melissa.

Pap thought for a moment before responding. "No, Brandon can draft the brief, you've already done the legal research and analysis. I want us to go on the offensive here."

"The offensive?" asked Pup. "Don't we first need to get past the motion to dismiss before we start going on the offensive?"

"No. That's the old by-the-book Oliver and Cromwell way. But we're not Oliver and Cromwell. We're Peters and Peters. And we blow into a case like a hurricane. It says so right on our website.

"And that's what we're gonna do here. Melissa and Pup – and you too Chip – I want you guys to lead the charge. We'll file a cross-motion to their motion. We'll ask for an order appointing us guardians of all the chimpanzees in all the zoos we're suing. And we'll also ask for an order declaring the case to be a class action. On behalf of all the apes in zoos in New York State."

"That's a great plan" said Melissa. "Hortescue won't know what hit him."

"He'll go ape" said Chip.

"Okay" Pap concluded as he stood up. "Let's all get to work. We're gonna blow into this case like a Goddamn hurricane."

Chapter 15

JUSTICE NEVA WRIGHT

"All rise" shouted the no nonsense court clerk as the judge entered the courtroom. "The New York Supreme Court for the County of New York, Justice Neva Wright presiding, is now in session. Please be seated."

As soon as everyone was seated, she continued: "Counsel, please stand and note your appearances."

Transcript of Hearing:

Mr. Peters: Patrick A. Peters and Prescott U. Peters of Peters and Peters for the plaintiff.

Mr. Horvath: Hortescue Horvath the Fourth, Sheppard Sherman the Third, Lawrence Lindgren the Second and Franklin Stein the First for the defendant.

The Court: "Frankenstein?"

Mr. Horvath: No, Your Honor. Franklin Stein. Ms. Franklin Stein.

The Court: Well, Ms. Stein, you are welcome here. It's nice to see a woman attorney among so many male attorneys.

Mr. Horvath: We actually have several female attorneys in our firm.

The Court: How many?"

"Mr. Horvath: Well, there's Ms. Stein. And there are one or two in our Corporate Department. And I believe we have another two in our Trusts and Estates Department.

The Court: That's quite impressive, Mr. Horvath. Last time I looked, Oliver and Cromwell had over 200 attorneys. So, Ms. Stein, are you the only woman litigator in your firm?

Ms. Stein: Well, yes, I believe so Your Honor. But Oliver and Cromwell is a very old firm. It was started back in Medieval times. So we're a bit old-fashioned, it may take a while before we get totally caught up with modern times.

The Court: I can see that. Well, I hope you're getting good experience and that they're allowing you to play a useful role in this case."

Ms. Stein: I am Your Honor. They let me carry all the exhibits to court.

The Court: I guess that's a start. By the way, Mr. Horvath, I don't understand why your client needs four lawyers in the courtroom. When I was trying cases – it wasn't all that long ago – I rarely had another attorney with me. Our clients could barely afford to pay for one lawyer to represent them. Who is your client, by the way?

Mr. Horvath: The Wildlife Conservation Society. It operates three of the zoos involved in this case: the Bronx, the Brooklyn and the Staten Island zoos.

The Court: And you're being sued by a lady named Katy Kong? Which of those zoos does she work at?"

Mr. Horvath: Actually, Katy Kong is an ape. She lives at the Bronx Zoo. Very happily, I might add. She's never voiced any dissatisfaction with her care and surroundings. Or her food, she loves the food.

The Court: Mr. Peters, you've brought a lawsuit on behalf of an ape?

Mr. Peters: Yes, we . . . .

The Court: I hope you're not going to bring him to court. There wouldn't be any place for him to sit.

Mr. Peters: Your Honor, our client Katy Kong is a she. And she's not an ape. Well, she's in the ape family but she's a chimpanzee. Chimpanzees are extremely smart. Ninety-nine percent of their genes are the same as yours. I mean ours. You and I and everyone in this courtroom. Even Mr. Horvath and his three amigos; ninety-nine percent of their genes are the same as Katy Kong's.

The Court: Why does your client have two names. I mean, a first name and a last name. Don't animals usually have just one name? Like my dog, his name's Zeke. Just plain Zeke. No last name.

Mr. Peters: Here's the story, Your Honor. The zoo named her Katy. Just one name, like Zeke. You can see that name on the plaque in front of her cage. But now she has a boyfriend. A fellow chimp, his name's Kong. Now, it seems that Kong is an alpha male, very aggressive, he more or less runs the chimp house. He is unquestionably the leader of the apes. I mean the chimps. And so they started referring to him as King Kong.

The Court: So Katy married him and became Katy Kong?

Mr. Peters: Well, they weren't married by a minister or priest or anything. But they live together. Like a common law husband and wife. So there's no problem if they engage in monkey business.

(The Court addresses her clerk)

The Court: Ms. Grimm, I see a large stack of papers in front of me. What are they all about? I hope I don't have to read 'em all.
By the way, counsel, the lady there is my court clerk, Ms. Grimm. Greta Grimm. She'll help move things along. If I were you, I'd try to stay on her good side.

Ms. Grimm: Okay, we have three motions to deal with. The first . . . .

The Court: The case just started. How can we have three motions already? Why do you lawyers always insist on filing so many motions? Don't you appreciate that I have other cases to deal with?

(Lengthy Silence)

Ms. Grimm: The first motion is a motion to dismiss filed by defendant. The other two motions were filed by plaintiff. A motion to have their firm named guardian of the chimps in the zoos operated by defendant. And also a motion to have the case certified as a class action.

The Court: A class action? A class of apes? I'm not all that conversant with the law in this area but I don't recall ever having seen a class action case involving apes.

Mr. Horvath: Your Honor, I suggest you deal first with our motion to dismiss. If you grant that motion – and I'm sure you will, there's no precedent for a lawsuit, let alone a class action, on behalf of apes. Then you won't need to deal with the motions filed by plaintiff, they'll be moot.

The Court: What do you mean plaintiff's motions will be moot? I still have to decide them, don't I? And besides, shouldn't Mr. Peters be allowed to argue his motions, just like you're arguing yours?

Mr. Peters: Your Honor, I don't mind if Mr. Horvath wants to argue his motion first. Even though he's only the fourth, he can still argue his motion first. And I'm even happy if you want to consider his motion before you move on to our motions.

The Court: Very well. The court appreciates it when attorneys accommodate one another. Makes it easier for the court. Thank you Mr. Peters.

* * * *

Hortescue Horvath walked to the podium and spent the next fifteen minutes explaining – without the slightest trace of humor or amusement – that there was absolutely no precedent for allowing animals, let alone apes, to file lawsuits. In fact, he explained, the few precedents on point all rejected the argument that animals had the same right to file lawsuits as humans. He then commenced his conclusion.

* * * *

Mr. Horvath: So, Judge Wright . . . .

The Court: Justice Wright. You should know that Mr. Horvath. In New York, Supreme Court judges are called Justices.

Mr. Horvath: You're right, Justice Wright. My mistake. Most of my cases are in federal court and the judges there are just called judge.

The Court: Those federal judges all think they're the cat's pajamas. Just because they've got a fancier courthouse and get to hire more law clerks, that doesn't make them any better than us.

Mr. Horvath: I agree, Judge . . . I mean Justice Wright. They're no better than the judges . . . ah, justices, in this courthouse. Anyway, as I was about to conclude . . . .

The Court: I know what you were about to conclude, so there's no need for you to conclude. You don't think there's any precedent for this lawsuit. I got it twenty minutes ago. So now I'd like to hear what Mr. Peters has to say. He's been waiting here patiently while you drone on and on and keep referring to me as Judge Wright.

Mr. Peters: Thank you, Your Honor. Mr. Horvath is correct that the only two cases that have considered this issue have resulted in a dismissal of the complaints. But those cases are not dispositive because they were based on an incomplete record and a fatal error in how they were filed.

Let me address the filing error first. All the cases cited by the zoo were brought by the chimps themselves. Everyone knows a chimpanzee cannot file a lawsuit. It couldn't even sign its name to the complaint.

We have cured that problem here. That's why we filed our first motion – the motion to appoint our law firm guardian of the chimps in question. Once you grant that motion, we will file an amended complaint with a new caption: the plaintiff will be Peters and Peters as Guardians of Katy Kong et al.

The Court: You want your law firm to be the guardian of all those apes? Where you gonna put 'em? Do you have room in your office for all of 'em?

Mr. Peters: We're not seeking to become the physical guardian of Katy and the others. Just guardian ad litem. Guardian for purposes of this lawsuit. That kind of guardianship gets approved all the time. For infants, for example, and mentally incompetent persons.

Now, I don't mean to suggest that Katy Kong and the other chimps are mentally incompetent. To the contrary, they are quite intelligent. I may have mentioned this already but they share ninety-nine percent of the same genes as Mr. Horvath. Not only Mr. Horvath but Mr. Sherman, Mr. Lindgren and Ms. Stein as well. In fact, that could be why the zoo needs four lawyers, it doesn't want to be outsmarted by our client.

The Court: I see your point, Mr. Peters.

Mr. Peters: Now, here is the second reason the cases Mr. Horvath relies on are not dispositive. In none of them was there a record regarding the mental and human capacity of the animals in question. There was simply no evidence on that crucial issue.

Here, we are prepared to develop a record that will show that Katy Kong and the other members of the class are intelligent, autonomous human beings. With the same hopes and fears, and the same capacity to suffer, as humans. We will also prove that they resent being imprisoned in cages in zoos and would prefer to live free on a wildlife preserve. Preferably in Florida, where the weather is more like home. They hate the winters in New York.

The Court: How do you plan to prove all that?

Mr. Peters: We will present an expert, Doctor Doolittle – he's the country's leading expert on primates. Primatologists they're called. Doctor Doolittle is the top one in the field. He . . . .

Mr. Horvath: This is ridiculous. No expert can refute what we all know: apes aren't human . . . .

The Court: Mr. Horvath, Mr. Peters didn't interrupt you when you were carrying on about chimpanzees not being humans. I think you should show him the same courtesy.

Mr. Horvath: I'm sorry Judge.

The Court: Justice. How many times do I need to remind you? Mister Peters, you may continue.

Mr. Peters: I'm pretty much finished, Your Honor. If you approve our guardianship motion, our firm will have standing to bring this lawsuit on behalf of Ms. Kong and her colleagues. So, I think you should hold the zoo's motion to dismiss in abeyance until we've had a hearing at which we can present evidence from our expert. At that point you'll have a full record on which to make a ruling on the motion to dismiss. Thank you, Your Honor.

(Defendant's Counsel approaches the podium)

The Court: I don't think I need to hear any more, Mr. Horvath. I believe the procedure suggested by Mr. Peters is the right one. So here's what we're gonna do.

I'm going to grant the motion to have the Peters firm appointed Guardian *ad litem* for the chimps. They will only be guardian for purposes of maintaining this lawsuit. They don't have to take the chimps home or to their office. And they're not responsible for feeding them. It's not that kind of guardianship.

Second, I'll hold your motion to dismiss – as well as the class action motion – in abeyance pending the evidentiary hearing. Mr. Peters can have this Doctor Doolittle testify and you can cross-examine him. And put on any evidence you have in opposition.

Once we've concluded that hearing, I'll either grant your motion to dismiss or deny it and certify the case as a class action. After all, if I conclude that Katy Kong is competent to bring this lawsuit, there's no reason why the same shouldn't apply to all the other chimps.

Ms. Grimm will now meet with you both and determine a schedule for the hearing. As I said earlier, try to stay on her good side. That'll be all.

* * * *

As Justice Wright rose and left the bench, Pap looked at Pup and winked.

Horvath quickly packed his briefcase, looked at Sheppard Sherman, Lawrence Lindgren and Franklin Stein, gave a tight smile and shrugged his shoulders.

Horvath didn't mind that Justice Wright was requiring a hearing. Hearings, he told himself, were good. They required lots of preparation time and lots of time in court. And time spent on the case meant money in the bank for Oliver and Cromwell. The firm would do quite well on this case, that was the important thing. His partners would be pleased.

Chapter 16

LADIES DAY

The day after the hearing before Justice Wright, Pap called Pup and Melissa into his office to discuss the case.

"What do you think is the biggest thing we learned in court yesterday?" he asked.

"Well" said Pup "it basically confirmed our view that Justice Wright will be a good judge for this case. She seems surprisingly open to our argument."

"Yeah, that's true" said Pap. "But in terms of going forward, I don't think it's the most important thing we learned."

Melissa spoke up. "I think we learned that Justice Wright isn't all that fond of those blue-bloods at Oliver and Cromwell. And that she likes women lawyers."

"Bingo" said Pap. "Melissa's exactly right. Justice Wright not only likes to see a woman lawyer in the courtroom, she likes to see her play a meaningful role in the case. Not just carry the exhibits back and forth to court."

"If I weren't so little, you'd probably have me doing the same" Melissa said.

"Well, somebody's got to carry the exhibits to court and back" said Pap. "Can't be me, I need to keep my hands free so I can speak with the press.

"But look, here's what I'm thinking. Pup, why don't we have Melissa handle the testimony of Doctor Doolittle. Let Justice Wright see that our women lawyers have real responsibility."

"You said women lawyers. That's plural" said Melissa. "Have we hired another woman since yesterday?"

"Ha!" said Pap. "I think Melissa's trying to dodge my question. Which is, why not have her put on Doctor Doolittle?"

"I've never done that before" said Melissa. "I'm not sure you want my first time in court to be an examination of our most important witness on an issue where, if we lose, the case is over."

"Nonsense. I know you can do this. There's gotta be a first time for everything and this is the perfect first time for you. If you do a good job representing an ape, we might even let you represent a human some time."

"Well, I don't . . . ."

"Look, Melissa" Pap continued, "you'll be in front of a friendly judge who'll be rooting for you to do well. And because she'll be rooting for you, she'll listen extra carefully to what Doctor Doolittle has to say."

"I think Pap's right" said Pup. "You've already met with Doctor Doolittle twice and the two of you seem to get along very well."

"Maybe Melissa grew up on a farm like Doctor Doolittle" said Pap. "Maybe she even talked to the farm animals."

"Melissa grew up in Brooklyn" said Pup. "There haven't been any farms there since the eighteenth century."

"I just think" said Melissa, "that Doctor Doolittle likes me because I listen to what he has to say and don't smirk. He could tell that Pup was dubious about all this animal communication stuff."

"Probably so" agreed Pup. "But look, Melissa. I can help you prepare a Q and A for him and then we can do a practice run the day before the hearing. And once you get through the first few questions in court, you'll begin to fell comfortable."

"What if that jerk Horvath keeps objecting and interrupting, trying to throw me off?"

"Won't happen" said Pap. Judge Wright is not going to allow that stiff-necked, humorless bastard to distract you. He may try to but the judge is going to shoot him down."

"What do you say, Melissa? "said Pup. "Will you do it?"

"Sure. Sounds like a good plan."

* * * *

Three weeks later, Pap, Pup, Melissa and Doctor Doolittle got out of their livery car in front of the Supreme Court building. As they headed for the long row of steps leading up to the courthouse entrance, they were suddenly face-to-face with two groups of protesters. All of the protesters were wearing ape-faced Halloween masks.

One group carried placards reading "FREE THE CHIMPS." The other half had placards saying "APES R US." The two groups were engaged in back and forth chants of "Free the Chimps" followed by "Apes R Us."

The chanting was continuous. "Free the Chimps." "Apes R Us." "Free the Chimps." "Apes R Us."

One of the reporters observing the demonstration recognized Pap and called out to him. Telling Pup, Melissa and Dr. Doolittle to go on up to the courtroom, Pap walked over to the reporter. It was Miranda Marvello of Fox 10 News with a cameraman in tow.

"Mister Peters" she asked over the din of the demonstration, "can you tell our viewers why your firm brought this lawsuit?"

"Sure, Miranda. As you know, our firm always stands up for the little guys, especially when they are fighting for their rights against an uncaring, unscrupulous business. Well, these chimpanzees are classic little guys and they are being denied their freedom by being held against their will in zoos throughout the City."

"How do you know they're being held against their will? And wouldn't you agree the zoos probably treat them extremely well."

"The zoos never stop to think that these chimps might not want to be locked up in cages with people coming by and watching everything they do all day. They don't have an ounce of privacy. Would you want to be in their shoes?"

"I don't think chimpanzees wear shoes" said Miranda.

"Maybe boots" said Pap. "I've seen some of them walking around the zoo in those heavy work boots like construction workers wear."

"Seriously" insisted Miranda, "we can't just have dozens of apes roaming the streets of Manhattan like they're part of some horror movie."

"They should be permitted to roam free in nature preserves. There are two large preserves in Florida that are terrific. That's where we'll send them when we win this case. The chimps will feel much more at home there."

As Pap started to move toward the courthouse steps, Miranda shouted another question. "Isn't this just a publicity stunt?"

Pap was furious. "Miss Marvello, Peters and Peters doesn't do publicity stunts."

"But you held a press conference the day you filed the lawsuit."

"Of course we did. How else could we publicize what we're doing for these chimps. I'm sorry Miranda, but I've gotta go. Justice Wright always starts right on time and I don't want to be late."

And with that Pap bounded up the long row of steps and into the courthouse. Once inside he passed through the security line and headed for Justice Wright's courtroom, where he joined Pup and Melissa at the counsel table. Dr. Doolittle was seated behind them in the first row of the spectator section.

* * * *

There was a very long wait. Justice Wright was notorious for never starting on time. Finally her clerk, the imposing Greta Grimm, strode into the courtroom and immediately took charge.

Transcript of Proceedings:

Court Clerk: All rise. The New York Supreme Court in and for the County of New York, Justice Neva Wright presiding, is now in session. Please be seated. Counsel, please note your appearances for the record.

Mr. Peters: Patrick Peters, Prescott Peters and Melissa Muffett for the plaintiff.

The Court: Miss Muffett, what a pleasant surprise. It's nice to have you with us. I hope you'll be participating in the hearing.

Mr. Peters: She will, Your Honor. She will be conducting the examination of our expert witness, Doctor Doolittle.

The Court: Excellent. I'm looking forward to it.

Mr. Horvath: Hortescue Horvath, Sheppard Sherman, Lawrence Lindgren and Franklin Stein for the defendant.

The Court: What happened to all those seconds, thirds and fourths? Don't you want to include them for the record?

Mr. Horvath: I don't believe so, Your Honor. We'll keep it short and simple today.

The Court: I certainly hope so. Now, as you all know, I agreed to hold this hearing before ruling on defendant's motion to dismiss. I believe the issue before us today is whether the chimps and apes in the three zoos operated by defendant should have the same right as humans to file a lawsuit. Is that correct?

Mr. Peters: Yes, but we're not talking about their right to file any conceivable lawsuit. We're not talking about them pursuing their second amendment rights or bringing a lawsuit seeking a refund on a bunch of rotten bananas. We're only talking about their right to bring a lawsuit challenging their detention by defendant. It's a very narrow question.

Mr. Horvath: Your Honor, that's just the problem with this case. Mister Peters may claim it's a very narrow lawsuit seeking only narrow relief. But mark my words, if this case is allowed to proceed it will open the cages – I mean the floodgates – for all kinds of lawsuits in the future.

If these apes can sue to protest their so-called detention by defendant, then they would also be allowed to sue to demand better food. Or better reading material. Or they could sue demanding the right to own guns. Maybe even assault weapons. Imagine if all the apes in all the zoos in the city were allowed to carry assault weapons and went around shooting at anything that moved. That would be . . . ."

The Court: Mister Horvath, you're getting a little ahead of things here. This case isn't about the next case. It's about this case. It's only about whether the chimps your client is holding in its zoos - perhaps against their will – can pursue a lawsuit challenging their detention. That's all this hearing is about and that's all I plan to decide. Whether they're in fact being held against their will is a separate question. We would have to address that at a trial on the merits when – I mean if - I deny your motion to dismiss. Now, Mister Peters and Miss Muffett, are you ready to proceed?

Mr. Peters: We are Your Honor. We call our primatologist expert, Doctor Doolittle. My colleague Miss Muffett will conduct the examination.

The Court: Dr. Doolittle, please take the stand and Ms. Grimm will swear you in.

Ms. Grimm: Please state your full name and raise your right hand.

The Witness: Dr. Doolittle.

Ms. Grimm: Perhaps you didn't hear me. I said your full name, not just your last name.

The Witness: Klint Kwak.

The Court: Klint Kwak? I thought you were Doolittle?

The Witness: I am. My birth name is Klint A. Kwak. But my professional name is Dr. Doolittle. So I'm Klint Kwak dba Dr. Doolittle.

(Witness is sworn in)

Direct Examination by Ms. Muffett:

Q: Good morning, Dr. Doolittle. Please tell us how you came to acquire the Dr. Doolittle name.

A: Well, I've been talking to animals all my life. Ever since I was a young boy growing up on a farm in Vermont. We had animals of all kinds: dogs, cats, horses, cows, goats and more. I always loved talkin' to 'em while I was doing my chores. Later, when I started up my practice and clients learned that I could talk with animals, they started calling me Dr. Doolittle. After the veterinarian in that children's book. It stuck and so I decided to make it my business name.

Q: You have several academic degrees, I believe?

A: Yep. Undergraduate degree from the University of Vermont, I majored in Agriculture. Then a Masters in Anthropology from the State University of New York, Albany, and a PhD in Primatology from there as well.

Q: And have you published articles in your field in academic journals?

A: Yes, over twenty. They're listed in my CV. I would've written more but my practice is a full-time job and it keeps me really busy. Doesn't leave much time to write scholarly articles.

Especially since you have to put all those footnotes in the articles. I hate footnotes.

The Court: I agree with you on that, Dr. Doolittle. Attorneys are always putting footnotes in their briefs, like they're writing some pretentious law review article. It's a waste of time. I never read them.

Q: Speaking of your practice, Dr. Doolittle, what does it encompass?

A: Almost anything involving communication with animals. I've probably communicated with over five thousand animals during my career.

Q: What do you talk with them about?

A: It depends on what I'm hired to do.

Q: Could you give the Court some examples of what you're hired to do?

A: Well, take farm animals, as that's where I first started getting into the field. Farmers frequently want to know why one of their cows isn't producing much milk. So, if the vet hasn't been able to find a physical problem, I meet with the cow and try to find out what's bothering her.

Q: What about horses?

A: Oh, that's a big part of my practice. Race horse owners always want to know why their horse doesn't do better in big races. So, I gotta talk to the horse and see what the problem is. Diet? Exercise? Nerves? I need to get to the bottom of what's bothering the horse.

Q: I believe you also get hired in divorce cases?

A: Absolutely. Justice Wright, you'll appreciate this. I'm frequently brought into divorce cases as a court-appointed expert to figure out which party gets the dog. Seems like most divorcing couples always have a dog and they always fight about who gets to keep it. They sometimes fight about the dog more than about who gets the kids.

Q: So do you go and talk with the dog?

A: That's the only way to do it. You just gotta go and talk with the dog and see what it wants. And then I report that back to the court, they almost always take my recommendation. No judge wants to be in the doghouse for awarding the dog to the wrong spouse.

Q: Okay. So now let's talk about chimpanzees. How much experience have you had with them and with other members of the ape family?

A: Apes are right up my alley. I've been studying and talking with them for years.

Q: Can you give us some examples?

A: Sure. Over the past couple of years I've served as a court-appointed expert in three cases in upstate New York involving chimpanzees. All three cases involved claims by animal rights groups – such as PETA and the Nonhuman Rights Project – that chimps being held on small farms were entitled to file writs of habeas corpus. So I got to know the chimps in those cases.

Q: What did you observe in those cases?

A: My observations in those cases confirmed my long-held view that chimpanzees are remarkably intelligent and sophisticated creatures with highly developed social, cognitive and communicative skills. They have families, friends, interests and emotions just like humans. That is, by the way, consistent with what you find reported in the vast literature on chimpanzees.

The Court: You mean all those long-winded articles with dozens of footnotes?

A: Right. You can usually just read the first page and get the gist of the article. I usually skip the rest.

Q: So when you were observing the chimps in those cases, what specifically did you observe that reinforced your long-held view?

A: Well, perhaps the most striking thing I discovered was how much their leisure time activity mirrors that of humans. For example, Tommy – he lived on a farm near Albany – had a stereo. He spent lots of time listening to music. He loved those old songs about dogs, such as "How Much is that Dogie in the Window?" Tommy had always wanted to have a dog. There was also a song about chimps that he loved: "Daba Daba Daba said the Chimpy to the Monk." He played it all the time. But Tommy's favorite was "Hold That Tiger." He was terrified of tigers.

Q: Sounds like he really appreciated good music. Now, what about the chimp who lived near Buffalo?

A: That was Kiko. Now Kiko loved television. Had a TV set up in his barn. Didn't much care for the news but he loved football. He was a huge Buffalo Bills fan, watched all their games. He kept hoping they would get back to the Super Bowl.

Q: And the third case, didn't that involve a chimp near Binghampton?

A: Actually two chimps lived there, Hercules and Leo. They also had a TV but they mostly watched movies. Mostly animal movies, such as Tarzan, they loved the old Tarzan movies. Planet of the Apes was also a favorite.

Q: Dr. Doolittle, I haven't asked you about Spider Monkeys. There are several of them being detained at the Staten Island Zoo. Are they comparable to chimpanzees in terms of intelligence and the other characteristics we've been discussing?

A: Oh yes. If anything, they could be even smarter than chimpanzees. Their native habitat is the rain forests of Central and South America. There are no rain forests on Staten Island, at least none that I'm aware of. What a shame all those Spider Monkeys are forced to live on Staten Island.

The Court: I've always felt that way abut the humans who live there.

Q: Dr. Doolittle, you said Spider Monkeys could be more intelligent than chimpanzees. Can you give us the basis for that belief?

A: The Staten Island Zoo is home to one of the most famous Spider Monkeys in history. He's pretty old, so they call him "Grandpa." Well, Grandpa is quite clairvoyant. He can predict the outcome of sporting events, such as tennis matches.

Q: You can't be serious.

A: Dead serious. You may have even read about it in the paper. A few years ago, 2010 I think it was, Grandpa accurately predicted the outcome of six out of nine tennis matches at the

U.S. Open. He does the same for baseball games, such as predicting the winner of the so-called Subway Series between the Yankees and the Mets. The gamblers always look for his prediction before placing their bets.

Q: Sounds like he could be useful in political campaigns.

A: He is. The zoo spent a lot of time publicizing his predictions in the 2012 primaries. He was far more accurate than the professional pollsters.

Q: So Dr. Doolittle, based on your experience as well as the scholarly literature on the subject, do you have an opinion as to whether chimpanzees and spider monkeys are sufficiently intelligent beings that they should have the right to pursue a lawsuit to seek release from their captivity?

A: Yes. They are intelligent and autonomous beings, and they express the same feelings, joys and fears as human beings. They should have a right to be heard regarding their captivity.

Q: No further questions Your Honor.

The Court: We'll take a ten-minute break before Mr. Horvath begins his cross-examination. Mister Peters, you have quite an accomplished associate there. You should give her a raise.

Chapter 17

CHIMP SPEAK

After everyone had re-assembled following the break, Greta Grimm opened the door to Justice Wright's robing room and beckoned her in.

"Please be seated" the judge said as she took the bench. "Mister Horvath, you may cross-examine Doctor Doolittle."

Cross-Examination by Mr. Horvath:

Q: Mr. Kwak, I'd like to ask you about . . . .

The Court: Mr. Horvath, the witness has testified that his business and professional name is Dr. Doolittle. I think we should refer to him as Dr. Doolittle in this courtroom. You may call him whatever you wish when you're back in your office with your colleagues.

Q: Very well. Dr. Doolittle, I want to ask you about those Spider Monkeys in the Staten Island Zoo. Particularly the one they call Grandpa. The one who predicts the outcome of sporting events and primary races.

A: Sure. What's your question?

Q: How does anyone know what his prediction is? Surely they don't just go and ask him?

A: Well, they've developed procedures for this. Take tennis matches. They take two tennis balls. The name of one opponent goes on one ball, the other opponent on the second. They put both balls in front of Grandpa and wait to see which one he picks up first. The name on that ball is the projected winner.

Q: So Grandpa's not really choosing the winner of the match. He's just choosing which of the two balls he wants to play with.

A: That's where you're wrong. Each ball is clearly marked with the name of one of the players. The balls are placed name up, so Grandpa can plainly see the two names. So he's not just choosing a ball, he's choosing a ball with a particular player's name.

Q: And you believe Grandpa is cognitively thinking that the player who's name is on the ball he chooses is the player who will win the match?

A: Certainly. Why else would he choose that ball over the other ball?

Q: All right, let's put aside tennis balls. Let's talk about political forecasting. The primary in 2012 that you referred to.

A: Sure. What's your question?

Q: My question is, how does Grandpa go about predicting the winner of the primary? Let's say it's New Hampshire and there are five candidates on the ballot. How does Grandpa go about predicting the winner? Do they put all the names on tennis balls and see which ball he chooses?

A: Oh no. For tennis it's easy to get Grandpa to participate. He loves tennis. But he's not very fond of politics. Thinks most politicians are baboons – not very smart and also quite greedy.

Q: Baboons aren't smart?

A: No sir. They're not at all like chimpanzees and Spider Monkeys. That's why nobody is trying to give them legal rights.

Q: Okay, so Grandpa thinks politicians are baboons. But how does he go about projecting a winner in the primary?

A: You see, because he doesn't like politics, they need to give him an incentive to participate. The incentive is bananas. His favorite food. So, say there are five candidates on the ballot in New Hampshire. They take five bananas and put the name of a candidate on each of them. Then they put the bananas in front of him. Name facing up. Whichever one he picks up first is his choice as the winner.

Q: So Grandpa really is just picking up a banana. He could pick up any one of 'em. It's all just fortuitous.

A: That's where you're wrong, Mr. Horvath. Grandpa is looking at the array of bananas, each bearing a different name. He only picks up the one with the name he likes best. And he's generally been right. None of the pollsters even came close to him in 2012. You can look it up.

Q: I think I'll move on, we're not getting anywhere. Ms. Stein, may I have a copy of the complaint. Mr. Kwak – I'm sorry, Dr. Doolittle – I'm looking at paragraph 24 of the complaint. It states that plaintiff – the chimp – and the other chimps and Spider Monkeys in the zoos operated by defendant are being held against their will. The complaint goes on to demand that they all be released from this alleged involuntary confinement so that they can be sent to a wildlife preserve in Florida.

A: What's your question?

Q: My question is, how do you know they're being held against their will?

A: I don't. At least not yet.

Q: You're saying all these members of the purported class may not in fact be held against their will?

A: I suspect a majority of them are. But I won't know until I talk with them. That's what I explained when Ms. Muffett was asking me questions. My job is to communicate with the chimps and find out what they think about their confinement.

Q: So what will you be communicating with them about?

A: Pretty much everything. How do they like where they are? Are they getting enough food? Enough exercise? Are they able to spend time with their family and friends? Are their medical needs being attended to? By the time I'm finished I'll have a pretty good idea of whether they'd rather be somewhere else, like a wildlife sanctuary.

Q: Aren't you just going to come back and tell us that all of them are being held against their will? That they all want to go to this wildlife preserve in Florida?

A: Oh no, not at all. I suspect a few of them might be quite comfortable where they are. Especially the ones who aren't particularly adventuresome. Take that fellow Kiko on that farm near Buffalo. He was perfectly happy, particularly since he had his own TV where he could watch all the Bills' games. He had no desire to live elsewhere, especially on a wildlife preserve where there would be no TV.

Q: So when and where will you meet with these apes?

A: I'll begin as soon as Justice Wright gives me the go-ahead. And I'll talk with them right where they are. You don't have to bring 'em in like its a deposition or something. I'll talk with them in their present environment. Just like I did with Miss Katy.

Q: Like you did with Miss Katy? You've already talked with that chimp? Without the Court's permission? Without allowing the Zoo's counsel to be present?

A: Sure, I . . . .

Mr. Horvath: Your Honor, this is absolutely outrageous. Dr. Doolittle had no right to go snooping around our zoo, talking with our inmates – I mean animals – without the zoo having the right to have its counsel preset. Or its expert, to make sure Dr. Doolittle is accurately reporting what that chimp said.

The Court: You mean you have your own expert in animal communication? Seems to me you are conceding that humans can indeed communicate with animals.

Mr. Horvath: The zoo makes no such concession. Its attendants may talk to the animals every day but they don't communicate with them. Anyway, my point is that this was an improper ex parte contact with a witness and so Dr. Doolittle's testimony on this matter should be stricken and plaintiff should be sanctioned.

The Court: Mr. Horvath, Katy – or "that chimp" as you keep calling her – is the plaintiff. Her attorneys, and now her Guardian ad litem, is the Peters firm. They didn't need my approval to have their expert speak with their client. And you have no right to demand that they speak with Katy in your presence. That would violate the attorney/client privilege.

So, as far as the Court is concerned, there was nothing improper about what Dr. Doolittle did. Why don't you ask him what he found out when he spoke with Katy? I'm sure we would all like to hear his answer.

Mr. Horvath: But Your Honor, we're now getting into the merits of plaintiff's claim. Their claim of wrongful detention. I thought this was just a hearing on whether that claim could even be advanced, or whether, as we believe, it should be dismissed.

The Court: It seems to me, Mr. Horvath, you're trying awfully hard to prevent Dr. Doolittle from telling us what he learned when he spoke with Miss Katy. If you don't wish to ask him, I will.

Q: Okay. So Dr. Doolittle, when you snuck into the Bronx Zoo and spoke with that chimp without anyone else present, what did it tell you? That only you can relate because nobody else was present?

A: I didn't sneak into the zoo. It was open to the public. I went in like any other visitor. And I spoke with an attendant in the chimp house who showed me where I could find Katy. I invited him to stay with me while I spoke with her but he was busy. Said it wasn't necessary, people always try to speak with the chimps.

Q: How long did you meet with that chimp?

A: Only about half an hour. I want to talk with her more, but that half hour was sufficient to tell me what I needed to know.

Q: And what was that?

A: That the plaintiff in this case, Miss Katy, is in a very abusive relationship with her boyfriend. The big guy, Kong. At first, when he was wooing her, he was nice and sweet. But over time he's grown extremely domineering and abusive. Beats her, steals her bananas, won't let her mingle with the other chimps. She is utterly miserable. Desperately wants to get out of there. She'd move to a sanctuary in Florida in a heartbeat.

Q: You expect us to believe that?

A: Certainly. I'm under oath to tell the truth. Why would I lie?

Q: But we've no way to determine if what you've told us is true. I mean, whether what you say that chimp told you is true.

A: Have your own expert meet with her. I'm not the only animal communicator in the country.

Q: But any of you so-called animal communicators could meet with an animal and then come into court and say here's what it told me — and there's no way on earth anyone can determine whether what the communicator said is true.

A: I'm sorry but you're wrong again. All you have to do is examine my record. I can have Mr. Peters' firm provide you with a list of all the divorce cases where I was appointed by the court to determine who should get the dog. Then go talk with some of the dogs. All of them if you like. You'll find that all of them wound up where they wanted to be.

The Court: We need to take a lunch break now. I don't know how much longer you plan to be with this witness; I can devote another hour to this case but I have another matter at three o'clock. If an hour isn't sufficient, you'll have to come back another day. Let's reconvene at two.

* * * *

At two fifteen Greta Grimm walked into the courtroom, shouted "All Rise" and Justice Wright came in and took her seat on the bench.

Transcript of Heraring:

The Court: Mr. Horvath, if you have further questions for this witness you may proceed.

Mr. Horvath: No Your Honor, we have no further questions of this witness. However, we move to strike his testimony regarding his conversation with the chimp. Its captivity is not the subject of this hearing. The only issue before the Court today is whether plaintiff should be allowed to pursue this lawsuit. So Dr. Doolittle's conversation with the chimp – which we have no way of knowing whether what he said it told him is true - is irrelevant to the question before the court today. So we move to strike that portion of his testimony.

Ms. Muffett: Your Honor . . . .

The Court: Ms. Muffett, there's no need for you to respond. The motion is denied. Mr. Horvath, you opened the door – you might have even opened the cage – for that testimony. You specifically asked Dr. Doolittle how he would determine whether the chimps were being held against their will and he proceeded to tell you. You cannot strike testimony you elicited.

Mr. Horvath: Well, that's not . . . .

The Court: Motion denied. Let's move on. Ms. Muffett, do you have anything further to present?

Ms. Muffett: No, Your Honor.

The Court: Mr. Horvath, is there anything you wish to present on this issue?

Mr. Horvath: Not in the way of evidence. Our real argument is a legal argument. As we spelled out in our brief in support of the motion to dismiss . . . .

The Court: The Court is well aware of your legal argument. We have read your brief in support of your motion. And your reply brief in support of the motion. And your brief in opposition to plaintiff's Guardianship motion. And your brief in opposition to the class action motion. We've even read your sur-reply briefs in opposition to those two motions, even though sur-reply briefs are not allowed in State court. Maybe they're allowed over there in Federal court where the judges all have two or three clerks each. Here it's just me and Ms. Grimm who have to wade through all the briefs you and your colleagues file.

Now, if there is no further evidence to be presented, the Court is prepared to issue its ruling. I always find that the best time to issue a decision is immediately after I've concluded the hearing. I will never be more familiar with the issue than I am then.

So, the Court finds, based on the evidence presented at today's hearing, that plaintiff Katy, as well as the other chimps and Spider Monkeys in the three zoos in question, are entitled to pursue this lawsuit. To be more precise, I find that because the chimps and Spider Monkeys are intelligent and – Ms. Muffett, what was that other word Dr. Doolittle kept using?

Ms. Muffett: Autonomous. Intelligent and autonomous.

The Court: Right. Because they are intelligent and autonomous beings who, like humans, have feelings, fears and emotions, it is appropriate for their Guardian ad litem – the Peters firm – to bring an action on their behalf contesting their detention. Whether or not they are being unlawfully detained is an issue for trial. Today's ruling does not address that question.

Ms. Muffett, if you will submit an Order to chambers, Ms. Grimm will see that it gets signed and filed. Anything else before we depart?

Mr. Horvath: Your Honor, when will we get your full written opinion?

The Court: You just got my full opinion. And as soon as the court reporter has the transcript completed, you will have a written copy of it.

Mr. Horvath: But we . . . .

The Court: That will be all. Good day.

* * * *

Pap and Pup immediately turned to Melissa and congratulated her on her performance.

"Melissa" said Pap, "I'd love to give you a hug but I think I'd probably get in trouble with the EEOC. But you were terrific. Great job.

"But now we've got to get downstairs. You and Pup order up a car and then take Doctor Doolittle down. Try to keep him away from the press. I'll deal with them. I can't wait to tell them Peters and Peters won a ground-breaking decision on animal rights. It'll be on all the news shows tonight and the papers tomorrow. The firm's gonna' be famous."

Chapter 18

TORTS "R" TOURISM

Two weeks after the final day of the chimps trial, Pap and his public relations consultant, Jack Boks, were in Hartford for a meeting of the General Assembly's Committee on Economic Development.

As Democrats controlled the General Assembly, the Committee was chaired by a Democrat, Sam Snake, an attorney with the Bridgeport law firm of Snake, Rabble and Rolle. Pap knew Snake from their days together in the New York District Attorney's office when they were just out of law school. While Snake opted to move to Connecticut so that he could eventually go into politics, Pap opted to stay in New York City so that he could eventually make a lot of money.

The Committee's ranking Republican member was Assemblyman Kit Sink from Stamford. Sink was a partner in the firm of Sink, Ore and Swinn. When Pap had met with Chairman Snake about his plan, Snake had taken him to meet with Assemblyman Sink. Sink and Snake agreed that Pap's plan had merit and should be presented to the entire committee.

Chairman Snake called the committee to order. "Good morning everyone. I'm glad all members of the Committee could be here for this hearing. I think we will all find it most interesting."

After introducing Pap to the committee, he turned to Pap and said: "Patrick, I know you've met Assemblyman Sink from Stamford, our ranking minority member, who is on my right. I don't believe you know the other members, so let me briefly introduce them.

"On my left is Assemblyman Raff, Rick Raff. He's from Hartford where he's a partner in the firm of Riff and Raff.

"Next to Assemblyman Raff is the other Republican member of the Committee, Gino Garibaldi. Mr. Garibaldi is a solo practitioner in Waterbury.

"Now, next to Assemblyman Sink is Assemblywoman Bea Ware from New Haven. Just to show you that we don't discriminate against non-lawyers, Ms. Ware is a businesswoman. She owns a chain of funeral homes in the New Haven area. It's a very successful business I might add."

"That's because demand never seems to fall off" said Ware.

"Last but not least, next to Assemblywoman Ware is Assemblyman Motley, Marion Motley, from Bridgeport. Assemblyman Motley is a partner in the Motley Crew firm in Bridgeport."

"Mr. Chairman" said Assemblywoman Ware, "sorry to interrupt. But how did it happen that everyone on the committee except me is a lawyer?"

"I think the leadership in the General Assembly wanted people on this Committee who don't know anything about economic development. If we started having economic development in the state, there would be no reason to raise taxes. And so, the leadership concluded, who knows less about economic development than lawyers."

"I see their point of view" said Ware. "I also see that our witness today is a lawyer. So let me see if I've got this straight: a lawyer who knows nothing about economic development will be presenting a plan for economic development to a group of lawyers who know nothing about economic development."

"Exactly" said Chairman Snake. "So let's not waste any time. I think we should get started. Patrick, I see that you have someone with you that you would like the Committee to hear from after you speak."

"Yes I do" said Pap. "Next to me is a gentleman who has been working closely with my firm on the proposal I am about to present. His name is Boks, Jack N. Boks. He's a partner in a high powered public relations firm in Stamford. Stamford, as I'm sure everyone here knows, is the hub of corporate business in Connecticut. Assemblyman

Sink, I know you're from Stamford, you undoubtedly know Mr. Boks' firm."

"No, I don't believe so" said Sink. "Mr. Boks, what firm are you with? I thought I knew everyone in the PR business in Stamford."

Chairman Snake nodded to Boks to indicate that he was free to respond. So Boks said:

"My firm is Boks and Socks. We're fairly new. Right now we're operating out of a room over Buddy's Body Shop in the Springdale section of Stamford. My partner, Sam Socks, handles our corporate PR. It's mostly for small businesses. Delis, pizza parlors, hair salons, businesses like that. I try to focus on politicians and celebrities. They seem to have the same needs and concerns, I think of them as pretty much interchangeable."

"How long have you been in this business?" asked Sink.

"Three months. As I said, we're just getting started."

"What did you do before you started up this high powered PR firm in a room over Buddy's Body Shop?"

"I traveled a lot. Actually, I traveled all over the world."

"Doing what?"

"Well, I was in the circus."

"What did you do in the circus?"

"I was a clown."

"A circus clown?" said an astonished Assemblyman Raff.

"Sure, a circus clown, what's wrong with that? I was the lead clown for Ringling Brothers, Barnum and Bailey. But as you know, it recently closed down. After more than a century in business. One hundred forty-six years to be precise. A damn shame."

"Say" said Assemblyman Sink, "I think I may have seen you perform. My wife and I took our kids to the circus when it was at Madison Square Garden a couple of years ago. They turned the lights way down and someone rolled out a large brightly painted wooden box. There was a long drum roll and then all of a sudden the top popped open and out jumped a clown dressed in red, white and blue."

"That was me" said Boks. "That's how I always made my entrance."

135

"But how did the top happen to pop open just as you were jumping out of the box?"

"There's a button I pushed just before I sprang to my feet. It's all about timing. If I jumped up too quickly, my head would hit the top of the box, that really hurt. I must have sustained a couple dozen concussions hitting my head like that over the years."

"Well" said Assemblywoman Ware, "I hope you haven't had any long-term affects from all those concussions. Like loss of brain cells or something."

"No, not at all. My mind is just as fine today as it was when I was in the circus."

"We're getting a little off-track here" said Chairman Snake. "But what I think the committee would like to know is how you happened to go into public relations after the circus closed down. And you couldn't jump out of that box any more."

"Well" Boks began, "when the circus closed down, I had to find a new career. I thought about becoming a surgeon, but didn't think I could get through medical school. Same with becoming a lawyer. I understand you have to pass some sort of an examination to practice law."

"It's called a bar examination" said Assemblyman Snake.

"Right" said Boks. "And I wasn't sure I could ever pass it, I'm not good at remembering things."

"Probably from all those concussions" said Assemblywoman Ware.

"Right. Anyway, after I ruled out becoming a lawyer or a surgeon, I said to myself: Jack, what is it that you're good at? And my answer was: making people happy. And I thought, that's what pubic relations folks do. They may not wear a costume or paint their face like I did - well, at least not that I know of - but their job is to make their clients happy. I realized I was sort of doing public relations all those years in the circus, so this was a natural fit."

The room was silent for several moments. Finally, Chairman Snake spoke up. "Patrick, you were always pulling rabbits out of hats when you were trying cases in the DA's office. I'm glad to see you're still doing the same in private practice."

"Actually" said Assemblywoman Ware, "I think he's just pulled a Jack out of the box."

"Right" said Snake. "I stand corrected."

After a short pause, Snake said "Okay, let's move this hearing along. Patrick, why don't you explain your plan to the Committee. Although none of us knows the first thing about economic development, I'll give everyone on the Committee an opportunity to ask you questions about your plan for economic development. After that, we can hear from Mister Jack in the Box."

So Pap proceeded to give a lawyer-like presentation of the idea he had presented to Congressman Earmacher over lunch at the Hay Adams. He started with the sad state of the economy in the State's three large cities – Bridgeport, Hartford and New Haven. And the fact that all three cities housed a federal courthouse but none of them saw much in the way of big money lawsuits that would bring teams of lawyers to town.

Pap then told the committee about California. That in a five-month period, over one hundred lawsuits had been filed in the state on behalf of consumers claiming some sort of deceptive advertising. And that those cases had been filed in California only because California had a broad consumer deception law that encouraged the filing of such lawsuits.

Pap pointed out that those cases were frequently filed as class actions, where the stakes were unusually high, and so both sides would retain large law firms. Those firms would, in turn, assign several lawyers and a paralegal or two to the case. So the city where the case was filed would receive the economic benefit of two large teams of lawyers decamping there for weeks at a time.

Saving the best for last, Pap told the story of how Marshall, a tiny town in east Texas, had reinvented itself as a favorable venue for patent litigation. And how patent lawyers around the country began filing their cases in Marshall. Two hundred and thirty-six patent cases had been filed in Marshall in a single year!

That litigation explosion, Pap said, had reinvigorated the town. New hotels went up. New restaurants opened. Scores of jobs in construction were created, followed by scores of jobs for hotel and restaurant workers once the new buildings were completed. And all of this was accompanied by an avalanche of new business for bars, fitness centers, message therapists, coffee bars and upscale prostitutes.

Pap went on to explain how lawyers who were out of town on a big case operate.

"After court is over for the day, they first need to revive themselves with a grande latte. Then they head to the hotel's fitness center for a work-out, before they get a message to ease their tension, following which they go out for a lavish dinner on the client before they head for a bar in search of a hook-up. The hook-up is, of course, on the lawyers' own dime, although sometimes they manage to find a way to pass it on to the client.

"So" Pap concluded, "if Connecticut adopts the new consumer protection law my firm has drafted, these lawyers with their big cases will start coming to Connecticut. They will bring their entourage of people to Bridgeport, Hartford and New Haven. Those cities will enjoy an economic renaissance. If this isn't economic development I don't know what is."

"Patrick, I want to thank you for this very thoughtful plan" said Chairman Snake. "We've been struggling for years to find a way to jump-start the economy in those three cities. Despite the fact that all but one member of this committee is a lawyer, none of us ever thought of the angle you're proposing."

"That's understandable" said Pap. "You are all small time lawyers doing . . . I'm sorry, I mean small town lawyers. Your practices are focused on everyday issues – real estate sales, divorces, getting your friends' speeding tickets quashed, finding ways to avoid taxes, that sort of thing.

"If you haven't represented large corporations in a large litigation or large corporate deal, you'd have no way of knowing what that kind of practice is like and the economic impact it can have. These big firms hire kids just out of law school and pay them a hundred and sixty thousand a year. And the pay goes up quickly in the following years; by the time you make partner you're probably gonna make a million a year.

"Now, a firm's gotta have a lot of big cases and big corporate deals to afford salaries like that. And they do. They have tons of big cases and deals. I don't know why Assemblywoman Ware thinks lawyers don't understand economic development. I can assure you that lawyers in big city firms know all about economic development, they engage in it every day.

"But here's the important thing for you to remember. When the big case happens to be out of town, the firm can hardly expect its lawyers to abandon the lavish lifestyle they've become accustomed to and start living like you guys do. When they go out of town, they need the same first class accommodations and services they've become used to at home."

"I can see that" said Chairman Snake. "We could never expect attorneys from a big city firm to stay at our only hotel in Bridgeport, 'May's End' it's called. Actually, it's really just a motel, it's not a real hotel."

"What's wrong with 'May's End'?" demanded Assemblyman Motley. "I have lunch there all the time. And I've even stayed there several times, it's perfectly fine."

"Assemblyman Motley" asked Assemblyman Sink, "why would you have need of a motel in Bridgeport? You live in Bridgeport."

"Mister Sink" said Motley in a huff, "you tight-ass Republicans never have any fun. We Democrats in Bridgeport may not be as rich as you and your fellow Republicans in Stamford and Greenwich, but we know how to have fun. And 'May's End' is a nice place to have fun."

"To tell you the truth" replied Sink, "we've got a place like that in downtown Stamford. 'Quick Tricks' it's called. And that's all it's good for. You wouldn't want lawyers from fancy out-of-town firms staying there."

"It's the same in Waterbury" said Assemblyman Garibaldi. "Right in the old downtown area, there's a dive called 'Inn and Out.' That's I-N-N, two n's. Been there for years."

"There's a place like that in New Haven" said Assemblywoman Ware. "'One and Done' it's called. They cater to seniors."

"Now that we seem to be taking an inventory" said Chairman Snake, "what about right here in Hartford? Any hotels like that?" he asked as he looked at Assemblyman Raff.

"Oh sure" Raff answered. "'Quicken Moans.' It's just a few blocks from here. I'm surprised you don't know about it."

"Ha ha" said Snake. "But now I think we've exhausted the matter of the need for new hotels in our cities. Let's move on. Who has a question for Mr. Peters?"

"I do" said Assemblywoman Ware. "Mr. Peters, I'm an undertaker, not a lawyer, so I don't know anything about the kinds of cases you hope your legislation would attract. Can you give us some idea of the kinds of cases that are going to bring lawyers from around the country flocking to Connecticut?"

"I'm glad you asked that, Assemblywoman Ware" said Pap. "You wouldn't believe the huge number of lawsuits filed by consumers over the past few years. Almost any labeling or advertising claim can lead to a lawsuit by a consumer.

"Take food products. They are the source of more than half the cases. As you know, all kinds of foods are now promoted as 'healthy' or 'nutritious.' And 'all natural', that's really a big claim these days. But sometimes the product contains a small amount of an ingredient the foodies deem bad, such as trans fats. So the plaintiffs argue that the presence of that ingredient makes the advertising false."

"What are trans fats?" asked Assemblyman Garibaldi.

Pap had no idea what trans fats were. So he replied: "Trans fats are fats that are undergoing a transition. They're transitioning from good fats to bad fats. That's why tort lawyers have been bringing dozens of cases complaining about trans fats in foods promoted as healthy."

Pap went quickly on before anyone could reply. "Now there's an interesting case involving Fruit Hoops. The company that makes 'em was sued in a class action on the ground that consumers are deceived into believing that Fruit Hoops contain actual fruit. Not just a fruit flavor but actual fruit.

"And there's also a big case involving yogurt. Zhobani was sued for falsely promoting it's yogurt as Greek when it's actually made in Turkey."

"Well" said Assemblyman Garibaldi, "if it's not made in Greece it shouldn't be called Greek Yogurt. That would be like calling sausage Italian Sausage when it's actually made in Bulgaria."

"Bulgarian sausage would appeal to me" said Assemblywoman Ware. "I don't see why you're making fun of it."

"If Bulgarian sausage is made in Bulgaria, it can't be genuine Italian sausage" insisted Garibaldi. "Ask any Italian."

Ignoring this exchange, Pap continued. "When I met with Congressman Earmacher, I told him about a case involving Junior Mints. It's a class action case. The plaintiff claims the package is only filled to fifty-seven percent capacity, yet comparable candies – such as Milk Duds and Good n Plenty - are filled to seventy-five percent capacity."

"Milk Duds are much better than Junior Mints" said Assemblyman Raff. "I'm glad to hear you get your money's worth with them."

"I prefer Good n Plenty" said Assemblyman Motley. "Been eaten 'em since I was a kid. Mints are for sissies. They're probably popular in Westport and Greenwich."

"I hope the plaintiffs don't win all of these cases" said Assemblyman Garibaldi. "A lot of the claims seem like they could be implausible." Garibaldi was a Republican and Republicans didn't believe in frivolous lawsuits. Unless they brought them.

"It's certainly true that some of the claims in these cases are implausible" said Pap. "But it's not a matter of which side wins. The important thing is that the case – and the hundreds of other cases just like it – were brought. Doesn't matter if they're good cases or frivolous cases. What matters is that they were brought. And sadly, they were all brought somewhere else. We want them to be brought in Connecticut.

"So" Pap said as he shifted into his most dramatic voice, "if you pass this consumer protection legislation our firm has proposed, you can tell tort lawyers across the country that Connecticut is open for business. Tell them our welcome mat is out for them.

"Pass this legislation and they will come. The lawyers will come. And come and come. And when they come we'll have a bunch of nice new hotels and restaurants for 'em. No more nights at 'Quicken Moans' in Hartford or 'One and Done' in New Haven. No more crummy lunches and dinners at 'May's End' in Bridgeport. In fact, Assemblyman Motley will now have no trouble getting a table for lunch there. Or a room for the evening.

"Let me end by saying that my colleagues and I at stand ready to assist you in any way we can with respect to this legislation. We greatly appreciate your interest in this matter. Thank you for your time and attention."

"Are there any questions for Mr. Peters?" asked Chairman Snake.

"I'd like to hear from Mr. Boks" said Assemblyman Sink. "We can pass all the consumer protection laws we want, but unless lawyers from around the country know about them and start filing cases here, nothing much is going to happen. I want to know what he thinks we can do to make that happen."

"Before we do that" said Snake, "let's take a ten-minute recess. We've been going at this for some time.

"And Patrick, I hope your Mr. Boks is going to give us some real specifics, we don't need the usual PR generalities. Remember, this is economic development we're talking about. We need specifics. Especially since none of us on the committee knows anything about economic development."

Chapter 19

THE TORTE STATE

"I always hold my breath when we take a break" Chairman Snake said when the hearing resumed. "People go back to their office and find other things to do. Check their Facebook page, send out selfies, play computer games, whatever. Anyway, this is a pleasant surprise. Thank you all for coming back."

"We couldn't wait to hear what this clown – I'm sorry, former clown – has to say" said Assemblyman Raff.

"I'm sure we'd all like to hear what Mr. Boks has to say" said Snake. "So why don't we just proceed. Mr. Boks, I believe the question you were asked before the break was: if we pass this consumer protection statute, what can we do to make sure attorneys across the country know about it and start filing cases here?"

"Right" said Boks. "I've been thinking about this ever since I first met with Mr. Peters a couple of months ago."

"Did you meet him in your office above the body shop?" asked Raff.

"Yes. In fact, that's how Mr. Peters found out about me. He had brought his car – a BMW I think it was – in for some body work. Someone had nipped his front bumper in a parking lot. He saw my sign out front and came up and spoke with me. I get a lot of clients that way. You see . . . ."

"Okay" said Chairman Snake, "let's keep on track here. The question is not how you get your clients, but what are your ideas for bringing all those lawyers to Connecticut?"

"Okay, sure. First of all, it's obvious we would need a massive national advertising campaign. Full page ads in The New York *Times*, the *Wall Street Journal*, maybe The Washington *Post*. And also in lawyer's publications, like The American Lawyer and The National Law Journal. But it can't be just ads. We need stories. We need to generate stories for newspapers and the national media about Connecticut's broad new consumer protection law. And about how hospitable Connecticut is to lawsuits brought to protect consumers from deceptive advertising."

"You think a handful of news stories and ads are gonna do the trick?" asked a skeptical Raff.

"No, of course not. Remember how that town in East Texas – Marshall, I think it was – went about turning itself into a mecca for patent lawsuits? It literally re-invented the town. Got a friendly judge appointed to the federal court there. Recruited the state's best patent lawyer to start filing patent cases there. And it undertook a massive public education campaign to inform its citizens of the need to honor the rights of patent owners and to punish those who infringe those rights. It was a total reinvention of the town. The town became synonymous with the protection of patent rights."

"So how would we go about doing that here?" asked Assemblywoman Ware.

"You've got to think big" said Boks. "Go into this in a totally big way. So big that lawyers around the country will have no choice but to take notice."

"Okay, but how do we do that?" insisted Ware.

"You've got to re-brand the state. Starting with the state's nickname. Right now we're 'The Nutmeg State', right?"

"Right" said Ware.

"Well, on D-Day we'll change our name to 'The Torte State.' That's tort with an 'e' on the end. Nutmeg is a food, so we need to make it a food kind of torte. So it's tort with an 'e' on the end."

"But Connecticut's always been known as 'The Nutmeg State' " said Assemblyman Raff. "People are proud of that."

"What's there to be proud of. I'll bet nobody has any idea why we're known as 'The Nutmeg State.' And besides, who uses nutmeg anyway? It's only used on eggnog at Christmas time. Anyone ever just sit down at a table and eat nutmeg?

"Furthermore, tortes – that's the edible kind – are much more inclusive than nutmeg. Inclusiveness is really important these days. If you think about it, nutmeg's use is basically limited to upper class folks with low cholesterol – upper class people are the only people with low cholesterol – who put it on eggnog at their Christmas parties.

"But tortes, now that's a different matter. Everybody likes tortes. And the reason is that there are so many different flavors, you can always find one you like. Chocolate, strawberry, lemon, cherry, apricot, rhubarb – you name it. There's a flavor for everyone."

"Rhubarb tortes?" said Assemblyman Garibaldi. "I've never heard of rhubarb tortes. And besides, nobody I know likes rhubarb anyway."

"I'm afraid you're wrong, sir. When I was in the circus, all the trapeze artists ate rhubarb. Said they felt like flying after they ate it."

"People wanna feel like they're flying, we've got marijuana" said Assemblywoman Ware.

"Maybe we could have marijuana tortes" said Assemblyman Sink.

Boks cut back in, this was getting off track. "But listen, we can't just change our designation to 'The Torte State.' We've got to announce it and publicize it. We need to do it strongly, in a way that gets noticed. Let everyone know the state's been renamed 'The Torte State.' To do that, we need to start with the 'Welcome to Connecticut' road signs.

"You'd change them?" said an irritated Assemblyman Motley.

"You bet. The new signs will say 'Welcome to Connecticut. The Torte State'."

Boks went hurriedly on. "You know what's on those signs now? The Governor's name. And every time we have a new Governor they have to take down the old signs and put up new ones. Every four years they gotta replace all those signs. You have any idea how much this must be costing the state?

"And here's another thing. You know how many of those signs there are? Thirteen thousand and seven. Thirteen thousand and seven signs have to be taken down and replaced every four years."

"Mr. Boks" interjected Assemblyman Sink, "how do you know we have thirteen thousand and seven 'Welcome to Connecticut' signs posted throughout the state?"

"I counted 'em. I might have missed three or four but that number is pretty close."

"You can't have . . . ."

"Now, as I was saying" Boks continued, "all those signs gotta be replaced every four years. Unless, of course, the Governor gets re-elected to a second term. Which should never happen here, we haven't had a decent governor since the 1970's."

"Mr. Boks, I'd be careful if I were you" warned Assemblyman Motley. "Most of the members of this committee are Democrats. We're perfectly happy with our current governor, Governor Tacksett. He's been great at increasing taxes. We like him because he can always find something new to tax."

"Speaking of taxes" said Assemblyman Garibaldi, "didn't I just hear something about a new tax on bird feeders? I think that's crazy. You already pay a sales tax on bird feeders when you buy one."

"Yes" said Motley, "but that sales tax is just a one-time tax. Once you own the bird feeder, there's no more taxes to collect. But Governor Tacksett has come up with a great idea. He plans to impose a use tax on the bird feeder once it's up and running. A tax based on the number of birds that use it each month."

"That's crazy" said Garibaldi. "There's no way to determine the number of birds that use the feeder."

"I'm sorry but you're wrong" said Motley. "You're ignoring video cams. We can get video cams installed in everyone's back yard. The video cam focuses on the bird feeder and feeds the recording to a computer and the computer counts the number of birds visiting the feeder each day. We can program the computer to spit out a record of the total number of birds using the feeder each month."

"What if the same bird visits the feeder twice the same day? Wouldn't that be double counting?" asked Assemblywoman Ware.

"Each visit counts as a new use of the feeder" answered Motley. "That's the beauty of the idea, it maximizes revenue. This is why we love Governor Tacksett. He can always find a way to tax it."

"Well, that's your view" said Boks. "My view is that the Governor and I should have changed places a few years ago."

"That's not . . . ." stammered Motley before Boks cut him off.

"Anyway, lets get back to the new road signs. Changing those signs is gonna be national news. The media will love it. The great state of Connecticut is changing its name from 'The Nutmeg State' to 'The Torte State.' They'll want to know why we're doing this. And we'll tell 'em. Connecticut is now 'The Torte State' because it has opened its doors to tort lawyers from around the country. Our welcome mat is out to lawyers of all kinds, especially to tort lawyers.

"You see" Boks continued, "we're not just talking about a new law. We're talking about a total re-branding of the state. We're backing up our words with actions."

"Do you honestly believe . . . ." said Assemblyman Raff before being cut off.

"But that's just the beginning" Boks interrupted. "We need to take several other steps to make the state known as 'The Torte State.' Such as our state flower. Anyone here know what our state flower is?"

Only Assemblywoman Ware raised her hand. "Mountain Laurel" she said. "The state flower is the Mountain Laurel. It's an evergreen shrub with a beautiful white flower in early summer."

"That's right" said Boks. "But there's no reason to keep the Mountain Laurel as the state flower once we re-brand ourselves as 'The Torte State'."

"I don't believe there's a tort bush" said Ware.

"No, but there's a Tortuosa tree. That's Tortuosa: T-O-R-T-U-O-S-A. It's in the willow family. Willows are great, they grow well in our climate. So now, when we tell the world we've become 'The Torte State', we can say we're also adopting the Tortuosa tree – which, of course, will eventually be known as the Tort tree - as our state flower."

"But it doesn't have a flower" said Ware. "Willow trees don't have flowers."

"I wouldn't get hung up on flowers" said Boks. "Flowers on shrubs, particularly Mountain Laurel, last a week at most. The rest of the time there's no flower. The Tortuosa tree is a tree, not a flower. It stays green from Spring until late Autumn. Makes a far better horticultural symbol than a Mountain Laurel.

"And now, think of all the things we can do to promote the Tortuosa tree, also known as the Tort tree. Take Arbor Day. Everyone's always being encouraged to plant a tree on Arbor Day. Well, we get every nursery in the state to stock Tortuosa saplings. Then we encourage everyone in the state to show their state pride by planting one. And we get all the schools in on the act. The little saplings will be easy to plant, so even children can plant them. So, thousands of Tort trees will get planted around the state on Arbor Day. The media will eat this up.

"In fact" Boks continued excitedly, "we could even have contests to see which town can plant the most Tort trees on Arbor Day. Encourage all the towns to compete. The Governor could then have a big ceremony with the mayor of the winning town. That would make all the national news, especially if a small town – let's say Goshen – wins. Imagine the Governor going from Hartford to meet the First Selectman of Goshen to present him or her with the award for planting more Tort tress than any town in Connecticut. The story's irresistible."

"But what if . . . ."

"And speaking of contests" continued Boks, "we could also have contests for torte baking. Torte bake-offs. We pick a festive summer holiday – say the Fourth of July or Labor Day – and have a series of torte bake-offs in every town in the state. We could have a panel of distinguished citizens sample all the entries and declare the winner.

"But that's not all. Once we see that it's working, we could expand it to a statewide contest. All the local winners could come to Hartford, stay in one of those nice new hotels you're gonna build, and compete in the state finals. Have the Governor or Secretary of State determine the winner."

"You couldn't have a state official, especially the Governor, pick the winner" said Assemblyman Raff. "What Governor is gonna want to decide that the tortes from, say Greenwich, are better than the tortes from Bridgeport? No Governor could ever do that."

"Okay, so we get some famous people other than politicians to do the judging. Plenty of movie stars live in Connecticut, we could get them to do the judging and have their picture taken with the winner. Movie stars always like to have their picture taken."

"This all sounds pretty ambitious" said Assemblyman Raff. "You're throwing everything into this except the kitchen sink."

"I resent that" said Kit Sink.

"I'm not done yet" said Boks. "There's one more thing we can do."

"What's that?" asked Chairman Snake. "I can't think of anything you've left out."

"Bridgeport" said Boks. "We need to change it's name. To Bridgetort."

"That's ridiculous" shouted Assemblymen Snake and Motley simultaneously.

"Our city's been known as Bridgeport since it was founded" said Snake. "And by the way, Mr. Boks, the founder of your circus – P.T. Barnum – once lived in Bridgeport. We even have a museum devoted to him, The Barnum Museum it's called. Barnum would never want to have the city renamed."

"You don't know that" responded Boks. "I doubt you ever had a chance to ask him about it, he died in 1891."

"Okay, but you couldn't have asked him either. You have no way of knowing whether he would support your idea."

"I'm afraid you're wrong, Chairman Snake. Barnum would have loved the idea. Old P.T. was an entrepreneur. Always creative. His watchwords were 'ingenuity and innovation.' Ingenuity and innovation, that's why he was so successful. And by the way, he absolutely loved tortes. Ate 'em by the dozen. That's how he got so fat."

Assemblyman Motley was beside himself. "Bridgeport has a huge harbor on Long Island Sound. Ships of all kinds come in and out of that harbor. Bridgeport has long been a port town. Which is why we call it Bridgeport."

"Well, now its gonna be a tort town" said Boks matter of factly. "You want to let Bridgeport continue to wither and die? Or do you want it to be re-invented and rejuvenated as a destination city? Just like everything else we've been talking about today, its gotta be re-branded. Formerly Bridgeport, now Bridgetort. You think that won't get the attention of the national media? You think that won't show our commitment to being a welcoming state for lawyers?"

"Say" interrupted Assemblyman Garibaldi, who was suddenly getting caught up in Boks' ideas. "How about a tort museum?"

"What on earth would be in a tort museum?" asked Assemblyman Raff.

"We could put some stuffed tort lawyers in there" suggested Assemblywoman Ware.

"That's one possibility" said Garibaldi. But I'm thinking more about artifacts from famous tort trials. Maybe we could even get Nalph Rader involved. He's the most famous tort lawyer in the country. He wrote that book about the old Chevrolet Corvair, 'Unsafe At Every Speed.' I'll bet he could even get one of those cars for a display."

"As a matter of fact" said Assemblyman Sink, "Rader grew up in Connecticut. And even though his office is in DC, he still keeps a house in Winsted. I'm sure we could convince him to help us start a museum."

"What a great idea" said Boks. "Wish I'd thought of it. Now, look at what we've got if you put everything together. Connecticut is now 'The Torte State.' The state flower is now the Tortuosa tree, Tort tree for short. Tort trees will be planted by the thousands across the state every Arbor Day. And every summer, we'll have torte bake-offs in towns across the state. And every road sign at the state's border will announce 'Welcome to Connecticut, The Torte State.' And as a tourist attraction we'll have a National Tort Museum. With this total re-branding of the state, the plan's guaranteed to succeed."

"I'm afraid we're out of time" announced Chairman Snake.

Wrapping up the hearing, he said: "As you can all see, there's a huge upside here for everyone. New hotels and restaurants. Hundreds of new jobs in construction and hospitality. Fancy lawyers from law firms across the country coming to Connecticut. And Patrick will no longer have to go to another state to file his cases. And Mr. Boks, maybe you could get yourself a nice office in downtown Stamford. Move out of that space over the body shop."

"That's the plan" said Boks. "That's how I drew it up."

"We'll take this matter up among ourselves at our next meeting" said Assemblyman Snake. "Until then, we stand adjourned."

Boks jumped up, without hitting his head, to get in the last word. "I think everyone should go and have a nice torte for lunch. Maybe apricot, I think they're the best."

Chapter 20

MEET THE PRESS

In early June, Pap and Pup walked down the long steps of the New York Supreme Court building at Foley Square in lower Manhattan. They were joined there by Chip and Lydia, who had come downtown from the firm's Fifth Avenue office. Pap and Pup had left an hour earlier to file the two lawsuits, one in New York Supreme Court and the other next door at the Federal courthouse.

Pap counted at least a half dozen reporters waiting at the foot of the steps, along with several photographers and cameramen. He did a double take as he saw that two of the reporters were holding up signs. Jeb Jablonsky of the New York *Post* held a sign saying "WELCOME BACK LYDIA." Mort Kaplansky of the Daily News held a similarly-sized sign saying "LYDIA, WE'VE MISSED YOU."

As they approached the swarm of reporters, Miranda Marvello of Fox 10 News thrust a microphone in front of Lydia and asked: "Miss Lowlace, you seem to have attracted quite a crowd. What exactly is going on?"

Quickly grabbing the mic, Pap said "You'll all have a chance to ask Miss Lowlace your questions. I'm sure you would rather hear from her than from me, but I need to first explain what's behind the two lawsuits we just filed. That should help speed things along."

"You filed two lawsuits?" asked one of the reporters, a frumpy lady wearing an ill-fitting outfit that could only have been purchased at a down-market thrift shop. "That makes three lawsuits for this lady in the past couple of years."

"I'm sorry, we haven't met" said Pap. "What did you say your name was?"

"I didn't. But I'm Hannah Wringer of Eyewitness News. Channel Three. I cover the courts, state and federal."

"Nice to meet you, Miz Wringer" Pap said as he nodded to her. "I believe what I am about to say will answer your question." He then began addressing the assembled group.

"I'm Patrick Peters and the fellow on my left is my brother Prescott Peters. As most everyone here knows, we're the founding partners of Peters and Peters. Our firm specializes in hard-hitting, ground-breaking lawsuits – mostly class actions – against corporate wrongdoers. Today I want to tell you about two humdinger cases we just filed on behalf of our client, the lovely and talented Lydia Lowlace, against two companies that have shamelessly exploited her.

"Now I'm sure some of you remember when, a couple of years ago, we stood at this very spot and I told you about the case we had just filed on behalf of Miss Lowlace against a club owner who operated a series of gentleman's clubs where Miss Lowlace was employed as a dancer.

"I see that Mister Jablonsky and Mister Kaplansky both remember that day. Jeb and Mort, thank you for your welcome back signs. I know Miss Lowlace is deeply touched by your greetings."

"Mister Peters, sorry to interrupt" said Jablonsky. "But Mort and I are hoping that we could each get a photo of ourselves with Miss Lowlace. After the press conference is over, of course. We think our wives would like to have a memento of how we earn our living."

"We can certainly arrange that, Jeb" said Pap. "I'm sure a photo of each of you with Miss Lowlace is exactly what your wives would want.

"Now, as many of you know, that lawsuit we filed some two years ago had an enormous impact on our client's life. Not only did Peters and Peters win that lawsuit on behalf of Miss Lowlace, we also won it on behalf of an entire class of plaintiffs, for whom Miss Lowlace was the class representative."

"Mister Peters" interrupted Hannah Wringer, "I'm sorry to quibble but you didn't actually win that case. You settled it. The defendant settled with you before the case went to trial."

"Miz Wringer, you are correct. I can see that Channel Three picked the right reporter to cover the courts. Technically speaking, we did not win the case, it did end in a settlement. But those clubs settled the case because they knew they were going to lose the case if it went to trial. As a result of that settlement, Miss Lowlace and the members of the class received numerous substantial benefits, some financial and others non-financial. That's a win in my book.

"Now, as I started to say before Miz Wringer interrupted, that settlement changed our client's life. She was discovered by *Playboy* magazine, which made her its Playmate of the Month last October. That in turn opened new horizons for her.

"Miss Lowlace is now modeling lingerie for two well-known brands, Barely Enough and Victor's Little Secret. Well, Victor's Little Secret isn't a well-known brand yet, it's just now preparing to put out its first catalog; but it will feature Miss Lowlace, she will be their top model.

"Now, you'll probably not be surprised to hear what happened next. Greedy companies that couldn't wait to profit off of Miss Lowlace sprang into action. They had no interest in profiting honestly off of Miss Lowlace, like the two lingerie companies who hired her to showcase their wares. I suppose you could say they were showcasing Miss Lowlace's wares as well.

"In any event, some companies have chosen to profit dishonestly off of Miss Lowlace by using her likeness to promote their business without her knowledge or consent.

"The first company to do so is the subject of the lawsuit we just filed in the courthouse at the top of these steps. The company is Aegean Love; it's owned by a shady Greek businessman named Ambrose Lambros. The company operates three strip joints in the Metropolitan area: Sins of the City here in Manhattan; Sugardaddy's Place, in Long Island City; and Empty Laces over in Jersey City. Each of these clubs has been running ads using photos of Miss Lowlace that appeared in *Playboy* last October.

"Now, I want you to know that Miss Lowlace has nothing to do with those lowlife strip joints. This Lambros fellow is shamelessly using photos of Miss Lowlace that appeared in *Playboy* to promote his strip clubs. This is a clear violation of the New York laws on privacy and publicity. Those laws flatly prohibit the use of our client's photograph for commercial purposes without her permission. Peters and Peters is not about to stand by and allow that to happen.

"Now, the second lawsuit, which we filed next door in federal court, involves an even more sinister scheme. A California video game company known as Erotic Arts created a video game called Bunny Hop. Actually, its an adult video game, but if any of you have teenage boys they're probably playing it right now. Even if they're in school.

"This game uses the face and body of Miss Lowlace, as well as other former Playmates of the Month, in a game who's object is to see which player can 'score' with the most *Playboy* bunnies. Each bunny has a score attached to her. I'm proud to say that Miss Lowlace comes with the highest score attached to her image. If you score with her you've hit the jackpot, so to speak.

"But of course neither Miss Lowlace nor any of the other Playmates who serve as avatars in this game gave their consent to be so used. They did not agree to it. They did not consent to it. And they are not being compensated. So, we are pursuing this case as a class action on behalf of all the Playmates who are being used as avatars in this shameful video game. Peters and Peters will not rest until this game is over and the bunnies have won.

"My colleagues have copies of both of the complaints, and will disseminate them before you depart. Now, I'll be happy to take any questions you might have. Mr. Jablonsky, I see you have your hand up."

"If I may, I have a question for Miss Lowlace."

"Sure. I thought some of you might want to hear from her. Here, Lydia, why don't you take the mic."

"Miss Lowlace, I'm Jeb Jablonsky of the New York *Post*. You may remember me from that press conference a couple of years ago. Could you tell us, what was it like going from being a lap dancer in those three gentleman's clubs, as Mr. Peters described them, to being a

Playmate of the Month? And having all those wonderful pictures of yourself in the magazine?"

"Well, Mister Jabosky, it wuz real nice. That magazine takes real good care of you. And they's always doin' somethin' to make you look your best in those pi-chers. All my friends said they's never seen me look so good. I specially liked it when they poured all those red and yellow leaves on me – Autumn leaves I think they called 'em. They kind of tickled. So now when I see Mister Chip there, he always brings in some leaves and . . . ."

"Lydia, sorry" said Pap "but I think you've answered Mister Jablonsky's question. We need to give everyone a chance to pour some leaves on . . . I'm sorry, I mean a chance to ask you questions."

"Miss Lowlace, Miranda Marvello of Fox 10 News. I think our viewers will be most interested in your appearance in the Bunny Hop video game. How did you wind up being in that game?"

"That's watt I'd like to know, Miss Miranda. I didn't know nothin' 'bout no video game. But then my friend Honey, Honey Combe, she worked with me at Bottoms Up, Tops Down and Below the Belt, she's my best friend. She said her little brother sees me in a video game. Not the Bunny Hop game, Honey's little brother is a good kid, they wouldn't let him play no video game with *Playboy* bunnies runnin' round half naked.

"It wuz a different video game he wuz playin'. Grand Theft Trucker I think it wuz called. Honey says I was an aviator or somethin' in that game. So when I's havin' lunch with Mister Chip there – he took me to that fancy twenty-somethin' restaurant. Told me how it wuz a speakeasy back during pro-bition.

"He tells me all about pro-bition. He's real smart, he didn't go to Yale like Mister Peters – that Mister Peters, the one that's smarter than this one – but he, Mister Chip that is, he went to Dartmouth. He wuz a quarterback or somethin' on that football team. Anyways, when we wuz havin' lunch I told him, Mister Chip, about this here aviator thing in that video game.

"And Mister Chip he tells me they can't do that. Can't use me as an aviator without payin' me. So he and Mister Peters – this one here, the one who didn't go to Yale cause he's not as smart as the other one

– they sent some sort of letter to that Grand Theft outfit and gave 'em the watt for. Told 'em they had to stop usin' me as an aviator. And they does. They stops right away. They even sent Mister Peters a hu-nert and fifty thousand dollars; it wuz for compasation they said.

"Now, Mister Peters he says I deserve a hu-nert thousand of that. He says if it wuz okay with me they wuz keepin' the other fifty thousand as their fee, and I says tha's fine with me. I have lunch with Mr. Chip at that fancy restaurant and next thing I knows they's givin' me a check for a hu-nert thousand dollars. So it's okay with me if they keeps the other fifty thousand.

"I knows that Mister Peters and the other Mister Peters, the one that went to Yale, and Mister Chip, they's all fine lawyers. If it weren't for them I'd still be workin' at Bottoms Up and Tops down. Maybe even Below the Belt, but I never liked that place so much as the other two. And I wouldn't 'a been no Playmate in *Playboy* magazine or modelin' ladies underwear for them two fancy underwear brands. So like I said, its okay by me if they keep that fifty thousand.

"Well then, after I gets that money – they coulda' mailed it to me but Mister Chip there he brings it to me. Brings it to me in person. Mister Chip he's always lookin' out for me and takin' care of me. Anyways, he brings me that money and we had us a nice little celebration.

"And then after our celebration he tells me 'bout my pi-ture bein' used in this Bunny Hop thing. But its even better, he says, cause lots of other Playmates is also aviators in this here Bunny Hop and so now we can file this here class action. Anyways, to answer your question, I got no idea how that outfit decided to make me an aviator in this Bunny Hop thing. I guess you'll have to ask them."

Leaning into the mic, Pap said "Okay, Miz Downes, I see you have your hand up."

"Yes. Miss Lowlace, I'm Pat Downes from 1010 WINS. Why do . . . .."

"Ten ten wins watt?" asked Lydia. "Ten ten sounds like a tie. How can it be a win?"

"Ah, nobody's ever looked at it that way before" said Downes. "But let me explain it for you. WINS is the name of the station, it's our call letters: W-I-N-S. And ten ten is the place on the radio dial where you can tune into us."

"Thanks" said Lydia, "tha's real helpful. I 'preciate it. Now what wuz your question again?"

"Actually I hadn't asked it. But here it is: Why do you think these three clubs are using your photo in their advertising? You think they want their customers to think you work at those clubs?"

"Well, that sure might be. You see, when I worked at them other clubs last year, and they wuz cheaten' us out of our wages and tips – them tips wuz really important to us, that's how we made most of our money. And so I 'splained all that to Mister Peters here, this Mister Peters, I 'splained it to him first. Then he tells me to 'splain it to the other Mister Peters, the smart one who gone to Yale. I reckon it wuz that Mister Peters who says we should file the lawsuit.

"So then, when we's filed that there lawsuit against them clubs, we had that press conference. Right here it wuz. The same place we's standin' now. And it wuz at that press conference that my friend there, Mister Mort, asks me how I chose Peters and Peters to be my lawyers. Then, after I answered Mister Mort's question, we wuz done and I went home and got dressed for work. I sure couldn't go to work wearin' that nice navy blue outfit Mister Chip got for me.

"Well, next thing I knows that press conference is on the news. Maybe it wuz on your station, that ten twenty thing. And that night Phil, he's the bartender at Bottoms Up where I wuz workin' that night, Phil says: 'Lydia, you sure looked great at that press conference wearin' that nice navy blue suit an' all'.

"Then, a couple a days later, Phil says 'Lydia, have you noticed we's startin' to get a better clientele ever since you wuz on TV in that press conference? Lots of professional types. Not the usual lowlifes from New Jersey and Long Island.' And I tells Phil, that's right, I seen that too. Now we's startin' to get lots of guys in nice suits, just like Mister Chip wuz wearin' the first time he came to Bottoms Up.

"And you know watt? By the time we had that there trial before that nice judge, I mean justice – Mister Peters, the one that's gone to Yale – he told me that in New York judges in this here court are not called Judge, they's called Justice. Anyways, by the time we had the trial with that nice Justice Leghetti – I always could remember his name cause it rhymes with spaghetti – all three clubs wuz doin' real good. Better than they ever done before.

"So I reckon this here Greek fellow, I reckon he figured that my pi-ture in the news brought in lots 'a business for Bottoms Up and Tops Down – not so much Below the Belt, things never much improved there – I reckon he thought my pi-ture could bring in new business for his clubs. So he just takes one of my pi-tures from *Playboy* and puts it in ads for his clubs. Without even askin' me if it's okay.

"See, here's the thing. His clubs aren't classy clubs like the ones I use to work at. I don't want my pi-ture associated with lowlife places like Sins of the City. Or that one on Long Island, Sugardaddys. And certainly not any club over in New Jersey. But that Greek fellow he just took my pi-ture and used it without tellin' me. If Honey, that's my fiend Honey Combe, hadn't showed me them there ads I wouldn't never have known 'bout all this. So tha's why I think he's been usin' my pi-ture in those there ads."

"We might have time for one more question" said Pap.

"Miz Lowlace, Hannah Wringer here from Eyewitness News. You referred a couple of times to a Mister Chip from Peters and Peters. Who is he and what exactly is your relationship with him?"

"Well, you see . . . ."

"I think we've run out of time" said Pap as he took the mic out of Lydia's hand. "As you can imagine, with two brand new lawsuits we've got quite a lot of work to do. My partner Prescott has copies of the two complaints for you, please take them with you when you leave.

"Thank you all for coming. We'll let you know when we have any developments to report.

"And Mister Jablonsky and Mister Kaplonsky, you can get those photos with Miss Lowlace now. Then you can take 'em home to your wives."

Chapter 21

WRIGHT AND WRONG

In October, Pap and Pup met in Pap's office to discuss the appeal of the chimps case.

"It's too bad New York has this crazy procedure where virtually every decision a trial judge makes can be appealed before the case is over" Pap said. "If we could try the case before it reached an appellate court, I think we could win it. Justice Wright seems favorably disposed to our argument."

"Yes, that's a real shame" agreed Pup. "But there's nothing we can do about it. We're stuck with New York procedure."

"Anyway" said Pap, "the argument is two weeks away. We need to get ready for it. You're our law guy, you should argue it."

"No, Pap, I think you should. There's not much law involved, just that one Appellate Division case and two lower court cases. The zoo's entire argument is based on those three cases. Even you know enough law to deal with three cases."

"Very funny" said Pap.

"Seriously" Pup continued, "we both understand our position as to why those three cases are not dispositive. But I'm sure the judges will go well beyond the rulings in those cases. They're going to want to talk about the implications of our argument. The issues that would come up next if they allow this case to proceed."

"What kind of issues?"

"Well, if chimps can sue for wrongful detention, what else can they sue for? What other civil rights would they have? That kind of thing."

"Pup, you can answer that stuff as well as me."

"No I can't. I don't really believe in this case the way you do. And I would take all those questions seriously. They're legitimate questions and, if we respond honestly, we don't have good answers.

"You think we have a good answer to questions about whether the First Amendment applies to apes?

"You, on the other hand, will be much better at deflecting questions like that. Maybe even making a joke out of them. You'll be good at that."

"In other words, you don't want me to actually answer the questions? Just find a way to avoid them?"

"Exactly."

"But where will that leave us?"

"It will leave us not having to face up to the implications of our position. We can't allow the court to focus on what this case might lead to in the future. That's a path to disaster."

"So, you think I should deflect all those questions? Try to turn them into some sort of joke?"

"Right. It's our only hope."

"Okay" said Pap. He knew Pup was probably right. "I'll do it. But listen, you and Melissa need to make a list of the questions they might ask. Give me the list and I'll start thinking about how to answer them without saying anything."

* * * *

The appeal was before the First Department of the New York Supreme Court's Appellate Division, an intermediate appellate court. The First Department, generally considered the leading court in the Appellate Division, was housed in a fine old courthouse on East 23rd Street, just across from Madison Square Park. The courtroom itself was magnificently ornate.

As Pap and Pup exited the subway and headed across Madison Square Park, they ran into a large group of demonstrators. The demonstrators were wearing the same ape-faced Halloween masks, and carrying the same "FREE THE CHIMPS" and "APES R US" placards, as they had the day of the hearing before Justice Wright. The police were doing a good job of keeping the protesters confined to the park and not spilling onto Madison avenue.

"My God, Pup, look at that" Pap exclaimed as they reached the Madison Avenue side of the park. Spaced along the eastern edge of the park were a series of tiny cages. In each cage, a protester dressed in an ape-like coat and wearing an ape-faced mask sat hunched over, knees bent up to their chin, in an extremely uncomfortable-looking position.

When a couple of reporters started to approach, Pap waved them off. This protest, particularly the ape-suited people hunched over in cages, seemed a bit over the top. Commenting on it would not lead to anything good.

"We need to sign in and then get into the courtroom" Pap told the reporters. "They always do the roll call of cases right on time. We can't afford to be late."

* * * *

Katy Kong versus Wildlife Conservation Society was case number eight on a very long docket. Each side had initially been given fifteen minutes for argument. But Justice Feinstein, the presiding Justice, announced that due to the long docket, the allotted time was being cut to ten minutes per side.

As the zoo was the appellant, Hortescue Horvath the Fourth went first. Horvath had no trouble presenting the zoo's argument in the allotted time. He simply argued that Justice Wright's decision was contrary not only to common sense – "everyone knows that apes are different from humans" – but to the only three cases that had ever considered the issue. All three cases had disallowed the lawsuits. Aside from one of the justices suggesting that Katy Kong should be referred to as a "chimpanzee" and not an "ape," Horvath faced no difficult moments during his ten minutes in front of the court.

Pap was not so lucky.

"Your Honors" he began, "Patrick Peters for the plaintiff. In the hearing below, Justice Wright . . . ."

"Counsel" interrupted Justice Slocombe, "there are only three cases that have ever considered this issue and all three of them disallowed the claim. Why should we depart from those rulings?"

Although he had never appeared before any of the five judges before, Pap had no trouble attaching a name to each of them. "Justice Slocombe, those cases are not dispositive. The only appellate case is the Fourth Department case; that case did not involve the issue we face here.

"The question in that case was whether a chimp could seek a writ of habeas corpus. The court correctly held that habeas corpus is only available when the petitioner seeks to end his or her confinement. Kiko, the plaintiff in that case, only sought to improve the conditions of his confinement. As Mister Horvath correctly said, everyone knows habeas corpus is never available in that situation."

"But Counsel" said Justice Hokem, "the other two cases, the one involving that chimp Tommy and the one that involved the pair of chimps, dealt with the precise issue we have in this case. The courts in those cases held that chimpanzees are – and I quote - 'fundamentally different' from humans. They do not have - and again I quote – 'neither legal rights nor legal duties.' Those rulings are precisely on point."

"I'm sorry Justice Hokem, but I don't believe they are. There was no record in either case. The courts just issued rulings based on their own views and prejudices.

"Here, in contrast, we have a fully developed record. We have the testimony of one of the foremost primatologists in the country. Justice Wright's decision was not based on her own experience or views or prejudices. Rather, it was based on the primatologist's expert testimony regarding the intellectual and psychological properties of chimpanzees. And, by the way, that testimony was unrefuted."

"Counsel" said Justice Bokem, "put aside the precedents. What I want to know is, if we sustain Justice Wright's ruling, where will this end? Are we going to face an endless parade of lawsuits brought by animals?"

"Justice Bokem, all that is before this court is a very narrow case brought on behalf of a class of highly intelligent chimpanzees and Spider Monkeys who seek to move out of their confinement to a nature preserve. That is the only case before this court."

"But Counsel" continued Justice Bokem, "if chimps and Spider Monkeys can bring lawsuits, why can't other animals?"

"They'd have to prove they were intelligent and autonomous beings, with the same feelings and emotions as humans. If they can prove that, they can sue. But there's a lot of animals that probably couldn't meet that test. Alligators, for example. And sloths. I doubt a sloth could qualify as an intelligent, autonomous being."

"What about my dog?" asked Bokem. "His name is Barrister, by the way. And he's just as smart as any chimpanzee. Why couldn't he sue me, just like your chimps are suing the zoo?"

"Why would he sue you, Justice Bokem? Are you mistreating him? Abusing him? If so, maybe someone should be able to sue you on Barrister's behalf. But so long as you are treating him well, you have no reason to fear a lawsuit by Barrister."

"Counsel" said Justice Menendez, "we understand that Justice Wright's ruling is limited to chimpanzees and their attempt to end their confinement. But if they have the right to sue to end their confinement, why couldn't they also sue on any number of grounds? For example, to demand better food? Or to be let out of their cage once a day?"

"Justice Menendez, if Katy and the other members of the class prevail, they'll be allowed to move to a nature preserve in Florida. There will be no cages and no limit on the amount of food they can eat. So those issues will never arise. Give them their freedom and they won't need to pursue any other rights."

"What about other rights the chimps might claim?" said Justice Slocombe. "Humans are entitled to all sorts of rights under the Constitution. Do chimpanzees get all those same rights?"

"Well, Justice Slocombe, they should certainly be entitled to their rights under the First Amendment. Freedom of speech, freedom of assembly – chimpanzees are certainly entitled to that. They should be able to say whatever they want to say without fear of retribution. And they should be able to enjoy the freedom to assemble. Peacefully of course, we don't want them engaging in demonstrations that get out of hand."

Justice Hokem jumped in. "What about Second Amendment rights? What if they insisted on the right to bear arms? Pistols or rifles or, God help us, those semi-automatic assault rifles?"

"Well, they'd have to go through a background check, just like everyone else. I don't see a problem there."

"You want all the apes in New York City zoos to have access to guns?" asked an astonished Justice Bokem. "Running around the zoos playing cowboys and Indians and shooting at each other? Maybe even at the guards? Someone could get hurt."

"Well, there are laws against that sort of thing. They couldn't just go around shooting indiscriminately, they'd get arrested."

"Where would we put 'em after we've arrested 'em" asked Justice Slocombe. "We couldn't put 'em in regular jails, in with real people. We'd be setting ourselves up for a rash of inmate lawsuits complaining about the ape in their cell. The ape smells bad. Has poor hygiene. Isn't potty trained, that kind of thing."

"That's not a problem, Judge Slocombe. The zoos can set up monkey jails. In situ, so to speak. They've already got plenty of cages. Easy to set a few aside for a monkey jail."

"Counsel" said Justice Hokem, "what about voting rights? Would Katy and the other members of the class have the right to vote?"

"Sure, Justice Hokem, so long as they have a photo ID."

"How would we ever get them registered and issued photo IDs?" asked Justice Bokem.

"That can all be worked out" said Pap. "New York does a good job of issuing photo IDs. I'm certain the State can work something out here."

Justice Feinstein, who had not posed a single question to Pap and who had been scowling the entire time, finally spoke up.

"Mister Peters, I think you've already gone over your allotted ten minutes. We need to conclude this argument and move . . . ."

"We haven't gone though all the amendments with him" interrupted Justice Slocombe. "I'd like to hear what he has to say about the applicability of other amendments . . . ."

"Especially the Fifth Amendment" said Justice Hokem. "I'd like to know if he thinks chimpanzees have the right to remain silent during a criminal investigation."

"Don't forget the Fourth Amendment" added Justice Bokem. "Would they have the right to avoid unreasonable searches and seizures? Would the zoo be prevented from searching their cages for contraband without a warrant?"

"These are all . . . ." said Pap before being interrupted by Justice Feinstein.

"Mister Peters – and I address this to my esteemed colleagues as well – this has been a fascinating case. But it is not the only case on our docket. We cannot spend all day on it, much as some of you might want to. We've got eight more arguments to get through.

"So, thank you Mister Peters and, uh, Mister Horvath. Now, we need to move on. We'll take the case under advisement."

* * * *

Four months later the court issued its decision. Ruling unanimously, it concluded that Justice Wright was wrong.

The key paragraph in the ruling read as follows:

"Chimpanzees are fundamentally different from human beings in the eyes of the law. Since they cannot bear any legal duties, or be held legally accountable for their actions, it would be inappropriate to confer on them the same rights as are accorded to humans."

And so ended the case of Katy Kong versus the Wildlife Conservation Society of New York.

Executives at the three zoos breathed a sigh of relief. Oliver and Cromwell collected a ton of money from their client. And Pup told Pap "I told you so."

Chapter 22

HAZEL NUTT

A month earlier, Pup and Melissa were in the firm's conference room with their client Hazel Nutt, who's deposition was being taken in the Corny Flakes case.

Pap never participated in depositions. He hated them; he found them boring and was always falling asleep. During one deposition when he was at Rogers and Autry, the opposing counsel woke him up to announce that he was about to ask Pap's client a controversial question and he thought Pap might want to object to it. So it was generally left to Pup and one of the associates to deal with all depositions.

Colonel Mills, the maker of Corny Flakes, had retained the high-powered firm of Cravat, Swine and Hoare to represent it. Cravat, which prided itself on the lean staffing of its cases, brought only two lawyers to the deposition: Elliott Hess, the firm's top litigation partner, and Jay Edward Hoover, an associate.

After the court reporter had sworn in the witness, Hess began the examination.

Examination by Mr. Hess:

Q: Good Morning, Ms. Nutt. As you know . . . .

Mr. Peters: Mr. Hess, I'm sorry to interrupt you before you even begin, but the witness holds a PhD and is a licensed

168

psychologist. We'd appreciate it if you would address her as Dr. Nutt, not Ms. Nutt.

Q: Certainly. Dr. Nutt, may I ask you . . . .

A: Actually my professional name is Dr. Hazel Nutt, not Dr. Nutt.

Q: Your first name is part of your professional name? That's really unusual. Most doctors are just known by their last name. Dr. Kildare. Dr. Jeckell. Dr. No, that kind of thing.

A: I do use just one name. Hazelnutt. It's all one name. Dr. Hazelnutt.

Q: Why don't you just call yourself Dr. Nutt, that would be more traditional?

A: There's already one Dr. Nutt, my husband, Dr. Nathan Nutt. He's a pediatrician. One Dr. Nutt is enough. Two would be nuts. It would be confusing to our patients.

Q: Surely the two of you have separate offices?

A: Oh, certainly. But we both work out of our house in Scarsdale. My husband's office is near the front of the house. Patients enter through a door on the west side of the house. The waiting room is our children's old play room. It was full of toys – puzzles, legos, dolls, action figures, knives, guns, rifles, all the usual stuff. So, we didn't even have to make any changes to it except to put in a couple of chairs for the parents.

Q: And your office, where is it?

A: It's on the east side of the house. But the patients have to go around to the back door to enter, there's no door on the east side. And unlike Nathan, I don't have much of a waiting room, its just an old broom closet with a chair and tiny table. We took out all the brooms.

Q: I think I got it. Your husband is Dr. Nutt. He's a pediatrician and his office is on the west side of your house. You, Dr. Hazelnutt – all one word – are a psychologist. Your office is on the east side of the house but your patients have to go in through the back door.

A: Correct. But see, the fact that we both practice in our house is why I had to change my professional name. When I first started out seeing patients, I just used my last name, Dr. Nutt. But so did my husband. He was also Dr. Nutt. We had mothers with sick kids showing up in my waiting room, all jammed into that broom closet.

At the same time all the rich ladies with their various neuroses were showing up in my husband's waiting room, which was full of all those guns and rifles, they were having nervous breakdowns on the spot. Then everyone would realize they had come in the wrong door and would have to change places. It was like a nut house for a while.

Q: You mentioned rich ladies with neuroses. Are they your primary clients?

A: Yes.

Q: Could you elaborate a little?

A: Well, Mr. Hess, I'm sure you can imagine it's tough being a rich lady in Scarsdale with a big house and a designer garden. These ladies have a hard time coping and yes, they have a lot of neuroses. My job is to help them.

Q: Okay, but exactly what do you do for them?

Mr. Peters: I think this is getting into matters of Dr. Hazelnutt's professional treatment. I don't see how it is relevant to the case.

Mr. Hess: I don't want to belabor this, but Ms. Nutt – I mean Dr. Nutt, Dr. Hazelnutt that is – has brought a multi-million-dollar lawsuit against our client and seeks to to be the representative of a class of Corny Flakes purchasers. I think I'm entitled to some leeway to explore her professional credentials.

Mr. Peters: Dr. Hazelnutt, if you can answer the question with a general statement, you can do so. But you are not required to get into details about your professional practice. In fact, all your discussions with you neurotic patients are covered by the doctor/patient privilege.

A: Oh, I would never betray the confidence of my patients. Like what they tell me about their sex lives. They're always telling me about their sex lives. Or the lack thereof, that's their most frequent complaint.

Mr. Peters: I don't think Mr. Hess wants to hear about your patients' sex lives. Or their lack of a sex life. I think he just wants to know generally what you do to help your patients. If you can answer that without getting into the details of your interaction with them, you may answer.

A: Sure, I don't mind answering. You see, over the years I've developed a three-step process that I use with all my patients.

Q: A three-step process?

A: Yes

Q: And you use it with every one of your patients?

A: Sure. It seems to work, why would I change it from patient to patient?

Q: I can see you wouldn't want to change it. So, please tell us, what are the three steps?

A: Well, step one is you must be woke. Woke to your innermost feelings. Know them. Embrace them. And whatever you do, don't suppress them.

Step two is mindfulness. You must be mindful. Mindful of everything in the moment. Birds, bees, flowers, cars, trucks, noise, trash, pollution – be mindful of it all.

Q: I see. First be woke and then be mindful. These rich ladies pay you money to be told that?

Mr. Peters: I move to strike that remark. Mr. Hess, that was disrespectful. It was uncalled for.

Mr. Hess: I'll withdraw the remark from the record. But that doesn't mean I'm withdrawing it from my thinking.

Q: Anyway, let's move on to step three. What is step three?

A: Hazelnuts. Eat lots of hazelnuts. They are one of our most nutritious foods. They're full of vitamins and minerals. Vitamin E and Vitamin B-6. Magnesium. Potassium. Manganese. Fiber. And they've got lots of healthy fats, such as Omega-6 and Omega-9.

Q: You're a clinical psychologists and you push hazelnuts?

A: Certainly. You should eat them daily, Mr. Hess. Mr. Hoover too. They're loaded with anti-oxidants, which help prevent heart disease and lower your risk of cancer. They're truly a wonder food. That's why I have a framed picture of a hazelnut behind my desk. If my patients remember nothing more about what I tell them, they'll remember that picture of a giant hazelnut.

Q: Yes, I can see your patients are likely to remember that. By the way, do you tell them where to go to buy their hazelnuts?

A: Oh, they don't need to go anywhere. They can buy them from me and take them home with them when they leave. It's a patient service thing. They come to my office and leave their worries and neuroses with me. And they go home with a month's supply of hazelnuts. It's a win/win. The patient gets a nutritious healthy product and I get additional revenue.

Mr. Hess: Mr. Hoover, let's remember to suggest this to our management committee when we get back to the office. Maybe we could sell hazelnuts to our clients when they come in for legal advice.

Mr. Peters: Mr. Hess, we're here for you to ask questions of this witness. I think you should move on and drop your editorial comments.

Q: Okay, let's get to the nut of the matter. Dr. Hazelnutt, tell us how you came to purchase the new Corny Flakes line extension known as Berry Good Corny Flakes.

A: Well, it all started at a meeting of our Third Thursday Club. Fanny started telling us about the new Corny Flakes product and Faith, Kiki and I were getting excited. We . . . .

Q: Dr. Hazelnutt, we've got to take this a little slower, this is an important part if the case. First of all, did you say this was at a meeting of the Third Thursday Club?

A: Yes.

Q: What is that?

A: That's a club the four of us formed. Besides me there's Fanny, Fanny Pak. There's Faith Heeler. And Kiki, that's Kiki Keeler. We meet on the third Thursday of the month. We have dinner at the Spinning Wheels Bistro in Scarsdale.

Q: And you call it the Third Thursday Club?

A: Of course. That's because we always meet on the third Thursday of every month. That way it's easy to remember the date of the meeting. Third Thursday.

Q: What does the club do?

A: We rotate between two topics, health and wealth. We thought about calling it the Health and Wealth Club, but then how would we ever remember the dates of our meetings?

Q: Yes, I can see the wisdom of that. Now, what specifically do you do about these two topics, health and wealth?

A: We talk about 'em. As to health, how to keep it. As to wealth, how to get more of it.

Q: I assume this is just an informal club. You're not incorporated or anything?

A: No. But if we were, do you think we could deduct the cost of our dinner as a business expense?

Q: I doubt it, I'd have to ask one of my tax partners about that.

A: Could you do that? Four of us having dinner every month, twelve times a year. It adds up.

Mr. Hess: I don't think it would be proper for my firm to give you tax advice. Maybe Mr. Peters' firm could help you.

Mr. Peters: Thank you, Elliott, for the referral. We'll try to return the favor some time.

Q: Let's get back to Corny Flakes. Please tell us what was said at that dinner regarding Corny Flakes.

A: Okay. First of all, it was our January meeting. So health was the topic that time. We always start with health in January, that means it comes up again in March, May, et cetera. Now, as you may know, and as all the ladies in the Third Thursday Club know, I'm a fanatic about healthy eating. Except for chocolate eclairs, I love chocolate eclairs. Otherwise I stick solely to healthy foods.

Q: Could you just tell us the discussion about Corny Flakes?

A: That's just what I was getting to. Fanny, Faith and Kiki all know I only eat healthy foods and that a healthy breakfast is really important to me. Now, growing up, I loved old-fashioned Corny Flakes. But once I started paying attention to my diet, I realized there was nothing healthy about Corny Flakes. Maybe if you put some bananas or strawberries or blueberries on them they might have some nutritional value. But not if you just eat them plain, as I did growing up.

So, as we were all eating our grilled salmon – no sauce, just a little fresh lemon juice squeezed on top – Fanny started talking about the new version of Corny Flakes. She said Peter had just told her . . . .

Q: Who's Peter?

A: Fanny's husband, of course. Peter Pak. He works for that big advertising agency, Young and Olde. One of their clients is Colonel Mills. Well, Peter told her, Fanny, that Colonel Mills was coming out with a new version of Corny Flakes. They were trying to catch up with all the other breakfast cereals that were focusing on healthy ingredients.

This new product would be called Berry Good Corny Flakes and would have blueberries, thus making it a healthy breakfast food. Everybody knows blueberries contain anti-oxidants and that anti-oxidants are good for you. That's why I promote hazelnuts to all my patients, they're chock full of anti-oxidants.

Q: Dr. Hazelnutt, are you describing what Mrs. Pak, Fanny Pak, said her husband, Peter Pak, told her? Or are you describing what Fanny Pak told you and the other ladies at the meeting of the Third Thursday Club?

A: Both. They're the same. That's what Fanny said Peter told her and it's what Fanny told the three of us Peter told her. Why would they be different?

Q: And what Peter told Fanny, and what Fanny told you and the other ladies Peter told her, is that the new Corny Flakes line extension has blueberries in them?

A: Yes.

Q: Actual blueberries, in the cereal box itself?

A: Yes, where else would they put them?

Q: And you believed that? That there were actually blueberries in the cereal box?

A: Yes, why else would they be a healthy improvement over regular Corny Flakes? Everyone knows you can always buy some bananas or strawberries or blueberries and put them on your Corny Flakes. The trick was putting them into the cereal so you didn't have to go out and buy them separately.

Q: So then what happened?

A: Well, we finished our grilled salmon then had some chocolate eclairs for dessert. That's why we always have our dinner at the Spinning Wheels Bistro, they have wonderful chocolate eclairs. Rich and . . . .

Q: Dr. Hazelnutt, I didn't mean what happened next at your dinner meeting devoted to healthy eating where you all had chocolate eclairs for dessert. I meant what happened next regarding Corny Flakes?

A: Oh, I see. Well, when I got home I told Nathan, that's my husband Dr. Nutt, about the new healthy version of Corny Flakes. Told him I was going to get some the next time I was at Whole Foods. He said that sounded like a good idea and could I also get some for him. He said he was looking for a new breakfast cereal, he was getting tired of Cheerios, he's been eating them every day since he was eight.

Q: Okay, now let's talk about . . . .

The Witness: Could we take a short break so I can get some coffee? I always need caffeine to keep me going. And I also need some hazelnuts. I brought a can of them with me, I can pass it around if you like.

Chapter 23

BERRY GOOD CORNY FLAKES

When they came back into the conference room following the break, Dr. Hazelnut passed around a container of hazelnuts.

Elliott Hess took a handful and said "Thank you, Doctor . . . . whoa, I see this tin has a label on it, 'Dr. Hazelnut's Hazelnuts.' You have your own brand of hazelnuts?"

"Sure. I buy them wholesale by the bushel. Then I put them into half-liter tins. I print my own labels. When my patients come in for a session, I send them home with one of these tins. Just add it to their bill. It's been a great boon to my practice. Some patients come just for the nuts."

"You certainly have a most unusual practice" said Hess. "But let's get back on the record. Enough about the nuts."

Continued Examination by Mr. Hess:

Q: Dr. Hazelnut, before the break you told us that you learned about Berry Good Corny Flakes from one of the ladies at your Third Thursday Club. Did there come a time when you made your first purchase of them?

A: Yes. My first and last.

Q: When was that?

A: It would have been the Saturday after the meeting of the Third Thursday Club. That would make it the fourth Saturday of January. There were five Saturdays that month but only four Thursdays.

Q: That's nice to know. Now, where did you buy them?

A: I bought them at the Whole Foods store in White Plains.

Mr. Hess: Mr. Hoover, could I have that box of Corny Flakes. Let's mark this as Nutt Exhibit 1.

Q: Dr. Nutt . . . I'm sorry, Dr. Hazelnut, is this the product you purchased at the Whole Foods store?

A: Yes.

Q: And what was the reason for your purchase of this product?

A: I've already told you. I stopped eating Corny Flakes years ago because they were not particularly healthy. When I heard that Corny Flakes now had blueberries in them, I couldn't wait to try them.

Q: So you bought a box and tried them?

A: Actually I bought fifteen boxes.

Q: Fifteen boxes?

A: Sure. I knew I was going to like them. And, as I said before the break, Dr. Nutt – my husband, the other Dr. Nutt – asked me to get some for him as well. He was tired of Cheerios after forty years.

Q: Are you saying you bought separate boxes for yourself and Dr. Nutt?

A: Yes. I always pour the cereal out of the box and into a bowl. Nathan just grabs the cereal out of the box by his hand. Surely you don't expect me to eat the Corny Flakes in his box?

Q: Right. Now, what did you think you were getting when you bought those fifteen boxes of Corny Flakes.

A: Mr. Hess, I didn't buy fifteen boxes of Corny Flakes. I bought fifteen boxes of Berry Good Corny Flakes.

Q: Okay, but now answer my question. What did you think you were getting when you bought those fifteen boxes?

A: I thought I was getting fifteen boxes of Corny Flakes with blueberries added.

Q: Where on Exhibit 1 does it say that this product has blueberries in it?

A: Right there on the front. There's a picture of them. Corny Flakes in a nice white bowl with blueberries on top.

Q: Dr. Hazelnutt, please look at the panel on the right side of the box where the ingredients are listed. Do you see any mention of blueberries?

A: Whoever reads this stuff on the side panel of a box? People just look at the front of the box. And on the front it says "Berry Good Corny Flakes" and then there's the picture of the blueberries on the cereal. And there's this statement here (pointing): "Anti-oxidant Vitamins C, E and Beta-Carotene." Everybody knows that blueberries are antioxidants.

Q: You haven't answered my question about the ingredient list. Does that list include blueberries?

A: No, but as I said, nobody looks at an ingredient list on the side of a box. Or an ingredient list on any part of the box, for that matter. Who has time to do that?

Q: But you could have looked at it and seen that blueberries were not listed?

A: I could have stood on my head in the grocery aisle but I didn't.

Q: Okay, so let's go back to the front of the box. Do you see that statement in white letters in the bright blue box below the bowl of Corny Flakes?

A: Yes I see it.

Q: Would you please read it.

A: Okay, I've read it.

Q: I meant would you please read it out loud and into the record?

A: It says: "Blueberry natural and artificial flavoring."

Q: What does that statement tell you?

A: That it has blueberry natural and artificial flavoring in it.

Q: Are you aware this product does in fact have blueberry natural and artificial flavoring in it?

A: If you say so.

Q: And would you not agree this makes Berry Good Corny Flakes different from regular Corny Flakes?

A: Well, if there is no blueberry natural and artificial flavoring in regular Corny Flakes, that would obviously make them different.

Q: And that difference is why this product is called Berry Good Corny Flakes and has a picture of blueberries on the cereal?

A: If that's the difference, they should have shown artificial blueberry flavoring in the picture, not actual blueberries.

Q: How would they ever depict artificial blueberry flavoring in a picture?

A: That's their problem.

Q: Okay, let's move on. When did you discover there were no blueberries in your Corny Flakes?

A: When I opened the box and poured them out. Actually, I kept pouring them out, thinking that the blueberries must have all settled to the bottom. By the time I was done I had eighteen bowls of Corny Flakes on the counter.

Q: What did you do with those eighteen bowls of Corny Flakes?

A: I poured them all back into the box, of course. But not the last one, I kept that one out for my breakfast.

Q: And you ate them? Were they good?

A: Well, I didn't try them until the next day.

Q: Why not?

A: Well, when I finally realized there were no blueberries in the box, I realized I had to furnish my own if I wanted to have Corny Flakes with blueberries. Which of course I did, that's why I bought fifteen boxes of Berry Good Corny Flakes.

So, I had to take my car out of the garage and go to the store and get some blueberries. That was a nuisance, I don't mind telling you. Nobody had any blueberries. It was January, remember, and so it wasn't blueberry season. I had to drive all over Westchester County before I found a store that had blueberries. By the time I got home, it was time for lunch.

Q: Dr. Hazelnut, I redirect your attention to the side of the box with the ingredients list. Would you please read the statement at the bottom.

A: Okay, I've read it.

Q: I meant, please read it out loud into the record.

A: It says: "If you are not satisfied with the quality of this product, a prompt refund or adjustment of equal value will be made."

Q: Did you ask Colonel Mills for a refund or adjustment?

A: I did. I sent a letter to Colonel Mills and told them I had been deceived and was now stuck with fifteen boxes of Corny Flakes that I couldn't use.

Q: And did Colonel Mills respond?

A: They sent me a letter saying they were sorry I was disappointed.

Q: Anything else?

A: Yes, they included a coupon good for fifteen boxes of Corny Flakes.

Q: So they did exactly what they said on the box: they gave you an adjustment of equal value to your purchase price?

A: Yes, but then I would have had thirty boxes of Corny Flakes, all without blueberries, where would that get me?

Q: You could have sold them to your patients along with the hazelnuts. You'd have a real grocery store going.

A: I never thought of that.

Q: Did you take any other action beyond your protest to Colonel Mills?

A: I sent a letter to Jane Brody.

Q: You mean the food writer for The *New York Times?*

A: Yes, I thought she might write something about this.

Q: And did she?

A: Well, a couple of weeks later she mentioned in one of her columns that people were complaining that their breakfast cereal never had the fruits – mainly blueberries and cranberries – that were pictured on the front of the box. And she said we should stop buying the cereals, they weren't all that healthy, we should just buy real blueberries and cranberries. That was the healthy way to go. But that wasn't much help, I still had all those boxes of Berry Good Corny Flakes in my closet.

Q: What caused you to file this lawsuit?

A: Well, in February we had our regular meeting of the Third Thursday Club. That meeting was supposed to be devoted to wealth, but I told everyone we had to change the agenda and devote the meeting to health, specifically the problem with Berry Good Corny Flakes. If we have unanimous consent, we can change the agenda.

Q: And did something happen at that meeting that caused you to file this lawsuit?

A: Well, by the time we got to dessert . . . ."

Q: Chocolate eclairs again?

A: Yes. By the time we were eating our chocolate eclairs, everyone was hopping mad. All of us had bought some Berry Good Corny Flakes and we were all angry they didn't contain any blueberries. When we talked about what we should do, someone suggested a lawsuit.

Q: Who suggested a lawsuit?

A: Faith. Faith Heeler. Her husband Harold is a lawyer. So she knows about legal stuff. She said the only way to get the attention of a company like Colonel Mills is to sue it. And make the case a class action. That's the only way they would take the case seriously.

Q: How is it that you are the one who brought the lawsuit and not one of the other ladies?

A: Well, none of them would be allowed to bring the lawsuit. Faith's husband, Howard, is a partner in that big law firm, Oliver and Cromwell. She said Howard told her the firm would never approve of a partner's wife being a plaintiff in a class action lawsuit. It would be against the interests of most of their clients.

Mr. Hess: That doesn't surprise me. Oliver and Cromwell's a bunch of stuffed shirts. That was off the record by the way.

Mr. Peters: Ms. Muffett and I were at Oliver and Cromwell before we started up Peters and Peters. I don't think either of us are stuffed shirts.

Mr. Hess: I stand corrected. Everyone at Oliver and Cromwell except Mr. Peters and Ms. Muffett are stuffed shirts. Now, let's get back to the case

Q: What about the other two ladies, why couldn't they be the plaintiff? Was it because they just didn't think the whole thing was worth a lawsuit?

A: Oh no, they were both in favor of a lawsuit. But Fanny couldn't be the plaintiff. As I said earlier, her husband's advertising agency represents Colonel Mills. As for Kiki, her husband Karl, Karl Keeler, is an investment manager. He hates class actions. Told Kiki they can ruin a company and then all its investors, people like his clients, suffer.

Q: So that left you?

A: Yep, I was the only one who's husband could afford to allow their wife to sue Colonel Mills. And so I did. I thought it was important for me to step up to the plate, so to speak.

Q: Okay. So now, how did you happen to be represented by Peters and Peters in this case?

A: Well, over expresso and cappucino we talked about how we could find a law firm to represent us.

Q: You had expressos and cappucinos after your chocolate eclairs?

A: Of course. We certainly couldn't have them before we had the chocolate eclairs.

Q: Some health club.

Mr. Peters: Mr. Hess, things would move along faster if you refrained from interjecting these editorial comments. Dr. Hazelnutt's club is not on trial here. Your client is.

Mr. Hess: I hadn't realized that. Thanks for telling me.

Q: Now Dr. Hazelnut, how did it happen that you are represented in this case by Peters and Peters? Did they seek you out?

A: Oh no. It was while we were having our expressos and cappucinos. I asked how I could go about finding a law firm to take on the case. I think it was Fanny who first mentioned them.

Q: What did she say?

A: She said her daughter Penelope had gone to Dartmouth and knew a lawyer from there. Chip Pierpont was his name, I believe. Actually, the daughter didn't just know Mr. Pierpont. They had been lovers during her sophomore year. Penelope had then seen this same Mr. Pierpont on the news when his firm held a press conference about some stripper they were representing.

Q: So, you chose Peters and Peters to represent you because the daughter of your friend Fanny Pak had an affair with this Mr. Pierpont in college and the daughter then saw him on television representing some stripper?

Mr. Peters: She was not a stripper. Lydia Lowlace was a lap dancer. And yes, our firm successfully represented her in a class action last year.

Q: Could you please answer the pending question.

A: It wasn't just Fanny's daughter that suggested Mr. Pierpont's firm. Faith's daughter Helen, Helen Heeler, had gone to Wesleyan. And somehow she met Mr. Pierpont during her junior year and they had sort of a long-distance romance. Mr. Pierpont up in the wilds of New Hampshire and Helen down in Connecticut. But apparently they had quite a torrid romance. And then Helen also saw Mr. Pierpont on television with that stripper lady . . . I'm sorry, the lap dancer lady.

Q: So, that is . . . .

A: That's not all. You see, Kiki also has a daughter, Christine. Christine Keeler. She went to Vassar, over in Poughkeepsie. Somehow she had also met Mr. Pierpont and had an affair with him. I think maybe when he went to Wesleyan to see Helen he then went on to Poughkeepsie to see Christine. He sort of made the rounds, like a doctor.

Ms. Muffett: That's our Chip. We're all quite proud of him.

Q: And this is why you chose this law firm? One of their lawyers had bedded the daughters of the three other members of your Third Thursday Club?

A: Well, that convinced me he was a real go-getter. And if his firm could represent a lap dancer in a class action, why couldn't they represent me?

Q: So you hired this Pierpont guy? I haven't seen his name on any of the papers.

A: Oh no. I looked up the firm on the Internet. I looked at their website. Studied all their backgrounds. Then I saw this statement on the website: "Peters and Peters blows into a case like a hurricane." That's a direct quote. And that's what I wanted, a law firm that would blow into my case like a hurricane.

Mr. Hess: I have no further questions.

Mr. Peters: I have no questions.

Mr. Hess: Dr. Hazelnutt, thank you for your time. And thank you also for the hazelnuts.

The witness: If you send your wife to me for a counseling session, I'll send her home with a tin of hazelnuts. I won't even charge her for them. She can even have some of the Corny Flakes. I've got fourteen unopened boxes of 'em.

Chapter 24

THE BIG HEIST

In late October, a month after Dr. Hazelnutt's deposition, Pap and Pup were seated in federal court in Manhattan. At the opposite counsel table were Elliott Hess and Jay Edward Hoover of Cravat, Swine and Hoare. Presiding was Southern District of New York Judge Jervis Prudence. Judge Prudence was plainly perplexed by the motion papers in front of him.

Transcript of Hearing:

The Court: Gentlemen, when you were in front of me in July on defendant's motion to dismiss – which as you know I denied – this was a class action under New York law on behalf of consumers of Corny Flakes, that is, the new line extension of Corny Flakes, I forget what it's called. Now, all of a sudden, you want to turn it into a nationwide class action on behalf of consumers in all fifty states. I don't get it.

Mr. Peters: Your Honor, when we first filed this lawsuit, we wanted to make it simple. A class action on behalf of all consumers in New York State who purchased the new cereal – Berry Good Corny Flakes is its name, by the way.

As there is no federal law involved, we thought it would be simplest for everyone if we just alleged violations of New York law. To bring in the other forty-nine states with their variety of laws, we would have to carefully research the consumer protection laws of all those other states and recite them in the complaint. Peters and Peters is a small firm. We can barely get our arms around the laws of one state.

The Court: I appreciate that, Mr. Peters, but with your proposed Amended Complaint you are doing just that. You are invoking the statutory and common law of all fifty states. Did you suddenly add forty lawyers to your firm since you were here in July?

Mr. Peters: No, Your Honor, we're still the same little firm. Little but dynamic, I should say. It's just my brother and me and three associates. Three terrific associates, I might add.

The Court: I recall you telling me when you were here in July that your brother was the smart one in the firm. He went to Yale, I think you said.

Mr. Peters: That's correct, he . . . .

The Court: Well, your brother must be really smart if, in just a few weeks, he figured out the laws of the other forty-nine states that you're now invoking in your new Complaint.

Mr. Peters: Judge Prudence, without taking anything away from my brother – everyone knows he's the smart one, I only went to Fordham . . . .

The Court: I'm glad to hear that. That's where I went. Damn fine law school, we actually learned some law, not all that philosophical stuff they teach at Yale and the other Ivies. Anyway, you were starting to tell me how your brother figured out the laws of the other forty-nine states that you suddenly want to inject into the case.

Mr. Peters: My brother had a little help, Your Honor. From Mr. Hess and his firm. They're a lot bigger than us, they can throw a lot of lawyers into a case.

The Court: Why on earth would Mr. Hess's firm help out your firm in order to expand the scope of the case some fifty-fold?

Mr. Peters: Because they wanted a larger class of plaintiffs. They wanted the class to encompass not just New York consumers but all consumers of Berry Good Corny Flakes throughout the country.

The Court: I'm sorry Mr. Peters, you're not making sense. Why would Colonel Mills want to be sued by millions of consumers across the country rather than by just a few hundred thousand in New York State?

Mr. Peters: They want it to be a nationwide class action so they can make a nationwide settlement. They don't want to settle this case with New York consumers and then have forty other cases filed against them around the country. That was the deal Mr. Hess and I worked out. Nationwide class action, nationwide settlement.

The Court: Mr. Hess, is this true? I've never seen Cravat so anxious to settle a case, let alone expand it fifty-fold. You normally fight like the dickens, it drives your opponents – and the Court, I might add – crazy. This is unlike your firm.

Mr. Hess: Yes. Well, Your Honor, if you were expecting a nasty fight, I'm sorry to disappoint you. You see, after you denied our motion to dismiss, we took the deposition of the plaintiff, Dr. Hazelnutt. Now, Dr. Hazelnut may be a bit of a nut – she and her husband are both doctors, he goes by the name Dr. Nutt and she goes by the name Dr. Hazelnut – it's a bit of a nutty story, I don't want to take up your time with it. But anyway, based on Dr. Hazelnutt's testimony, we realized this case could go either way. We might win, we might lose.

The Court: Yes, that's generally the case. One side might win or it might lose. Same with the other side.

Mr. Hess: Your Honor, Colonel Mills could not afford to risk losing this case. Berry Good Corny Flakes was a major new product launch. They've already sold over nine million boxes nationwide. That's in just six months. By the time the case would go to trial, they would have sold four or five times that amount, maybe even more.

And if the case was certified as a class action here in New York, it would get widely noticed and all of a sudden we would be faced with dozens of lawsuits around the country. Colonel Mills would be facing lawsuits in forty or more states. So, I went to Mr. Peters with a proposal: expand the case to a nationwide class action and we will make an immediate settlement. Before any other lawsuits can be filed.

The Court: I see. So you offered to have your firm figure out the applicable laws of the other forty-nine states?

Mr. Hess: That's correct. But it wasn't that big of a deal. We defend class action cases all around the country, so we have a pretty good idea of the applicable laws in most of the states. And we don't believe all of those laws have to be listed in the complaint. Mr. Peters merely needs to have a list of them in case we send him an interrogatory asking what state laws our client is alleged to have violated.

The Court: But if you already know what those laws are, why would you need to ask that in an interrogatory?

Mr. Hess: Well, we probably wouldn't. But we want Mr. Peters to be prepared just in case someone were to ask.

The Court: I think I'm beginning to see what you fellows are up to. I certainly haven't read through all those papers you filed, I'm hoping I won't have to. So, Mr. Peters, why don't you walk me through exactly what it is you are proposing.

Mr. Peters: Sure, Your Honor. There are three motions before you. The first one is for leave to file an Amended Complaint. The Amended Complaint merely changes the case from a statewide class action to a nationwide class action. Our client, Dr. Hazelnutt, is still the representative plaintiff for the entire class.

The Court: Mr. Hess, I assume you have no objection to this motion? Especially since it seems to have been your idea.

Mr. Hess: That's correct, we have no objection to the filing of the Amended Complaint.

The Court: Motion granted.

Mr. Peters: The second motion is a motion for a determination that this case may proceed as a class action. We have attached Dr. Hazelnutt's deposition to our papers. Our brief shows that, based on the criteria for class actions, Dr. Hazelnutt is an appropriate representative of the class. Would you like me to run through those criteria and the reasons why Dr. Hazelnutt's claim satisfies them?

The Court: Good heavens no. I can readily guess what you're going to say about each of the criteria. Besides, going through the class action criteria is really boring. Anyway, Mr. Hess isn't contesting this motion either, am I correct?

Mr. Hess: That's correct, Your Honor. We agree this case can be certified as a class action on behalf of all consumers in the country who have purchased a box of Berry Good Corny Flakes and that Dr. Hazelnutt is an appropriate representative of that class..

The Court: Okay, that motion is also granted. I wish counsel in my other cases were this cooperative, it would make my life easier.

Mr. Peters: We like nothing better than to make the Court's life easier. Now, Judge Prudence, that brings us to the heart of the matter. The settlement agreement. It is attached to the third motion and we would like you to approve it

The Court: You will have to take me through its terms. As you know, I'm required to review it to make certain it's fair to all the members of the class. If you walk me through all the terms, I won't have to read it. Now, can I assume that Mr. Hess will not be objecting to any of its terms?

Mr. Hess: That's correct, Your Honor, we will not be objecting. Why would we object when we wrote it?

The Court: I see. Very well, Mr. Peters please proceed. I'm anxious to hear what a box of improperly labeled Corny Flakes is worth.

Mr. Peters: Okay, Your Honor. Let me start with the monetary aspects of the settlement. There are three parts to it. First, a fund of $4.6 million is being established for refunds to purchasers of Berry Good Corny Flakes. Everyone who has purchased a box of them will be entitled to a refund of 75 cents.

The Court: What if they purchased two boxes, do they get $1.50 in refunds?

Mr. Peters: No, Your Honor. The basis of the lawsuit is that, when consumers purchase Berry Good Corny Flakes, they believe they are buying Corny Flakes with blueberries added. But once they open the box and have their first serving, they know there's no blueberries in them.

The Court: I guess that makes Berry Good Corny Flakes just plain Corny Flakes.

Mr. Peters: Yes, you could say that. Anyway, once they see that the cereal does not have blueberries in it, there's no deception if they buy a second box. Mr. Hess was very insistent on this – nobody gets a refund on their second or third box of Berry Good Corny Flakes.

The Court: I see that. But how did you come up with a fund of $4.6 million to cover the refunds?

Mr. Hess: I can explain that, Your Honor, since it was my client's calculation. As of the date we negotiated the settlement, Colonel Mills had sold approximately 9.2 million boxes of Berry Good Corny Flakes. But we also know from some early tracking data – that's market research that tracks sales – that some households have purchased more than one box. In fact, we know that the average household has purchased one-and-a-half boxes Berry Good Corny Flakes.

The Court: Colonel Mills sells half-boxes of Corny Flakes? I don't think I've ever seen a half box of cereal in a store.

Mr. Hess: Of course not. That is simply an average. Some households have purchased one box, others have purchased two or three boxes, but the average is one-and-a-half. Now, if 9.2 million boxes have been sold and the average household has bought one-and-a-half boxes, that means 6.15 million households have purchased Berry Good Corny Fakes.

The Court: I was never very good at math, that's why I went to law school. How did you come up with that 6.15 million number?

Mr. Hess: 9.2 million boxes sold divided by 1.5 boxes per household. That means 6.15 million households. So we are offering each of those households a 75 cent refund. As Mr. Peters said, they only get a refund on their first purchase.

The Court: How did you come up with 75 cents as the amount of the refund? It's hardly worth anyone's time getting a check for 75 cents and having to take it to a bank and deposit it. And I can't think of any place that would cash a check for 75 cents.

Mr. Hess: Initially we offered to provide a 50 cent refund. That would have constituted about 13% of the $3.95 purchase price. A 13% refund seemed quite appropriate since nobody has to give back the Corny Flakes, they can still eat them. But Mr. Peters insisted on a refund of 75 cents. That brings the refund up to 19% of the purchase price, which is quite generous. Especially since they can still eat the Corny Flakes, everybody likes Corny Flakes whether or not they have blueberries in 'em. So, with a refund of 75 cents going to 6.15 households, that gives you the $4.6 million figure Mr. Peters referred to.

The Court: Are you saying that 75 cents times 6.15 million equals $4.6 million?

Mr. Hess: Yes. That's straight multiplication. I can have Mr. Hoover show you on his hand-held calculator.

The Court: That won't be necessary.

Mr. Hess: So, in short, anyone who qualifies as a member of the class can apply for a refund of 75 cents from this fund of $4.6 million we are creating.

The Court: How much money has Colonel Mills made from the sale of these Corny Fakes?

Mr. Hess: I can't tell you the amount of profit, but I can tell you the amount of revenue. They've sold 9.2 million boxes at $3.95 per box. That comes to $36.3 million.

The Court: Sounds like Colonel Mills made a lot of money on these fake Corny Flakes.

Mr. Hess: The Corny Flakes were not fakes. Just the blueberries. Well, they weren't really fakes, there just weren't any.

The Court: Colonel Mills sold $36.3 million worth of Corny Flakes to consumers who thought they were getting Corny Flakes with blueberries added. But there were in fact no blueberries. And so purchasers like Dr. Hazelnutt who wanted blueberries on their Corny Flakes had to go out and buy their own blueberries, correct?

Mr. Peters: That's correct. In fact, Your Honor, that's exactly what happened with Dr. Hazelnutt. When she discovered there were no blueberries in her box of Berry Good Corny Flakes, she had to drive all around Westchester County looking for a store that had blueberries. It was January and nobody had any, it took her the entire morning before she found some. So you can see the terrible consequences this fraud had on consumers who fell for the hoax.

Mr. Hess: It's not Colonel Mills' fault that none of the stores Dr. Hazelnut went to had blueberries in stock. People who buy regular Corny Fakes have always had to go out and buy their own blueberries if they want them on their cereal. Same for cranberries, some people like cranberries on their Corny Flakes. None of these consumers have ever complained.

Mr. Peters: But that was the whole point of Berry Good Corny Flakes. The expectation that . . . .

The Court: Gentlemen, we're getting off track here. We all know the new version of Corny Flakes was supposed to have blueberries in them but didn't. Maybe we should be calling them Corny Fakes. But let's get back to the settlement. Mr. Peters, I believe you said there were other monetary components to the settlement?

Mr. Peters: Yes. The second item of compensation is coupons. Every member of the class will receive a coupon good for the purchase of either Berry Good Corny Flakes or regular Corny Flakes. The coupon has a value of $3.95, the price of Berry Good Corny Flakes. So, with 6.15 million plaintiffs each getting a coupon with a value of $3.95, that's a total value of $24.3 million.

The Court: Why would a consumer who is part of the class want a coupon for Berry Good Corny Flakes? They're claiming they were deceived when they bought them thinking they contained blueberries. Surely they don't want a coupon for the same product?

Mr. Peters: The coupon will be for the new version of Berry Good Corny Flakes. Under the settlement, Colonel Mills must change the labeling on the Corny Flakes box. I was going to cover that later, after I finished with the monetary terms.

The Court: You might as well cover it now. I want to make certain there is value in those coupons.

Mr. Peters: Okay. Colonel Mills will be required to cease selling Berry Good Corny Flakes in their current package. They can still sell the product but only in a new package. Under the terms of the settlement, they will have two options.

Option one is they delete the picture of Corny Flakes in a bowl with blueberries on top. They can retain the current banner that's on the front of the box and says "Blueberry naturally and artificially flavored." But no picture of blueberries.

Option two is they can retain the picture but the words in the banner must be changed to include the statement "No blueberries included" or "For a real treat add your own blueberries." Either statement is fine so long as it's in the same size as the rest of the words in the banner.

The Court: Okay, that seems appropriate. Now, let's get back to the monetary aspects of the settlement. I think you said there were three? What's the third one?

Mr. Peters: Yes. Once you approve the settlement, an injunction against the old package will go into effect. But Colonel Mills will have about six million boxes of Berry Good Corny Flakes on hand that they will be prohibited from selling. So it has agreed to donate these boxes to a food bank. That's six million boxes at $3.95. That comes to $23.7 million.

The Court: Yes. Six million times $3.95 equals $23.7 million, I see that. By the time this case is over I'll be ready for a graduate course in mathematics.

Mr. Peters: There's still a few odds and ends I need to mention. For one thing, there's an additional benefit Colonel Mills has agreed to provide. All members of the class will receive a free one-year subscription to the company's newsletter "Starting Smart, the Better Way to Better Health."

The Court: I'll bet it suggests starting the day with one of their cereals.

Mr. Peters: And I'll bet it also suggests that, if you put blueberries or cranberries on top of the cereal, you'll be starting the day out really smart.

Mr. Hess: Colonel Mills is just trying to induce consumers to start the day with a healthy breakfast. I don't see what's wrong with that.

The Court: Someone's always trying to tell us all how to eat. Why can't they just let us eat what we want? I like a muffin or bagel for breakfast, nothing wrong with that.

Mr. Hess: Perhaps Mr. Peters would agree that my client can supply you with a couple of those coupons, that way you could get off to a smarter start to your day.

The Court: That won't be necessary, I'll stick with my muffins and bagels. But I'll tell you what. I'll see if they have some muffins made from whole wheat. According to my wife, whole wheat is very nutritious.

Now, let's get back to the financial terms. Mr. Peters, in all this discussion about the class, we've forgotten about your client, Dr. Hazelnut. What does she get under the settlement?

Mr. Peters: She gets $50,000.

The Court: What about the other benefits? Does she get the 75 cent refund and a coupon?

Mr. Hess: Your Honor, we did not specifically cover that in the settlement agreement. But in the spirit of compromise, I will be happy to stipulate that Dr. Hazelnutt is entitled to the 75 cent refund and one coupon. Now, for some reason, she went out and bought fifteen boxes of Berry Good Corny Flakes before she ever opened the first box. She wasn't too clear as to why she did that. But she still gets only one refund and one coupon. We're not going to reward her bizarre behavior by giving her fifteen coupons.

Mr. Peters: That's fine, I don't think Dr. Hazelnutt needs another fifteen boxes of Corny Flakes without blueberries.

The Court: I think we've covered everything we need to address. Mr. Peters, any other odds and ends we need to take up?

Mr. Peters: Well, there is one minor matter Your Honor. That's our fee. The settlement agreement provides that we are entitled to 30% of the total monetary value of the settlement. That would amount to $15.8 million.

The Court: $15.8 million? The entire class is only getting $4.6 million. Thirty per cent of that would be – let me see – this is very rough but I think it would be only $1.2 million, maybe $1.3.

Mr. Peters: Your math is correct but your input is not. There are three monetary components to the settlement: $4.6 million in refunds, $24.3 million in coupons and $23.7 million in gifts to food banks. That totals $52.6 million. And that's not counting Dr. Hazelnutt's $50,000 or her 75 cent refund. So, 30% of $52.6 million is $15.8 million. If Mr. Hoover has his calculator handy maybe he can confirm it.

The Court: Let me see if I've got this correct. Your client, Dr. Hazelnutt, gets $50,000. The members of the class all get a 75 cent refund and a coupon for a box of Corny Flakes, regular or fake blueberry. And your firm gets $15.8 million? Mr. Hess, is your client consenting to this enormous fee?

Mr. Hess: Your Honor, 30% is pretty much par for the course. Some firms demand 33%, sometimes more if the case has actually gone to trial. But in the spirit of getting this deal done quickly, Mr. Peters has graciously agreed to a fee of only 30%.

If this case wasn't being turned into a nationwide class action, we would be facing dozens of lawsuits by dozens of law firms, each of whom would be claiming 30% or 33% of any verdict or settlement. We'd end up paying far more than $15.8 million to opposing counsel. So, we'd rather pay that amount to Mr. Peters' firm now and get this entire matter behind us.

The Court: Well, gentlemen, if both parties agree on all this, who am I to stand in the way? So, I'm going to grant all the pending motions. The Amended Complaint may be filed forthwith. The case is hereby declared a nationwide class action, the members of the class will be all U.S. consumers who purchased one or more boxes of Berry Good Corny Flakes. And the settlement agreement is approved.

Mr. Peters, congratulations, it looks like your client did quite well. It also looks like your firm is the big winner here. It also appears that you were ably assisted by Mr. Hess and Mr. Hoover. If I were you, I'd take both of them out for drinks. If there's nothing more, we stand adjourned.

* * * *

As Judge Prudence left the bench, Pup leaned over and said to Pap "I hope you aren't planning to talk to any reporters downstairs, we won't be seeing any of this money for a while. We can't jeopardize . . . ."

"Of course not" said Pap. "We've gotta wait until all the orders are signed and the settlement is officially approved. We can't risk jeopardizing that fifteen point eight million. But I can't wait to tell Bill

Fund – the Lien On Me Fund guy - about this. He thought the case was a loser. Now, let's see when Hess and Hoover want to have that drink."

Chapter 25

WALL OF FAME

It was a Wednesday morning in early November, a few weeks after the approval of the settlement in the Corny Flakes case. Pap had called a meeting for 10:00 to brainstorm ideas for new cases.

"I hope everyone has had a chance to think about potential new cases" Pap began. "That's why I sent out the memorandum about this meeting . . . ."

"Okay" Chip interrupted heatedly, "who's the wise guy who put up all those pictures?"

"What pictures?" said Pap.

"The ones in the Worry Room. I'm sure you had something to do with it" Chip said as he glared at Pap.

"What's this all about?" asked Pup. "We don't have any pictures in the Worry Room."

"We do now" said Chip. "There's five of 'em on the wall behind the sofa."

"How do you know that?" asked Pap. "You always say you never worry. Only Pup and Melissa ever go there to worry about our cases."

"Well, there were five pictures there last night" said Chip.

"Maybe you should tell us what you were doing in the Worry Room last night, after everyone had gone home" said Pap. "Which one of our cases did you go there to worry about?"

"You know full well what I was doing in the Worry Room last night. I met Candy there at nine o'clock."

"What were you and Candy up to, meeting in the Worry Room at nine o'clock at night?" asked Pap.

"Well, when Candy saw the pictures we didn't get up to anything. She took one look at them and stormed out of the room. I've never seen her so angry."

"So what are these pictures anyway?" asked Melissa. "There were no pictures up the last time I was in there."

"They're photographs" said Chip. "Each one is signed with a personal message."

"But who's in the photographs?" insisted Melissa.

"Well" said Chip, "the first one is a photo of Lydia. It's one of the shots from *Playboy* when she was Playmate of the Month."

"You said there was an inscription?" asked Brandon.

"Yeah. It said 'To Chip with Love, Lydia.' "

"That's sounds nice" replied Brandon. "I'd love to have a signed photograph from Lydia, it would do wonders for my reputation."

"What about the other photographs?" asked Melissa.

"Well, the second one is Francoise. It's the same photo she gave me when she moved in with me. She signed it at the bottom: 'With All my Love, Francoise.' "

"Where did you say the photos are hung?" asked Brandon.

"In a row over the sofa. Francoise's picture is right next to Lydia's."

"Didn't you say there were five altogether?" asked Melissa. "This is getting interesting. Who are the other three?"

"Three girls I dated when I was at Dartmouth. The first was from Penelope. Penelope Pak. She also went to Dartmouth. We dated my sophomore year."

Pap said "I think Chip is being modest when he says they 'dated' while at Dartmouth. The way I heard it, they had a torrid love affair. Maybe her inscription sheds some light on this. How did she sign it, Chip?"

"It was kind of cute" said Chip. "Dearest Chip, First Love is Always the Sweetest. Love Always, Penelope."

Melissa was starting to catch on. "Isn't Penelope the daughter of Fanny Pak, one of the friends of Dr. Hazelnut? One of the ladies in that Third Thursday thing?"

"Right" said Pap. "And I believe that another member of that club also had a daughter who knew Chip."

"Sure" said Melissa. "Helen Heeler, I think her name was. Her mother was Faith Heeler. As I recall, Helen went to Wesleyan and Chip would drive down from New Hampshire every Friday and spend the weekend with her. This must have been after football season was over, you had to be at Dartmouth on weekends during football season, right Chip?"

"Yeah, I couldn't drive down to Wesleyan on the Friday before a Saturday game, I would have lost my scholarship."

"I didn't know you went to Dartmouth on a scholarship" said Pup. "I assume it was a football scholarship?"

"No" said Brandon, "Chip had a scholarship to study quantum physics."

"You're both wrong" said Melissa. "He had a scholarship in gender studies. The school thought he would bring an interesting perspective to the subject."

"Very funny" said Chip. "You all know I went to Dartmouth to play football. And chase women."

"Right" said Melissa. "But let's get back to Helen's photograph. What did she say on her photo?"

"She said 'Dearest Chip. Thanks for the Wonderful Memories. Love Always, Helen.'"

"So the fifth one" said Brandon, having finally caught on, "must have been that Keeler girl who went to Vassar."

"Yep" said Chip. "Christine Keeler. She was a typical Vassar intellectual, kind of cold and haughty, but she certainly loved to have a good time. And boy did we ever have some good times. When I drove down to Wesleyan on Friday – to spend Friday night and Saturday with Helen – I'd drive on over to Poughkeepsie on Sunday and spend the day there with Christine. By Monday I was totally exhausted. But it made for a nice weekend."

"So what was Christine's inscription?" asked Melissa.

"'My Dear Chip, I'll never forget those Sundays in my room at Vassar. With Love, Christine.'"

"That's quite a collection" said Pap. "I think we should view it as a sort of Wall of Fame."

"I don't get it" said Pup. "Other than their relationship with Chip, what's the connection with us? Why are these pictures up in the Worry Room?"

"You must be the only one not getting it" said Pap. "I can see Melissa and Brandon have figured it out. And they didn't even go to Yale."

"Sure" said Melissa. "All of them are connected not just to Chip but to our cases. Starting with Lydia. She was our first famous client. And she was a client because Chip brought her here from that strip joint where she worked."

"It was not a strip joint" said Chip irritably. "It was a gentleman's club. And Lydia and her colleagues weren't strippers, they were dancers. Well, lap dancers. And let me tell you, she did a helluva dance in my lap. But don't forget, when we got a settlement in that case, Pap told the judge how proud he was that our firm had brought justice to all the underpaid and exploited lap dancers in New York City."

"Yes" said Brandon, "the firm's always been proud of what we accomplished for Lydia. And some of us are envious of what Chip accomplished with Lydia."

"Let's get back to the wall" said Melissa. "According to Chip, next to Lydia is Francoise. Now Francoise is the one who tipped us off about that guy at the French mission to the UN, Pierre Dupre. It was Francoise who told us about Dupre's vulnerability. Pap passed that information on to the guys in DC and someone, maybe the CIA, who knows, put the squeeze on him to be our plaintiff in the suit against the Russkies. All of this was thanks to Chip's Francoise."

"Right" said Brandon. "And we all know about the three college girls and their role in the Corny Flakes case. They're the ones who mentioned Chip's name to their mothers when Dr. Hazelnutt was trying to find a law firm to take on her case against Colonel Mills."

"All right, I get it" said Chip. "Very clever. But why were all the pictures put on the wall in the Worry Room, just above the sofa for

God's sake? Candy's never going to meet me in the Worry Room again, she's absolutely furious."

"Well" said Pap, "maybe you'll have to stop violating the firm's Fornication Policy. I've talked to you about this before. The firm's Fornication Policy is embodied in an official firm memorandum authored by Pup and me. We sent it to everyone in the firm. It absolutely forbids fornication in the Worry Room.

"Now the Wall of Fame, besides its impact on unlawful fornication, is also an important record of the firm's history. And the role that you, Chip, have played in that history. You should be proud of that. Thanks to your many sexual escapades, the firm has grown and prospered.

"So, Chip, I think you should be proud of all that you have helped us to accomplish in so short a time. After all, we're barely a year old. I think the Wall of Fame is an appropriate way to salute your unique contribution to the firm's success. This afternoon, we should all convene in the Worry Room and salute the Wall of Fame with a champagne toast. In fact, I already have a bottle on ice, ready to go."

"I don't think Candy will participate" said Chip. "She's not crazy about those pictures."

Chapter 26

BRAINSTORMING

"Okay" Pap said. "Enough with the Wall of Fame. Let's get back to the subject at hand: ideas for new cases.

"Remember, there's two criteria here. First, its got to be a high profile case, one that will generate publicity and enhance the firm's reputation. Second, its got to be one where we can rake in some money. We're doing okay financially, but we could sure use a few more big winners like Corny Flakes.

"Brandon, let's start with you. Have you come up with anything?"

"Yes" said Brandon. "I've been looking into the Volkswagen emissions debacle. I'm sure you all know Volkswagen has admitted to installing software in its diesel-powered cars that allowed the car to evade emissions requirements. Basically, the cars had a pollution control feature that turned on when the car was undergoing pollution testing but turned off when the car was on the road."

"That's old news" said Pup. "There were scores of class action cases filed. I think I read that Volkswagen paid over fifteen billion dollars to settle those cases."

"That's right" said Brandon. "But most of the plaintiffs in those cases had purchased the smaller two-liter engine cars, mostly ones sold under the VW brand. Those buyers thought they were buying environmentally sensitive cars. They claimed – quite rightly – that they were deceived because, in actual use, the pollution control system automatically shut off. So their car was fouling the environment instead of saving the environment."

"I don't see where you're going with this" said Pup. "That ship has sailed and we weren't on it."

"Hear me out" said Brandon. "Some of the vehicles involved, Audis and Porsches, had larger three-liter engines. They were recalled too and the pollution control software was corrected so that the emissions control device was operative when the car was in actual use."

"So?" said Pup. "Audi and Porsche did the right thing."

"Maybe. But those Audi and Porsche buyers thought they were getting hot, fast cars – well, they were hot and fast when they first bought them, before they were recalled – were now saddled with slow, lumbering pollution-controlled vehicles. Who wants to drive a slow, lumbering Porsche just because it's good for the environment?"

"This is interesting, Brandon" said Pap. "Going against the grain. I like that. But what's the legal claim here?"

"I haven't fully worked that out yet. But certainly all those buyers test drove the car before they bought it. Who would ever spend all that money on a Porsche without first taking it out on the road to see how it performs? And that performance during the test drive – when the pollution control device was deactivated - is what the buyers thought they were getting. It was, essentially, the basis of the bargain.

"But now, all of a sudden, the car is recalled and force fed some software that activates a pollution control device when the car is in use. So now they've got a lumbering, everyday sedan instead of a hot, zero-to-sixty-in-two-seconds car. So, I'd say they've been defrauded."

"Brandon, you're a genius" said Pap. "Those Porches cost a lot of dough, we could sue Volkswagen for a return of the purchase price. Multiply that times all the Porches, and maybe even Audis that were recalled, we could be talking real money here."

"I don't know" said Pup. "How can we claim that Porsche buyers were defrauded when they had to undergo changes to a car that was cheating on emissions testing? Before the recall, those cars were illegal. In fact, Volkswagen was actually prosecuted for selling them. We can't represent clients who admit they wanted a car that cheated on its emissions testing."

"Pup, let's not get judgmental here" said Pap. "We shouldn't be criticizing the values of car buyers. Car buyers are buying cars. They want a sleek, fast car, they buy a Porsche. They want a slow environmentally-friendly car, they buy a Volvo. Or maybe a covered wagon. Covered wagons were environmentally friendly and people drove them all the way to the West Coast. But if they buy a Porsche, they shouldn't be stuck with a covered wagon."

"I agree we shouldn't be judgmental about car buyers" said Melissa. "My uncle has one of those huge Dodge Rams that look ridiculous in a suburban setting. But that's okay with me, I don't want to be judgmental, even though he always drives over everyone's lawn, he can't seem to keep the thing in the road.

"But look, Pap" Melissa continued, "what Pup is saying is that it would be against public policy to argue that someone is cheated when he can't drive a car that is itself illegal. Illegal because it's designed to evade emissions testing. No court would ever certify a class of car buyers when their claim is against public policy."

"You really think so, Melissa?"

"Yes, I really think so."

"Damn. Okay, I suppose Melissa's right. She always is. But holy Hell, Brandon, that was a terrific idea. Creative, inventive. That's our trademark. That's what we want Peters and Peters to be known for.

"But I guess we better move on. Chip, what about you? What have you come up with?"

"One of my friends from Dartmouth, James Pearson Morgan – I think he's related in some way to J. P. Morgan – is a first-year banker at Golden Slacks, that big investment banking firm. He and the seventy-nine other first year bankers are at their wits end. They consistently have one hundred to one-hundred-twenty-hour work weeks. And they have extremely long days, sometimes they work twenty hours a day. They can't even take Saturday or Sunday off.

"A couple of them came up with a survey about the state of their physical and mental health. All but one or two of them filled out the survey. Virtually everyone ranked themselves eight or nine on a ten-point scale when they first started at the firm. But now they're all down to about two or two-point-five. This is inhuman, they shouldn't be treated like that."

"I don't see any claim here" said Melissa. "No laws are being violated."

"What about all those New Deal laws – minimum hour laws, for example" said Chip.

"They don't apply to investment bankers working in plush offices on Wall Street and making a fortune" said Melissa.

"Okay, what about Blue Laws? Aren't there laws about making people work on Sundays?"

"There were fifty years ago" said Melissa. "Those laws have been off the books for ages."

"Chip" said Pup, how much do you think those guys are being paid?"

"I'm not sure."

"Well I am" said Pup. "It's well-known that Golden Slacks bankers have a starting salary of eighty-five thousand. And with their bonus – in those firms their annual bonus is sometimes more than their annual salary – I think the bonus brings their average compensation to one hundred fifty thousand or more. In their first year at the firm. They wanna make that kind of money, they gotta pay the price."

"Look, Chip" said Pap patiently. "I'm sure your J. P. Morgan guy and his colleagues have a legitimate gripe. But we're not in business to help a bunch of overpaid rich kids sue Golden Slacks. We're in business to help underpaid little people sue Golden Slacks.

"As a matter of fact, if we represented a class of little people in a case *against* Golden Slacks, we could make a lot of dough. But no judge or jury is going to feel sympathy for a bunch of kids making one hundred and fifty thousand dollars their first year out of college. So, forget about your friend at Golden Slacks. We've got bigger fish to fry.

"And speaking of fish to fry, it's food cases we should be looking for. Packaged foods sold nationwide by big food companies. Like Corny Flakes. That's the kind of case we need more of. Now, can one of you please come up with a new Corny Flakes case?"

Pup spoke up. "There's an interesting case that was just filed by Multilever, that big food and household products company that sells

Mellman's Mayonnaise. They just sued a competitor, Uptown Creek, for false advertising. Uptown Creek makes a vegan version of mayonnaise that it calls Simply Mayo. Because Simply Mayo doesn't contain any eggs – eggs come from chickens which . . . ."

"I never knew eggs came from chickens" said Pap. "When did that start happening?"

Ignoring Pap's interruption, which Pup knew was the only way to deal with him, Pup continued. "Eggs, of course, come from chickens. And chickens are bad in the vegan world. Which is why Simply Mayo isn't made from eggs. So, Multilever claims that Simply Mayo is not true mayonnaise because it isn't made from eggs and so is being falsely advertised."

"Do you think they'll win?" asked Pap.

"I think they will. Apparently the widely-accepted definition of mayonnaise is a product that's made from eggs. I believe there may even be a federal regulation on that point as well."

"Does it taste like mayonnaise?" asked Pap. "Melissa, you're into this health food stuff. Ever tried this Simply Mayo product?"

"No, but I can get some and try it this weekend. I always have a peanut butter, mayonnaise and cucumber sandwich on Saturday. But what if it tastes like real mayonnaise? I suspect it probably will."

"If it's not made from eggs then it's not real mayonnaise, at least according to Multilever" said Pup.

"But look" said Pap, "the big issue isn't how it tastes but how high its sales are. If it's just a niche product, appealing only to a few vegan nuts, the sales aren't going to be all that high. The case wouldn't be worth our while."

"Why don't we do a little investigating" said Pup. "Let Melissa buy some and try it on her peanut butter, mayonnaise and cucumber sandwich on Saturday. Then tell us what she thinks. And Brandon, why don't you dig into the sales data, see what you can find. See if its sales are large enough to warrant a class action lawsuit."

"Good plan" said Pap. "Now, anyone else come up with an idea? Melissa, we haven't heard from you yet."

"I just read about a case filed in California. A consumer bought some vanilla yogurt. Claimed she thought it contained real vanilla, but discovered that it only had vanilla flavoring."

"What's the difference?" said Pap. "Vanilla's a flavoring."

"Not necessarily" said Melissa. "According to the lawsuit, there is real, natural vanilla, which comes from the vanilla bean. The bean is only grown in a couple of African countries – I think Madagascar is one – so it is quite expensive. That pure vanilla extract we all have in our kitchen is the real thing. But it costs one hundred to two hundred dollars a gallon, that's why the bottle is so small.

"On the other hand, most vanilla flavored products are made from a flavoring that costs about fifty dollars a gallon. That's what's used in all kinds of products: yogurt, soft ice cream, coffee creamers, root beer. It's used in a really wide range of foods."

"But wouldn't vanilla flavoring be made from actual vanilla?" asked Pap.

"Apparently not" said Melissa. "There's some sort of fermentation process they use to make vanilla flavoring. Sometimes they even start with wood pulp."

"Wood pulp? Jesus" said Pap.

"But still, if it tastes like vanilla, what's the big deal?" said Pup. He didn't like where this was going. "We eat vanilla yogurt all the time. Priscilla and I put it on blueberries."

"You mean the blueberries that aren't in Berry Good Corny Flakes?" said Pap.

"Right" said Pup. "The kind Dr. Hazelnut had to drive all over Westchester to find. But the yogurt has a real vanilla favor. I can't imagine it tasting any more like vanilla than if it was made using real vanilla from those beans in Madagascar. So I can't see any claim here."

"Pup" said Pap, "the trouble is you're thinking like a reasonable consumer. We don't represent reasonable consumers, consumers who only care that the vanilla flavoring in their vanilla yogurt tastes like vanilla. We represent unreasonable consumers. Gullible consumers who believe what the labeling and advertising tells them.

"If they're told they're buying mayonnaise, they want real mayonnaise, not some egg-free vegan version. And if they're buying vanilla yogurt, they want real vanilla made from Madagascar beans, not some vanilla flavoring made from wood pulp. Even if it tastes like real vanilla and the wood comes from Madagascar."

"But Pap, if there's no difference in how either product tastes, who cares about . . . ."

"Our clients care" said Pap. "That's why they come to us. Or, if they don't come to us, we go out and find them. Like that Risotto girl we were going to use in that Wunderpants case."

"Rizzuto" said Melissa. "Pap, I've told you a hundred times, her name is Rizzuto. Risa Rizzuto. Now, she does eat a lot of risotto, so she's gotten a bit heavy. That's why everyone at Oliver and Cromwell started calling her 'Too Much Risotto Rizzuto.' "

"Okay" said Pap. "Now we couldn't use her before because the company that made Wunderpants went out of business before we could sue 'em. Damn inconsiderate of them.

"But I'll bet we could convince her to help us in one of these food cases. Risotto versus Uptown Creek, that has a nice ring to it. But if we do the vanilla case instead, we gotta figure out who to sue. Sounds like lots of food companies could be in the picture. Let's see what products and companies we could be looking at."

Glancing at his watch, Pap stood up and said: "Look, we've got to wrap this up. Congressman Earmacher's niece is coming in for lunch. Then I'm taking her to the U.N. to meet Andre Bonnet, the chauffeur who helped us in the case against the Russkies. Earmacher wants her to seduce Bonnet, then see if she can find out what the French are up to in North Africa.

"So, let's figure out if we want to pursue any of these two cases. If so, we can have Melissa recruit the Risotto girl as our plaintiff.

"In the meantime, I'll see you all later. I've gotta go start setting up the honey trap for Andre. Poor guy, I really liked him. But I think he'll have a good time with Earmacher's niece."

Chapter 27

STRIP CLUBBED

The trial against the three strip clubs operated by the Aegean Love company commenced on a Wednesday morning in late February. It was just two weeks after the unfortunate appeal in the Chimps case. Pap and the firm needed a win, they hated losing. Losing was almost as bad as not getting paid.

Pap and Chip were seated at the counsel table in New York Supreme Court along with their client Lydia Lowlace, who was wearing the smart navy blue suit Chip had given her for her first press conference three years ago.

Because the case was not a class action and the stakes were not particularly high, Pap decided that Chip would replace Pup as second chair on the case. He wanted Pup to focus on Lydia's class action case involving the Bunny Hop video game. Besides, Lydia had come to view Chip as more or less her personal attorney at Peters and Peters. Being Lydia's personal attorney carried with it certain fringe benefits which Chip readily embraced.

At the counsel table opposite were the attorneys for Aegean Love, Jack Jeckel and Harry Hyde. They were the only attorneys in the two-person Newark firm of Jeckel and Hyde.

Pap had run up against them when he was representing Lorner-Wambert in the Breath Magic case in Newark, when he was still at Rogers and Autry. Jeckel and Hyde seemed to have a habit of representing shady New Jersey companies, and Aegean Love certainly met that description. The company's president and sole shareholder,

Ambrose Lambros, was at the counsel table along with Jeckel and Hyde.

Pap felt right at home in this courtroom. It was the courtroom of Justice Charles E. Chan, the judge who had presided over the criminal case of the comedian Phil Crosby. That was the case where Pap had made his name at Rogers and Autry. Due to Crosby's huge popularity and Pap's clever antics during an outburst of firecrackers during closing argument, Crosby was acquitted - despite being plainly guilty of - assault and battery against two photographers at a charity dinner at which Crosby's wife was being honored.

Justice Chan's court clerk, Lance A. Lott, entered the courtroom and shouted "All rise." He then intoned: "The New York Supreme Court for the County of New York, Justice Charles E. Chan presiding, is now in session. Please be seated. Counsel, please stand and enter your appearances."

Transcript of Proceedings:

Mr. Peters: Good morning Justice Chan. Patrick A. Peters for the plaintiff, Lydia Lowlace. With me is my colleague Charles Pierpont.

The Court: Good morning Mr. Peters, and welcome back. I think it was this same time of year when you last appeared before me. The Chinese New Year starts on Friday, so I'm afraid we might have some of those fireworks again. You made extremely good use of them last time, I'm looking forward to seeing how you might use them this time.

Mr. Peters: Thank you, Your Honor. I had to think of something fast, they were driving me crazy.

The Court: Counsel for defendant, may I have your appearances.

Mr. Hyde: Your Honor, I'm Harry Hyde. My partner Dr. Jeckel and I practice in New Jersey, our firm is in Newark, but we have been admitted *pro haec* for this case. Our client, Aegean Love, is a New jersey company that we have long represented and they asked if we would represent them in this case.

The Court: Did you say your partner is Dr. Jeckel?

Mr. Hyde: Well, his name is Jack Jeckel, but all the lawyers in New Jersey refer to him as Dr. Jeckel so he's sort of embraced that name. But he's not really a doctor, he's a lawyer. There's a big difference.

The Court: I see. And who is the dour-looking gentleman with you at your table? He looks like he wishes he were somewhere else.

Mr. Hyde: Your Honor, this is Mr. Lambros. Ambrose Lambros. He's the owner and president of Aegean Love. And I can assure you, Your Honor, there is no place Mr. Lambros would rather be today than in this courtroom.

The Court: Before we start . . . . Oh, I see that my colleague Justice Leghetti just walked in and took a seat. Justice Leghetti, you are certainly welcome to watch this proceeding. I'd like to think you want to see how I conduct bench trials, but I suspect there must be some other reason you're here.

Justice Leghetti: Hello Justice Chan. Actually it was Mr. Romo's idea. That's my court clerk, Tony Romo. We had a trial involving Mr. Peters and this lovely lady a couple of years ago. Mr. Romo thought we should see how she's doing. He thinks it was our case that made her famous, we're kind of proud of that.

* * * *

Lydia turned in her seat and waved to Justice Leghetti and Tony Romo. Romo waved back and gave her a wide smile.

At that point, Justice Chan explained that, since neither side had filed a jury demand, he would proceed with a bench trial. And because it was a bench trial, there was no need for opening arguments. He hoped they hadn't spent too much time preparing openings. He then called for Pap to proceed.

Pap promptly called Lydia to the stand. He and Chip had worked together on an outline of her testimony and Pap had drilled her constantly on the need to answer the questions directly and concisely. He repeatedly told her that short and sweet answers were the best way to avoid trouble.

Lydia proved to be a surprisingly good student. She responded to Pap's questions with, for her, a minimum of digressions.

Pap walked her through her role in the lap dancers class action case and how that case had caught the attention of someone at *Playboy* magazine. And how her appearance in *Playboy* had led to considerable fame, offers of marriage and several business opportunities. Pap went on to establish that, while Lydia had accepted two such business opportunities – both involving the modeling of lingerie – she had quit her former job as a lap dancer and had no further connection with clubs of any kind.

Turning to the issue in the case, Pap had Lydia explain that she had never given permission for Aegean Love to use her photos to promote its clubs. In fact, her association with gentleman's clubs was a thing of the past. She wanted nothing whatsoever to do with Sins of the City, Sugardaddy's Place or Empty Laces. She was embarrassed and humiliated to be associated with such low-life clubs.

When Pap concluded his examination, Justice Chan announced that there would be a ten-minute break before cross-examination commenced. Lydia looked down at Pap and Chip, both of whom nodded their approval of her performance. When she looked back to Justice Leghetti, she saw him shoot her a quick smile. Tony Romo, however, was more demonstrative, giving her an enthusiastic thumbs up.

Please Pass the Torts

* * * *

Once everyone was back in place after the break, Harry Hyde rose to begin his cross-examination.

Cross-Examination by Mr. Hyde:

Q: Good morning, Miss Lowlace. I see you've been waving to that judge in the spectator section. Is he a friend of yours?

A: Justice. We's in New York State Supreme Court. The judges here they's called Justice, not Judge. You shoulda' known that.

Q: My practice is in New Jersey. We just call them judges over there.

A: Well, if you's gonna' be in these here New York courts, I think you should call 'em Justice. Even I knows that and I's not even a lawyer.

Q: Okay. But now will you answer my question. Is that Justice a friend or . . . .

Mr. Peters: Objection, this is irrelevant.

The Court: Sustained.

Mr. Hyde: But Judge Chan, if he's a friend of hers and he's also a friend of yours, that raises a question of bias. It could be a matter of disqualification.

The Court: Mr. Hyde, Justice Leghetti — and by the way Miss Lowlace is right, in New York we're called Justice, not Judge. You should know that if you're going to try a case in this court. In any event, Justice Leghetti is not the judge in this case, I am.

And I am not a friend of Miss Lowlace. Never even laid eyes on her before this case.

Mr. Hyde: Not even when she was Playmate of the Month? I'll bet you laid eyes on her then.

The Court: Maybe so, but you can't go around trying to disqualify every judge in New York who saw Miss Lowlace in the October issue of *Playboy* two years ago. Half the judges in New York would be disqualified. Maybe more.

Mr. Hyde: But see, you just acknowledged you know which issue she was in. October, two years ago, you said. She must have made quite an impression on you. And I can see she made quite an impression on your clerk, Mr. Lott. He's been looking at her spread in *Playboy* ever since Mr. Peters introduced it as an exhibit.

The Court: Mr. Lott is responsible for keeping custody of all the exhibits. I'm sure he was just making sure Plaintiff's Exhibit 1 was in its proper place. Now Mr. Hyde, we're not going to pursue this any further. Please move along to something relevant.

Mr. Hyde: Okay, but I want my objection noted for the record.

The Court: It's already noted. That's why we have a court reporter taking down everything that's said. Even if much of it is ridiculous.

Q: Very well. Now, Miss Lowlace, you've given lots of companies permission to use your photograph and likeness, have you not?

A: Are you askin' if I has or if I hasn't? It's confusin' when you say "have you not."

222

Q: I'm saying that you have given lots of companies permission to use your photo and image. Isn't that correct?

A: Sure, but I ain't never given permission to this here Aegean Love outfit or any of them clubs it runs.

Q: You gave permission to *Playboy* magazine to use all those photographs they took of you, did you not?

A: I told you it's confusin' when you keep sayin' "Did you not." Did I or didn't I, which do you wanna know?

Q: Did you give *Playboy* permission to use all those photographs it took of you?

A: Yes siree, how else could I be Playmate of the Month unless I let them use all those pi-tures they took?

Q: And those lingerie companies you're now modeling for. I think you testified that one is called Barely Enough. Is that correct?

A: Is what correct?

Q: That you gave permission to the company called Barely Enough to use your photo in their catalog?

A: Why that's the dumbest question you's asked me today. How could I be a model for their long . . . ah, underthings, I can't never remember that fancy name for 'em. How could I be a model for Barely Enough underthings unless I let 'em use my pi-ture? Dressed in their underthings?

Q: And the same is true, is it not, for the second lingerie company, Victor's Little Secret?

A: Is what not?

Q: Let me rephrase the question. Is it true that you gave permission to Victor's Little secret to use your photo – wearing their lingerie – in their catalog?

A: Well sure. As I was just sayin', how could I be a model for 'em unless I let 'em use my pi-ture wearin' their underthings?

Q: And isn't it also true that you gave permission to Mr. Lambros to use your photos to promote his three clubs?

A: Mr. Lambo, who's he? I don't know him.

Q: He's the gentleman sitting there next to Dr. Jeckel. He owns Aegean Love. You must not of been paying attention when I introduced him this morning.

A: Well, I was thinkin' 'bout that other fellow there, Dr. Jeckel. I kinda think I've heard of him, but I cain't remember when it was.

Q: I'm talkin' 'bout . . . sorry. I'm talking about Mr. Lambros. Didn't you give him permission to use your photos from *Playboy* to promote his clubs?

A: I's told you I don't know that there Lambro fellow. I never met him and I ain't never given him permission to use my pi-ture.

Q: Miss Lowlace, I'm showing you what we've marked as Defendant's Exhibit A. It's the agreement between you and Victor's Little Secret.

Mr. Peters: Objection, Your Honor. Miss Lowlace's contract with Victor's Little Secret is irrelevant. We agree that company has permission to use Miss Lowlace's picture and image to promote its lingerie.

The Court: I'll withhold ruling for the moment. Let's see where Mr. Hyde is going with this.

Q: You're familiar with this contract, are you not?

A: Are I not what?

Q: You recognize that contract, don't you Miss Lowlace?

A: I think I seen it before.

Q: In fact, you signed it, did you not?

A: Did I or did I not? Which is you askin?

Q: Miss Lowlace, turn to page eight please. There at the bottom of the page, is that your signature?

A: Yup, that sure looks like my signature. It's real purty, ain't it? I learned to write my signature in third grade, back in McKeesport, P-A where I's grew up.

Q: Yes, it's a real nice signature and we are very glad you wrote it so carefully. Now, Victor Little signed this contract as the president of Victor's Little Secret, did he not?

A: Did he not what?

Q: Did he not . . . oh, strike that, I'll start over. Victor Little signed this agreement on behalf of Victor's Little Secret and so the agreement was duly signed by both parties?

A: I don't know watt you means by "duly signed." Besides, I never met Mr. Little. See, he called me on the phone after he seen me in *Playboy*. And he tells me 'bout this new line of underthings they's gonna put out. Real sexy underthings for real sexy ladies. None of this plus-size stuff other underwear companies is startin' to sell.

And I tells him sure, I would be a model for his company, but could I first see the kinda underthings they wants me to wear. And he, that's Mr. Little, he tells me he'll have his lawyer draw up a contract and when I goes there to sign it he'll show me some samples of the underthings. Then, if I likes what I sees, I can sign the contract and I'll be in their catalog.

Q: I think the lawyer you're referring to is Mr. Pickens. Slimberty Pickens, everyone calls him Slim. His office is in Newark, just down the street from ours. Now, did you subsequently go to his office?

A: What do you mean by subquantilly?

Q: Subsequently. Oh, never mind. Did you go to Mr. Pickens office?

A: Yessir, I did.

Mr. Peters: Objection, Your Honor. This meeting and this contract are totally irrelevant to this case.

The Court: Mr. Hyde, where are you going with this? I don't see the relevance either.

Mr. Hyde: I'm about to show the relevance, Your Honor.

Q: Miss Lowlace, when you went to Mr. Pickens' office, did you sign this contract?

A: Well, like I asked Mr. Little when he called me on the telephone, Mr. Slim showed me some pi-tures of the underthings they was gonna sell. He also had a few samples he shows me. They's real nice, all white and lacy. Not really much to 'em. Now Mr. Slim, he says I can try them on if I wants, but I said no, I wasn't gonna' put on those underthings in a lawyer's office.

Q: But you signed the contract?

A: Yessiree, how else was I gonna be a model for Victor's Little Secret underthings unless I signs that contract?

Q: Would you turn to section four please, it's on page three.

A: Okay.

Q: And that section four is where you agreed that Victor's Little Secret could create and use photographs of you in its catalog?

A: Yes, I think that's watt is says there. That's watt Mr. Slim told me, he said that's watt this here part has to say in order for them to use me as a model for Victor's Little Secret.

Q: And now please look at the second paragraph of section four. Do you see that?

A: I sees a second paragraph here, yes.

Q: Would you please read it to the Court?

A: I ain't too good at readin' stuff out loud. Maybe you's oughta' read it for me."

Q: Okay. I'm reading from Section four, paragraph two of Defendant's Exhibit A:

"By this agreement, the party of the first part" – that's you by the way, you're defined as the party of the first part - "hereby agrees and consents to the use by Aegean Love and/or any clubs operated by said company of any and all photographs, images and sketches of her . . . ."

Mr. Peters: Objection. This is outrageous. This document was never produced during discovery, I've never seen it before. If this is Aegean Love's defense, it should have been turned over to us months ago.

The Court: Mr. Hyde, Mr. Peters has a point. Why wasn't this document turned over during discovery?

Mr. Hyde: Well, Mr. Lambros told us he thought there was a contract with Miss Lowlace but he could never find it. It was only this morning, after the trial started, that he remembered where it was. He contacted Mr. Pickens and Mr. Pickens retrieved it and brought it straight to court and gave it to me during the break.

The Court: Why didn't you at least show it to Mr. Peters then?

Mr. Hyde: Well, Your Honor, by the time me and Dr. Jeckel had read it the break was over and it was time for me to cross-examine the witness.

The Court: Mr. Hyde, that's the most preposterous story I've ever heard. And believe me, I've heard lots of preposterous stories.

I think we will take our lunch break now. That will give Mr. Peters time to review the document and discuss it with Miss Lowlace. I'm not excluding it yet, but I may well do so. Your failure to produce it during discovery is extremely troublesome. Mr. Peters, when we resume I'll allow you to examine Miss Lowlace about this document. I want to hear what she has to say about it before I rule on its admissibility.

Mr. Peters: Thank you, Your Honor. But in addition to examining Miss Lowlace about the document, I also need to examine Victor Little about it. He's the one who seems to have signed it for Victor's Little Secret. I ask that Mr. Hyde bring him to court this afternoon.

The Court: That's probably a good idea. Mr. Hyde, you may not represent Victor Little but please have him available this afternoon. We're adjourned. Be back at two-thirty.

Chapter 28

VICTOR LITTLE'S SECRET

Lance A. Lott emerged from the court's robing room and shouted "All Rise." After telling everyone to be seated, Justice Chan addressed the parties.

Transcript of Proceedings:

The Court: Mr. Hyde, I have a grave concern about the document you introduced during cross-examination. While it may indeed be relevant, there is no conceivable excuse for your not having produced it earlier. You may be able to pull stunts like this in New Jersey, but you can't get away with that in New York. My father always told me to watch out for New Jersey drivers, they ignore all the rules. He should have told me to watch out for New Jersey lawyers as well.

Anyway, as I said before the break, I will withhold ruling on this document until I've heard from Miss Lowlace, and perhaps Mr. Little as well, about its signing. But even if I decide to admit it, I will be sanctioning you and your firm, and perhaps your client as well, for failing to disclose it during discovery.

Mr. Lambros: Your honor, you can't blame me or my company for this. I told Dr. Jeckel about it the first time I met with him about the case.

Dr. Jeckel: Your Honor, you can't sanction me for this. I showed it to Mr. Hyde the day after I got it from Mr. Lambros. Mr. Hyde told me he would produce it to plaintiff's counsel but it appears he did not. Mr. Hyde's always doing stuff like that. I try to do the right thing and he goes behind my back and does something awful.

Mr. Hyde: Your Honor, that is not . . . .

The Court: I'm not about to listen to each of you fellows blame the other. As far as I'm concerned, you're all responsible. Dr. Jeckel, you may be as innocent as a new-born lamb but you are still responsible for what your partner does, even if it's behind your back. Maybe you need to keep a sharper eye on him.

But now let's move along. Mr. Peters, do you wish to recall Miss Lowlace to address this matter?

Mr. Peters: Yes I do, Your Honor. Miss Lowlace, will you please take the stand.

Redirect Examination by Mr. Peters:

Q: Miss Lowlace, you told Mr. Hyde this morning that you had signed three contracts giving companies the right to use photographs of yourself for their business. Is that correct?

A: Yes sir, tha's correct.

Q: And you said the first such contract was with *Playboy* magazine. Is that correct?

A: Yes sir, tha's correct.

Q: Were you represented by a lawyer when you signed that contract?

A: No sir, I wuz not. I wuz at their office in Cali-fornia. Los Angeles it wuz. All I knew wuz I wuz goin' out to Cali-fornia and when I got there I sees I wuz in Los Angeles. And then they puts me in this fancy hotel – I ain't never stayed in a fancy hotel like that before. And then the next day someone picks me up and takes me to this fancy office where I meet lots of people in nice suits and stuff.

Then they takes me to another room, I reckon it was some sort of studio cause there was lots of pi-ture takin' 'quipment there. And then they puts me in a dressing room and tells me to take off everything 'cept my underpants and then come out so's they can have a good look at me. Thank goodness I wuz wearin' underpants that day.

Anyways, I did watt they's ask. I guess they liked watt they seen since they told me to get dressed and come back to the office with them. And then this fellow in a suit says he's their lawyer and he gives me that there contract and tells me it's some sort of standard thing and all the Playmates have to sign it before they's in the magazine. So I fi-gered they knows watt they's doin' so I signed it. Right there in that office. In Los Angeles. Los Angeles, Cali-fornia.

Q: Okay, now the second contract you signed was with the company called Barely Enough. Is that correct?

A: Yes sir, tha's correct.

Q: And that was a contract where you agreed to model their lingerie and they, in turn, could take photographs of you in their lingerie and use them in their catalogs and advertising. Is that correct?

A: Yep, tha's watt it wuz.

Q: And were you represented by a lawyer when you signed that contract?

A: No sir, I wuz not.

Q: And why did you sign that contract without having a lawyer involved?

A: It wuz the same kinda' deal as that *Playboy* thing. 'Cept it weren't in Cali-fornia, it wuz in Brooklyn. And no one wuz wearin' fancy clothes like they wuz in Cali-fornia. They wuz a heavy-set lawyer wearin' a baggy suit and he tells me the company has lots of models who pose in the company's underthings and they all have to sign this here contract and so he hands it to me, the contract that is, tha's watt he hands to me, and says I should sign it. So I does and now I has my pi-ture takin' wearin' lots of their underthings and they sends me a check once a month. I sure don't mind gettin' a check once a month for havin' my pi-ture taken in their nice fancy underthings.

Q: So then you signed a third contract to allow someone to take photographs of you and use them in their business. And that was the company called Victor's Little Secret. Is that correct?

A: Yessiree, tha's correct.

Q: And that company is owned, insofar as you know, by a man named Victor Little. Is that correct?

A: Yes sir.

Q: And you signed a contract with that company, the contract Mr. Hyde showed you this morning. Is that correct?

A: Yep, tha's correct.

Q: Now, let's go through the circumstances surrounding the signing of that agreement. First of all, did you ever meet Mr. Little?

A: No sir. But I gets a phone call from him one day. He tells me he's seen me in *Playboy* and he likes watt he sees. Then he says he's startin' up a new line of ladies underthings . . . .

Mr. Peters: Lingerie.

A: Yes, tha's watt he calls it. Then he tells me this line of underthings will be for sexy women, not that stuff they's now sellin' for full-bodied women. I think they's actually fat women but Mr. Little he calls 'em "full-bodied" women. Then he tells me he thinks I'd be a perfect model for his stuff and would I be interested in bein' a model for his company, Victor's Little Secret he says it's called.

And I says well sure, if you wanna take pi-tures of me in your fancy underthings and then put those pi-tures in your catalog and send me a check every month then who was I so say no. So I . . . .

Q: Okay. Now let's go to the signing of the contract. Was Mr. Little involved in that?

A: No sir. Mr. Little he tells me he's the head of the company and he gots lots of folks to help him with details. He said he has this here lawyer, Mr. Slim . . . .

Q: You're referring to the lawyer known as Slim Pickens?

A: Yep, Mr. Slim. He has an office over in New Jersey, Newark I think it wuz. He calls me and asks me to come over to Newark and meet him in his office. He didn' send no car for me like they done in Cali-fornia, I had to buys a ticket on that there train that goes under the river. Now I sees when I gets to that office that I ain't in Cali-fornia no more. Actually, I ain't even in Brooklyn no more. I seems to be movin' down in the world. But Mr. Slim he's nice enough and he's got some young guy with him who is some sort of officer at the company. And then . . . .

Q: We need to go through this a little more slowly, Miss Lowlace. Please tell us what Mr. Slim, that's Mr. Slim Pickens, said at that meeting.

A: Well, it purty much wuz like the others where I signed those contract things. This fella from the company tells me Mr. Little is really lookin' forward to havin' me model his underthings. And then Mr. Slim, he says before I can be a model for Victor's Little Secret I needs to sign a contract. And he pulls out a contract and says this is a standard thing, everyone who models underthings – or even clothes, I suppose they must be some ladies who get their pi-tures taken wearin' clothes – all of them has to sign this here contract.

Q: Did Mr. Pickens or the fellow from the company say anything about using your image to promote a group of strip clubs in New York and New Jersey?

A: Why would they sez that? I wuz there to sign a contract to model underthings for Victor's Little Secret. I wuzn't there to talk about someone usin' my pi-ture to promote some low-life strip clubs.

Q: And so you signed the contract? Is that correct?

A: Yes sir, I did.

Q: And no one told you there was something in the contract giving Mr. Lambros and his company Aegean Love the right to use your photo and image to promote strip clubs?

A: No siree, no one says that.

Q: Would you have signed that contract if Mr. Slim or that other fellow had told you it also dealt with the use of your picture and image to promote strip clubs?

A: No siree, I wouldn't never a' done that. You see I's movin' on from things like clubs. That's watt I wuz doin' when I met Justice Leghetti and that nice Mr. Tony.

(Witness points to the back of the spectator section.)

But since I's been a Playmate in *Playboy* magazine, that stuff's all behind me. I's now got a nice job bein' a model for ladies underthings.

Q: One last question, Miss Lowlace. The contract Mr. Hyde showed you this morning had both your signature and also Mr. Little's signature. Did Mr. Little sign it when you were in Mr. Pickens' office?

A: No sir. Mr. Slim says Mr. Little wuz busy and could not be there but he would give the contract to him and get his signature after I signs it.

Q: So the first time you saw Mr. Little's signature on the contract was when Mr. Hyde showed you the contract this morning?

A: Yes sir, I never seen it 'til then.

Q: And they never sent you a copy of the signed contract?

A: No siree. But that's okay, watt was I gonna do with it if . . . .

Q: That's all for now, Miss Lowlace, thank you very much.

Mr. Peters: I now call Mr. Little to the stand. Mr. Hyde, I trust he's here or right outside the courtroom?

Mr. Hyde: Yes, Mr. Little will testify. Mr. Little, will you please take the stand.

(Ambrose Lambros approaches the stand.)

Mr. Peters: I called Victor Little, not Mr. Lambros.

Mr. Hyde: Mr. Lambros can explain.

The Court: I think we better swear in the witness before we go any further. Mr. Whoever-you-are, please face me and raise your right hand.

(Witness is sworn in.)

The Court: Mr. Peters, you may proceed. We're all anxious to see what is going on here.

Examination by Mr. Peters:

Q: Please state your full name. By that I mean your legal name, the name that's on your driver's license and your birth certificate.

A: I've never seen my birth certificate, but my momma always told me my name is Ambrose Lambros. I think she would know. That's the name that's on my passport and my driver's license.

Q: And who is Victor Little? Why did you take the stand when I called Victor Little to testify?

A: Well, I'm also Victor Little. And you asked for Victor Little to testify, so here I am.

Q: Could you explain how you can be both Ambrose Lambros and Victor Little?

A: Sure. I've had the club business for some time. But when I decided to branch out into lingerie, I didn't want to use the name of the company that runs the clubs, Aegean Love. That company was associated with strip clubs. And I personally was associated with Aegean Love, a strip club company. So I was known as a strip club guy. It was a guilt by association sort of thing. So I adopted the name Victor Little and called the new company Victor's Little Secret. That's a good name, don't you think?

Q: So you used the name Victor Little when you called Miss Lowlace to ask her to model for Victor's Little Secret?

A: Yes, of course. That's the name I use whenever I'm working on the lingerie business.

Q: This is a real business? You really are producing ladies' lingerie?

A: Certainly, that was the whole point of starting up a company under a different name.

Q: And you really do plan to use Miss Lowlace as a model for that business?

A: Of course. She'll be our top model. In fact, we plan on havin' our first photo shoot next week.

Q: Now Mr. Little-Lambros, when did you hatch this scheme to trap Miss Lowlace into signing a document that allegedly gives you the right to use her image and likeness to promote your strip clubs?

A: I didn't view that as a trap. It was just a matter of killing two birds with one stone, as they say.

Q: You better explain that.

A: Well, Bertie – he's one of my assistants at Aegean Love – he saw the spread of Miss Lowlace in *Playboy*. Of course, I saw it too, I have to read the magazine every month so's I can keep up with the latest lingerie fashions. Anyway, that spread on Miss Lowlace knocked my socks off. So, I started talking about recruiting her as a model for our lingerie business. And then Bertie – he works on the Aegean Love side of the business – when he hears this he decides to start using one of the *Playboy* photos to promote our clubs.

I only found out about it from Slim. Slim Pickens, he's the lawyer for both companies. When he was drawing up Miss Lowlace's contract for the lingerie business, he came to me and told me I may not know it but we were already using her photo to promote the clubs. He says we gotta protect ourselves by getting her consent for that. So he tells me we can kill two birds with one stone by adding a provision about the three clubs in the lingerie contract. Since the ads for the clubs will help spread Miss Lowlace's fame, we figured she'd have no objection.

Q: So you gave her the contract for the lingerie modeling work and simply added in the paragraph about using her photo and likeness for your three clubs?

A: Yep, that sounded like a good solution to me.

Q: But you never told her you had added in a provision dealing with the three strip clubs?

A: Well, I weren't there. Mr. Pickens was the one who met with her to sign the contract.

Q: But you didn't tell him to make sure he told Miss Lowlace about the extra provision dealing with the three strip clubs?

A: No sir, I did not. Do you think I should have?

Q: Thank you Mr. Little-Lambros. That will be all.

Mr. Peters: Your Honor, I move to exclude the contract, Defendant's Exhibit A. It is obvious that the provision pertaining to the use of Miss Lowlace's image to promote the three strip clubs was grounded in fraud and deceit. Moreover, with that contract excluded, Aegean Love has no defense to the Complaint. So I believe this case is now ripe for a ruling on the merits as to liability.

The Court: Mr. Hyde, do you have anything more to offer?

Mr. Hyde: No, Your Honor, we done offered what we had.

The Court: Very well, I'm prepared to issue a ruling from the bench. Let's take a ten-minute break before I do that.

* * * *

(Court resumes at 4:10 pm)

The Court: Miss Lowlace, on behalf of the courts of New York State and the fine lawyers who practice in this great State, I'd like to apologize for the terrible way you've been treated by these ruffians from New Jersey. It's shameful. Nothing like that should ever happen to a fine lady like you. You have a right to control the direction of your career as you see fit, without being exploited by every New Jersey lawyer who saw your spread in

Playboy. You can rest assured that here in New York we hold our lawyers to much higher standards.

Now, having heard the evidence offered by both parties, the Court rules as follows.

One: The addition of the provision in Plaintiff's contract regarding the usage of her image and likeness to promote Defendant's strip clubs was the result of fraud and deceit. That portion of the contract is therefore null and void.

Two: In light of that provision being null and void, Defendant has no defense to the allegations of the Complaint. The Court therefore awards judgment in Plaintiff's favor on her privacy and publicity claims under New York law.

Three: Defendant's counsel, the firm of Jeckel and Hyde, committed a flagrant violation of their duty to produce the Victor's Little Secret contract during discovery and are hereby sanctioned in the amount of five thousand dollars. Moreover, a copy of this decision will be delivered to the New Jersey Attorney's Disciplinary Committee. I may also send it to each of your mothers.

Four: I invite Plaintiff's counsel to submit its damages claim in writing in two weeks. Defendant will have two weeks in which to respond. If I cannot resolve the amount of damages on the papers, we will have an immediate hearing to set damages.

Mr. Peters, please submit an Order, on three days notice, for the Court's approval. That will be all. Oh, and Miss Lowlace, I see that Justice Leghetti is no longer in the courtroom. Will you please give him my regards next time you see him. We're adjourned.

Chapter 29

BUNNY HOP

In late May, three months after the trial in the strip club case, Pap, Pup and Melissa entered the federal courthouse at Foley Square and went upstairs to the courtroom of Judge Judith June. The judge was referred to by all the lawyers in New York City as "Judge Juney."

Judge Juney was widely viewed as the most attractive female judge, state or federal, in New York City. In fact there were rumors that the trim, dark-haired judge with a captivating smile had once been a waitress at a Playboy Club in the midwest. Judge Juney was nevertheless recognized as a smart, hard-working judge who gave close attention to all her cases.

Judge Juney had scheduled that day for oral argument on Pap's motion for summary judgment – meaning that no trial was necessary because, on the undisputed facts, they were entitled to judgment as a matter of law - on Lydia's case against Erotic Arts for its wrongful use of her image in its Bunny Hop video game.

Erotic Arts was a California company and was represented by its regular Los Angeles firm, Rivers and Jordan. Because they were a California firm, they had retained the New York firm of Stone, Colde and Freize as local counsel. At a few minutes after 10:00, Judge Juney took the bench and commenced the proceeding.

Transcript of Proceedings:

The Court: Good morning everyone. Before we proceed with the summary judgment motion, I want to ask plaintiff's counsel about the status of the class. Mr. Peters, how many ladies have opted in since I issued my order allowing the case to proceed as a class action?

Mr. Peters: Good morning, Your Honor. We sent a notice of your ruling to all twenty of the former Playmates who are used as avatars in the Bunny Hop game. All of them have opted to join the class, and have submitted the appropriate acknowledgment.

The Court: Okay, but how do I know that the twenty who opted in are actually the ones depicted in the game?

Mr. Peters: Every bunny in Bunny Hop has a name and a number. For example, Miss Lowlace is labeled "Lydia" and is Bunny Number One. Bunny Number Two is Melony Harmony, referred to in the game as "Melony." Bunny Number Three is Harmony Melony, and is referred to as "Harmony."

Now, Number Four is "Tiffany," Tiffany Topps. Number Five is "Buffy," Buffy Tones. Six is Kitty Katz. Seven is Honey Pye – that's spelled P-Y-E. Eight is Amber Waves. Nine is Irene Goodnight. Ten is . . . .

The Court: Okay, I get it. But I don't understand how parents come up with names like that. Are those their real names?

Mr. Peters: Well, those are their professional names, the names they are known by in their work. If their legal name is different, that's the name we used on the opt-in notification. For example, the legal name of Number Six, Kitty Katz, is Katherine

Katzenjammer, so the opt-in notice shows that as her real name and Kitty Katz as her professional name.

The Court: Very well. Let's proceed with oral argument on plaintiff's motion for summary judgment. Mr. Peters, please proceed.

Mr. Peters: I'll be fairly brief because our motion is fairly open and shut. First of all, all twenty members of the class appeared in *Playboy* magazine as Playmate of the Month within the past two-and-a-half years. Photos of them in various poses, and of course various states of undress, appear in a multi-page section devoted to the Playmate of the Month. Their heads and faces are very distinct.

The Court: I suspect other things are quite distinct as well.

Mr. Peters: You could be right about that, Your Honor. Some readers may look beyond their faces. But it's their faces and head shots that provide conclusive proof that their likeness is being used in the Bunny Hop game. All their legs and breasts and backsides may be nice – and I'd be lying if I told you they weren't nice – but it's their faces and hair that set them apart. So, if you compare a head shot of a Playmate to the head shot on the avatars in Bunny Hop, you can immediately see that the avatar in question looks exactly like her magazine counterpart.

The Court: Does the video game show more than head shots of the Playmates?

Mr. Peters: Yes it does. And if you make a close comparison of the body of a particular avatar and the body of her magazine counterpart, you'll see a striking similarity. I've studied this quite a bit and I can assure you that the body of each of the twenty bunnies in Bunny Hop is virtually identical to the body of her magazine counterpart.

The Court: I'll bet you ran up lots of billable hours making those comparisons.

Mr. Peters: Well, it was an important job. Somebody had to do it and I didn't think I should entrust it to one of the associates.

Now, if the Court, or one of your law clerks, wants to verify the comparisons, we have submitted a copy of each of the twenty *Playboy* magazines with our motion. And of course we have also submitted the video game itself. When you compare the magazine spreads to the avatars in the game, you will immediately see that they are essentially the same.

The Court: That might be a good job for one of my law clerks, probably Jake, I'm sure he'd make a very careful study of them. My other clerk is Naomi. She's a bit of a feminist, I don't think she'd be as interested as Jake.

Mr. Peters: Good idea. It'll give him a break from all that legal research law clerks have to do.

Now, the second point I'd like to make is equally undisputed. None of the twenty members of the class ever gave their consent, verbally or in writing, to the use of their photos and likeness in this game. Miss Lowlace so testified in her deposition and the other nineteen members of the class submitted affidavits saying they never consented. In fact, they weren't even asked for their consent. Now, turning to the law . . . .

The Court: Before you go any further, I need to understand how this Bunny Hop game works. I understand the avatars use the image and likeness of the twenty Playmates, but what happens in the game? How are the Playmates used? I believe I need to understand that in order to evaluate defendant's transformative use defense.

Mr. Peters: I'm happy to explain that, Your Honor. It took me a while to figure out how to play the game. But one of our associates, Mr. Pierpont, plays the game a lot and he showed me how to play it.

First of all, as I said earlier, each of the bunnies has a name and number. Number one is Lydia. Two is Melony. Three is Harmony, and so on. Now, the object is to "score" with as many of the bunnies as you can. When you score with one of them, you acquire a certain number of points. For example, scoring with any of the bunnies numbered eleven through twenty gets you three points. So, if you manage to score with all of them, you've earned thirty points.

Now, bunnies five through ten are considered more desirable. You score with one of them and you earn six points. For all six, that would get you thirty-six points.

Then you keep going up the ladder. Bunny Number Four, Tiffany, is worth seven points. Number Three, Harmony, is worth eight points. Number two, Melony, is worth nine. And if you succeed in scoring with Miss Lowlace, you've hit the jackpot so to speak - you get ten points.

The Court: I think I know what you get to do if you score with one of them. But what do you have to do to enable you to score?

Mr. Peters: Well, it's not easy, it takes a lot of determination and hard work. For example, to score with a bunny in the eleven through twenty group, you have to cross a wide river, climb a steep hill and walk without a coat through a snowstorm. To score with a bunny in the five through ten group, you've got to do all that plus surmount a six-foot stone wall and crawl under three feet of barbed wire.

If you do all that and also swim across a lake, you get to score with number four. Bike twenty miles after the swim and you get to score with Number Three. And then escaping from a pack of angry dogs gets you Number Two. And then finally, if you walk through a swamp infested with alligators you get to score with Miss Lowlace. It's a clever game, I'll say that.

The Court: So the first person to get to – I think I counted one hundred points – wins?

Mr. Peters: Yes. And gets to score with Miss Lowlace. That's as good as it gets.

The Court: I can see my law clerk, Jake, is going to want to try his hand at this. By the way, you haven't said anything about the bunnies. What are they doing during the game?

Mr. Peters: Well, they are cavorting about in various states of dress and undress, on the other side of each of the obstacles. So, if you're trying to cross the river, a bunny is on the far side. Of course, once you get across the river she then moves to the far side of the next obstacle. They're kind of cute when they run from obstacle to obstacle with everything sort of flopping about.

Now, unless you have any more questions about the game, I'll move on to my final point, which is the law.

Under the New York right of privacy law, which is embodied in section 50 of the New York Civil Rights Law, a person's name or likeness cannot be used for commercial purposes without that person's written consent. And the common law of New York and most other states provides that, in the case of celebrities – which these Playmates certainly are – they have a right of publicity, which means that a company cannot use their name, picture or likeness without their consent.

Now, at one tine there was some doubt about the applicability of the right of publicity doctrine to video games, but that law has now become settled. When the video game uses the name, photo or likeness of a celebrity without their consent, that is a violation of the right of publicity. A celebrity has the right to control the use of his or her image for commercial purposes. So when . . . .

The Court: Yes, I've read your brief and I'm aware of the legal authorities you rely on. At this point I think I need to hear from defendant regarding its basis for opposing summary judgment. But first let's take a short break. We need to give our court reporter a chance to catch his breath. And I think he's itching to take a look at all the magazines you submitted with your motion. Come back in ten minutes.

* * * *

The Court: Let's resume. Who will be arguing for defendant?

Mr. Colde: Your Honor, I'm Barry Colde of Stone, Colde and Freize here in New York. Mr. Rivers, Rush Rivers of Rivers and Jordan, will argue for Erotic Arts. He's been admitted *pro haec.*

The Court: Very well. Mr. Rivers, you may proceed.

Mr. Rivers: Thank you Your Honor. Before I get to our legal defense, I want to make certain the Court understands the vast personal and business opportunities our client's business model is opening up. Bunny Hop is only the first in a series of video games Erotic Arts plans to introduce. These games will open up a wealth of opportunities for young ladies – and, who knows, maybe older ones as well – across the country.

For example, we envision a similar game featuring lovely female cops from around the country. It'll be called Cop Hop. There will also be one for baristas. As you know, there's been an explosion of coffee houses in recent years and all of them seem to be staffed by beautiful young baristas. I think they plan to call it Latte Hop. And there are also lots of good looking women in politics today, so they're thinking of a game called Pol Hop.

The Court: Please don't tell me your client is thinking of one with female judges.

Mr. Rivers: Actually we are, Judge June. In fact, I understand you once worked in a Playboy Club in St. Louis. I believe I could get our client to include you in that game.

The Court: That was a long time ago. I needed money to put myself through college. But now I'm older and anyway I have to wear this robe all the time. I don't think your customers want to look at a bunch of older ladies wearing black robes.

Mr. Rivers: You wouldn't be wearing your robe in our game. In fact, you wouldn't be wearing much of anything.

The Court: I was afraid of that.

Mr. Rivers: But you see what I'm saying, Your Honor. Our client's product is opening up new possibilities for countless groups of women from all walks of life. Baristas. School teachers. Professors. EMS personnel. Housewives. And speaking of housewives, we will have separate games for various geographical areas of the country. New Jersey Housewife Hop, for example. Just like all those TV shows. So, I don't think this

Court would want to stand in the way of such an important expansion of opportunity for thousands of women across the country.

The Court: Mr. Rivers, this is all very interesting but it doesn't make what your client is doing legal. You want to have all those games featuring everyone from Playmates to baristas to policewomen, I think your client needs to get their consent before it puts them in one of those games.

Mr. Rivers: But if we asked for their consent they'd want us to pay 'em.

The Court: Precisely. That's the way things work. Erotic Arts may have great ideas for expanding its business, but unless it's willing to pay its subjects for the use of their image and likeness I don't see how it can legally sell the games. Now, do you have any defense to plaintiff's privacy and publicity claims? If so I'd like to hear it.

Mr. Rivers: Well, as we said in our brief, Erotic Arts has made a transformative use of the Playmates' magazine photos. It didn't just take their photos and put them in the game unchanged. As you know – well, maybe you don't, Mr. Peters didn't mention this during his presentation – but all the Playmates are wearing tall bunny ears throughout the game. Even when they have nothing else on, they are wearing bunny ears. Now, no Playmate of the Month has ever appeared in *Playboy* magazine wearing bunny ears. So we have transformed the Playmates into something they were not in the magazine. That's a transformative use.

The Court: Well, when I worked at that Playboy Club in St. Louis, we – all the waitresses that is – wore bunny ears. That's in addition to our costumes. We were fully dressed, I don't want you to get the wrong idea. Well, we weren't wearing suits or dresses or anything like that, it was more like a one-piece bathing suit. But everything was covered.

Mr. Rivers: I'm glad to hear that, Your Honor. Maybe we could have the judges in our game wear one-piece bathing suits if you think that would be more appropriate for ladies in the judiciary.

The Court: We're getting off track here, Mr. Rivers. My point is that none of the waitresses in that club in St. Louis were transformed by the rabbit ears. I was still Judith June. My friend Betty Beatty was still Betty Beatty. And I believe the same is true in Bunny Hop. Miss Lowlace is still recognizable as Miss Lowlace. And Irene Goodnight is still recognizable as Irene Goodnight. Even with the bunny ears.

We just heard Mr. Peters say he spent many enjoyable hours comparing the face and body of each of the twenty Playmates to the face and body of their real-life counterpart in the magazine. I'm going to have my law clerk Jake confirm that, but I don't believe there will be any question about his conclusion. There may, however, be a question about how much time he spends making the comparisons.

Mr. Rivers: But there's more than the bunny ears, Your Honor. All twenty bunnies are cavorting endlessly during the game – wading across streams, running up hills and climbing over stone walls as they are being pursued by the players. There were no scenes like that in their spreads in *Playboy* magazine.

The Court: That's not the point, counsel. It doesn't matter what they are doing in the game, it's that they are clearly recognizable while they are doing it. Lydia and Irene and all those other Playmates are recognizable for who they are as they are hopping all over the place during the game. Without much of anything on. In fact, that probably helps to make them more recognizable.

Mr. Rivers, unless you have another defense, I think I've heard enough. I don't see that Erotic arts has any defense to the privacy and publicity claims set forth in the Complaint. So, as soon as my law clerk has completed the comparison exercise I referred to a moment ago, I'll begin preparing my opinion. The opinion will grant plaintiff's motion for summary judgment. At that point I'll set the case down for a trial on damages.

Now Mr. Rivers, my suggestion is that you have a meeting with Mr. Peters and see if the two of you can work out a damages settlement so that we can avoid a trial. Mr. Peters seems like a reasonable lawyer to me. I'm certain he would be willing to take less via settlement than he would demand as damages after a trial. So I think your time would be better spent negotiating a settlement than preparing for a damages trial.

I'm also sure Erotic Arts has made quite a bit of money off this game. I know the sales have been good, all my male colleagues seem to have the game. They usually say it belongs to one of their kids, but if that's the case why do they have it in their chambers? Anyway, Erotic Arts should use some of the money it made off the game to pay those Playmates for the use of their photos and images.

And by the way, Mr. Rivers, if you do reach a settlement, your client will be better positioned to expand its business as you have suggested. Who knows, maybe a Latte Hop or a Judge Hop would prove even more popular than Bunny Hop. We're adjourned.

Chapter 30

MONEY HOP

In late August, three months after the hearing on the motion for summary judgment, Pap, Pup and Melissa were back in Judge Juney's courtroom in the federal courthouse in downtown Manhattan. At a few minutes after 10:00 am, Judge Juney took the bench and commenced the hearing.

Transcript of Proceedings:

The Court: Good morning everyone. Mr. Rivers, I'm gratified that you took my suggestion and worked out a settlement with Mr. Peters. I told you I thought he would prove to be reasonable.

Mr. Rivers: Actually, he wasn't the slightest bit reasonable. Every time we made an offer he kept demanding more. It was excruciating.

The Court: But you finally got there, that's the important thing.

Mr. Rivers: Yes, Your Honor. And I will say that, once Mr. Peters and I reached agreement on the terms, the other Mr. Peters, and that little lady there, they were most reasonable when it came to putting the deal into writing.

The Court: I'm sure that "little lady," as you called her, has a name.

Ms. Muffett: Your Honor, I'm Melissa Muffett and yes I was involved in writing up the settlement. And it's also true that I'm little. I think that's why Mr. Peters and his brother call me Little Miss Muffett behind my back. But I don't mind it, they're great to work for and they give me lots of responsibility.

Mr. Peters: We don't just call her Little Miss Muffett behind her back. We frequently call her that to her face. It's a term of endearment.

The Court: I'm glad to hear that. Now let's get to the settlement. I've read through it but there are so many numbers and calculations I couldn't keep them straight. And I could be wrong but it seems like the only parties who get any immediate money are your client, Miss Lowlace, and your firm. Is that correct?

Mr. Peters: Yes Your Honor, that's technically correct. But if you will allow me to walk you through the agreement, I believe you will see that it is imminently fair to all members of the class.

The Court: Very well. Please proceed.

Mr. Peters: I need to start with three basic numbers that underlie all the calculations.

First of all, the Bunny Hop game sold for an average price of $34.95 since it was first introduced eighteen months ago. Some sold for more, some for less, but that is the average price.

Second, Erotic Arts had sold 1.321 million games as of the time we negotiated the settlement.

Third, the total revenue from the sale of these games was approximately $46 million. So, Erotic Arts plainly did very well on this game.

Now, the next question is, how should the twenty Playmates depicted in the game be compensated? Mr. Rivers and Mr. Jordan wanted a flat fee per Playmate. But we believed the amount paid to them should be a percentage of each unit sold, so that their compensation relates directly to the sales of the game.

After considerable back and forth, we finally agreed on twelve cents per game sold. This was the hardest part of the negotiation. We initially proposed thirty cents per unit but Rivers and Jordan thought it should be more like five cents per unit. We finally compromised on twelve cents per unit per plaintiff.

The next calculation is simple math. Twelve cents per unit times 1.321 million units is $158,520. For the nineteen members of the class who opted in, that is what they will receive as compensation for past sales. If you multiply $158,520 by nineteen Playmates, that comes to $3,011,880.

Now Miss Lowlace, as the original plaintiff and the class representative, is entitled to far more than the other nineteen. It was her astuteness that uncovered the existence of this game. And she worked directly with our firm to bring this matter to court, including undergoing a grueling two-day deposition by Mr. Jordan. So, we agreed that Miss Lowlace would receive ten times the amount the other nineteen receive. Ten times $158,520 comes to $1,585,200. That is Lydia's share of the settlement. And by the way, the other members of the class are fine with the amount she receives.

Now there is a third financial component to the settlement. Because Bunny Hop has been so successful, Erotic Arts wants to continue selling it. They estimate that they will sell anther 3.3 million games over the next two years.

The Court: Isn't that almost three times the amount of their current sales? The 1.3 million you mentioned?

Mr. Rivers: I can answer that, Your Honor. Mr. Pitts – that's Bernie Pitts, the CEO of Erotic Arts – plans an aggressive advertising campaign. It will use the Playmates themselves in the ads. Now, this case has already received considerable publicity. And I'm confident Mr. Peters will see that the settlement is widely publicized. I've never seen an attorney so good at generating publicity as Mr. Peters. It's something to behold. So yes, with all the publicity and marketing my client does expect sales to exceed three million over the next two years.

Mr. Peters: Of course, Erotic Arts will have to pay for its ongoing use of the plaintiffs' photos and likeness. All except Miss Lowlace, she doesn't want to have any further affiliation with the game. So Erotic Arts will have to find a new number one bunny.

The Court: Or they could bring in a new Playmate as number twenty, and move everyone else up a notch.

Mr. Rivers: That's a very good idea, Your Honor. Maybe my client should put you on its Board of Directors and take advantage of your business skills.

The Court: I don't think I could get approval from the U.S. Judicial Conference. They're fussy about things like that.

Mr. Peters: We're getting a little off-track here. I was about to address the ongoing license arrangement.

The Court: Yes, please do so. I was just trying to be helpful.

Mr. Peters: So, going forward, Mr. Rivers and I agreed on an ongoing license fee of ten cents per unit sold. Now if you multiply 3.3 million units, the expected future sales, times ten cents per unit, you get $330,000 per plaintiff. And $330,000 times nineteen plaintiffs comes to $6,270,000. That's the total projected royalties to all nineteen Playmates over the next two years.

The Court: What about the new Playmate? Bunny number one, or twenty, or whatever?

Mr. Peters: They'll have to make a separate deal with her. She's not a plaintiff and is not part of the class. The $6.27 million only relates to the other nineteen members of the class.

So, the total financial recovery has three components. First is the payment to the nineteen plaintiffs for past sales; that's $3,011,880. Second is Miss Lowlace's royalties for past sales; that's $1,585,200. Third is the other plaintiffs' recovery of future royalties; that's $6,270,000. Adding up all those amounts we have a total compensation package of $10,867,080.

The Court: Yes, I see that. It's an impressive number and seems more than fair to the class members. But with a total compensation of $10.8 million, how can it be that none of the plaintiffs except Miss Lowlace receive any immediate financial recovery?

Mr. Peters: Well, it's due to the impact of our firm's fee. We are taking the standard 33%. That's 33% of the total financial settlement of $10.8 million. Actually, it's $10,867,080. 33% of that comes to $3,586,136.40. I told Mr. Rivers we would forget about the forty cents. So it's simply $3,586,136.

Now, that fee has to be allocated among all twenty plaintiffs. So it's a simple mathematical calculation: $3,586,136 divided by twenty equals $179,307. That's each plaintiff's share of our fee. For Miss Lowlace, that means that her $1,585,200 recovery is reduced by $179,307. That leaves her with a net recovery of $1,405,893. She gets that money now.

The Court: I think I see where you are going.

Mr. Peters: Yes, it's just a matter of math. The numbers are the numbers. Each of the other nineteen plaintiffs receive $158,520 for past sales. They'll also get another $330,000 on future sales, but those sales haven't happened yet. They won't earn that money until the sales occur. So, when you compare their $158,520 in compensation for past sales to their $179,307 share of attorneys fees, they are in the hole, so to speak, by $20,787. That amount will be paid off via the withholding of future royalties. But since those future royalties are projected to be at least $330,000, these ladies will quickly pay off this sum and start taking home some real dough.

The Court: Mr. Peters, I'm not sure if you're to be congratulated or condemned. This is the first class action settlement I've ever heard of where the class members all start off by owing money to the defendant.

Mr. Peters: My firm is pleased to participate in such a trailblazing settlement. We like to be on the cutting edge of things.

The Court: I still think you should have found a way to give the other nineteen plaintiffs some immediate recovery.

Mr. Peters: But we did, Your Honor. The settlement is chock full of immediate benefits for the other nineteen plaintiffs. Shall I go through them?

The Court: Yes. And they better be good.

Mr. Peters: They are good indeed. And, by the way, the nineteen other plaintiffs are all fine with the way the settlement is structured.

The Court: We'll get to their acquiescence later. For now, I need to hear about these immediate benefits. As you know, I have to determine whether the settlement is fair and reasonable for all members of the class, regardless of the fact that they may have consented to the terms.

Mr. Peters: Yes, I appreciate that Judge June. So let me run through the immediate benefits the nineteen members of the class – and in some cases Lydia – will receive. There are seven of them.

First, each member of the class will receive a $250 gift certificate for lingerie from Victor's Little Secret, a new line of sexy lingerie for sexy ladies. Second . . . .

The Court: What's this lingerie company got to do with this case? Why are they providing gift certificates to the plaintiffs?

Mr. Peters: Their CEO was involved in another case we recently prosecuted on behalf of Miss Lowlace.

The Court: Miss Lowlace was recently involved in another lawsuit brought by your firm?

Mr. Peters: Yes. To be honest with you, she was actually involved in two prior lawsuits we brought on her behalf. The first was two years ago in State court. It was also a class action. We brought it on behalf of Miss Lowlace and numerous other ladies who were dancers at Gentleman's clubs throughout the city. The dancers were being cheated out of their wages and tips by the unscrupulous club owners. The case got lots of publicity, you may have heard about it.

The Court: I'm afraid I've not heard about it. I generally don't follow lawsuits about strip joints.

Mr. Peters: They weren't strip joints, they were . . . .

The Court: Never mind. But I assume the gift certificates had nothing to do with that case.

Mr. Peters: Correct. The gift certificates stem from a second case in which we represented Miss Lowlace. This time the defendant, a Greek businessman named Ambrose Lambros, was the owner of a real strip joint – three of them in fact. Miss Lowlace had nothing to do with them but the Greek, that Lambros fellow, was using her *Playboy* photos to promote his clubs. We sued under New York law next door in New York Supreme. There was a bench trial earlier this year which we won. We then reached a settlement regarding damages.

The Court: This is all very interesting but I still don't see where the gift certificates come in.

Mr. Peters: As I said, it's very simple. You see, Mr. Lambros had two names. He was Ambrose Lambros and he was also Victor Little. And as Victor Little he started up a lingerie company called Victor's Little Secret. Miss Lowlace had been hired by Mr. Little as a model for his lingerie line. But she didn't know that Mr. Little was also Ambrose Lambros, the owner of the three strip clubs that were using her photo for promotion.

What happened was that Mr. Little used the Victor's Little Secret modeling contract to surreptitiously insert a provision whereby Miss Lowlace consented to the use of her photo and image to promote the strip clubs that Mr. Lambros operated under the name Aegean Love. Of course Miss Lowlace had absolutely no connection with those clubs and her consent was obtained by fraud and deceit.

The Court: I thought you said it was simple. Well it's not, it's more like a crossword puzzle. I'm not at all sure I followed it. Anyway, I still don't see how the gift certificates came into the picture.

Mr. Peters: Well, it's pretty simple. After we received a ruling on the merits of our privacy and publicity claims in that case, the case against Mr. Lambros and his company Aegean Love, we commenced settlement negotiations with Mr. Lambros' counsel, Jeckel and Hyde. As part of . . . .

The Court: Did you say Jeckel and Hyde? Is that a law firm?

Mr. Peters: Yes it is. Jack Jeckel and Harry Hyde, they're over in Newark. Both of them are lawyers. So their firm is a law firm. Anyway, at the time we were negotiating that settlement, we were getting close to a resolution in this case. Since the owner of the strip clubs, Ambrose Lambros, was also the lingerie maker Victor Little, we got him to agree that if and when we reached a settlement in this case, the Bunny Hop case, he would provide $250 gift certificates to all the members of the class. It only ended up costing him another $5000 - $250 times twenty members of the class.

The Court: I must say your firm and Miss Lowlace seem to be involved in lots of bizarre litigation. I hope you can keep track of it all. Now, let's get back to those other immediate benefits you alluded to. I think you said there were six more?

Mr. Peters: That's correct. The second immediate benefit is that each member of the class will receive three free Bunny Hop games. They can keep them as a souvenir or give them to friends and members of their family, such as their younger brothers. Remember, each game sells for $34.95, so that benefit is worth more than $100.

Third, each member of the class is entitled to a 15% discount on all video games they purchase from Erotic Arts. The company puts out a number of erotic video games. They make excellent presents for birthdays and Christmas.

Fourth, each of the nineteen plaintiffs - the nineteen who have an ongoing license with Erotic Arts – will each be featured for one month in all advertising for the Bunny Hop game. This includes traditional print advertising and also electronic advertising, such as the company's website. This will give the nineteen plaintiffs terrific exposure to all Erotic Arts fans.

The Court: I assume the exposure will include more than their faces?

Mr. Peters: I believe so, but that's up to Erotic Arts. But all of them certainly have assets worth exposing.

The Court: Right. Next?

Mr. Peters: Number five is a big one. All twenty plaintiffs, including Miss Lowlace, will, collectively, be the subject of a feature article in Vanity Fair magazine sometime in the next nine months.

The Court: I'm afraid to ask how Vanity Fair got in the picture. Was it involved in another one of your bizarre lawsuits?

Mr. Peters: No, Your Honor. But one of our associates, Chip Pierpont – that's him in the front of the spectator section, just behind Miss Lowlace – he has connections everywhere. I don't know how he does it. Well, that's not true, I know exactly how he does it.

In the case of Vanity Fair, he seems to have been on excellent terms with Nora Cross, the magazine's executive editor. Now Ms. Cross has a reputation of being difficult and a bit of a bully, but Mr. Pierpont was able to overcome that. He succeeded in convincing Ms. Cross that this case, and the Bunny Hop game as well, would be of great interest to the magazine's readers. The magazine agreed and we are now working out an agreement for the spread. The ladies won't be getting money for it, but the publicity from being in the magazine is huge for them.

The Court: Yes, I can see that.

Mr. Peters: That bring me to the final two items. Number six is a free copy of a book on nutrition and fitness. Everyone these days wants to know the latest on nutrition and fitness.

The Court: What's the name of the book? I may be familiar with it.

Mr. Peters: "Dr. Hazel Nut's" - that's all one word, hazel and nut combined. But the nut has two t's, so it's "Dr. Hazelnutt." The book's title is "Dr. Hazelnutt's Guide to Better Nutrition and Fitness."

The Court: I'm not familiar with it. Who is this Dr. Hazelnutt with two t's?

Mr. Peters: She was the plaintiff in one of our recent cases. It was a class action against Colonel Mills regarding its Berry

Good Corny Flakes cereal. Berry Good Corny Flakes was a line extension of regular Corny Flakes. The box showed a bowl of Corny Flakes with blueberries on top but there were no blueberries in the Corny Flakes. You had to go out and buy your own.

Now Dr. Nutt, sorry I should say Dr. Hazelnutt, was the lead plaintiff and got a lot of money from the settlement. So, when my brother Prescott asked her, she readily agreed to supply twenty copies of her book for the members of the class. I think it's probably the first twenty that have reached the hands of a reader.

The Court: You seem to have a knack for leveraging all of your cases. It's impressive. I can't wait to hear how you will leverage the settlement in this case into your next case.

Mr. Peters: I'll make a note to let you know. Maybe I should send you an email, it probably shouldn't be part of the record in this case.

The Court: Maybe you could put it in a Valentine card, that way it definitely wouldn't have to be part of the record.

Mr. Peters: Well, that could look . . . .

The Court: I was joking, I didn't think you would take it seriously. But you'd be surprised at the number of Valentine cards I get from lawyers. Anyway we need to move on. Please tell me what the seventh benefit will be. That's the seventh benefit in this case, not your next case.

Mr. Peters: Right, I gotta keep these cases separate. So in this case, the seventh benefit is that each plaintiff will receive a framed picture of Bernie Pitts, the Chairman and CEO of Erotic Arts. Each picture will be personally inscribed with a message from Mr. Pitts. It will be a great keepsake.

So in conclusion, Your Honor, you can see that with the past and future licensing payments and these seven additional benefits, this is an extremely fair and equitable settlement for all members of the class. I know that all of the plaintiffs are happy with it.

The Court: You may be right but I can't make a determination that it's fair and equitable until I hear from some of the class members. We'll break for lunch now. When we come back, I would like to hear first from Miss Lowlace. I'm a little concerned that she seems to be a professional plaintiff on behalf of your firm. If I am satisfied that is not the case, and that she is an appropriate class representative, I'd then like to hear from two of the other members of the class. I want to make sure they understand the settlement and believe it is fair to them.

Let's come back at 2:15.

Chapter 31

BUNNY TALK

At two-twenty Judge Juney took the bench and called the proceedings to order.

The Court: Mr. Peters, will you please have Miss Lowlace take the stand. I want to deal with her first. There's no need for you to examine her, I'll do the questioning myself.

(Witness is sworn in)

The Court: Good afternoon, Miss Lowlace. I have some questions I want to ask you. As I said before the lunch break, based on Mr. Peters' remarks this morning, I am a little concerned that you could be what we call a professional plaintiff. We don't allow class action suits to be brought by professional plaintiffs.

The Witness: I sure ain't no professional plaintiff. I wuz once a dancer in Gentleman's clubs and now I's a model. That's watt I's professional at.

The Court: Miss Lowlace, please wait until I ask you a question. That's the way we do it in court. You should know that, you seem to have a lot of experience being in court. Now . . . .

The Witness: I don't know how I's always end up bein' in court. Things just seem to happen and next thing I know I's back in court again.

The Court: Miss Lowlace, lawsuits don't just happen. Someone has to start them. And I'm trying to figure out why you seem to have started so many of them.

The Witness: Well, it all started when I's workin' at Bottoms Up.

The Court: Bottoms Up?

The Witness: That's the name of one of the Gentleman's clubs I use to work at. Bottoms Up, Tops Down and Below The Belt. All three wuz owned by the same company and us dancers worked a week at one club, then a week at another and so on.

Anyways, one night I wuz workin' at Bottoms Up and this nice fellow come in. It's that Mr. Chip there, the good lookin' fellow in the front row. We's had a nice conversation and we became real friendly and then, when we's back in my apartment, Mr. Chip, he tells me he's a lawyer. And I tells him ain't that somethin', I been wantin' to talk with a lawyer 'bout the sitiation at the clubs, the owners they's been cheatin' us out of wages and tips and stuff.

And Mr. Chip, he says they can't do that and next thing I knows, well, by then it wuz the next morning, he takes me to this nice office on Fifth Avenue and I meets Mr. Peters and then the other Mr. Peters – that one there (pointing). And the first Mr. Peters he says the second Mr. Peters is real smart, he gone to Yale. And before I knows it they's filed a lawsuit right down here at that other courthouse next door. And then we's havin' a press conference right outside and I's wearin' this nice blue suit Mr. Chip bought me at Lord and Taylors, it was the nicest suit I's ever had. Actually, it was the only suit I's ever had. Then they showed that there press conference on TV that night. Did you see it?

The Court: No, I didn't . . . .

The Witness: That's too bad, all my friends seen it. Anyways, we then has a lawsuit and Mr. Peters and the other Mr. Peters they worked out what they calls a settlement with the other side. By then they wuz some other clubs involved. You see, other ladies from other clubs joined the case and it was some kind of a classy action. And then we had some sort of hearing . . . .

(Witness waves to a spectator)

The Court: Miss Lowlace, who are you waving to? That's most inappropriate.

The Witness: Why that's Justice Leghetti back there with his sidekick Mr. Tony. I wuz just startin' to tell you we had some sort of hearing before Justice Leghetti – you see, in New York courts, judges are called Justice, not Judge. I learn't that from Mr. Peters, the smart one that gone to Yale. And so Justice Leghetti and Mr. Tony, I think they liked me and so I always wave to them when they come to see me in court. Anyways, that's how it happened that I wuz in court that first time. I think we done good. There wuz a settlement and me and all those other dancers we start gettin' what we's owed by the clubs. Don't you think that wuz a good thing we done?

The Court: Well, maybe so. But you seem to keep getting involved in one case after another.

The Witness: Well, as I said, stuff just keeps happenin'. After that case with Justice Leghetti I seems to have become a celerybrety, cause I then gets this phone call from someone at *Playboy* magazine and they wants me to be in their magazine . . . .

The Court: We don't need to hear how you got into *Playboy* magazine. What I'm interested in is all the lawsuits you've gotten yourself into.

The Witness: That's watt I's gonna tell you. After I's had all them there pi-tures in *Playboy* I gets a call from Mr. Chip. He wants to celebrate my bein' in *Playboy* and so he takes me to that fancy twenty-somethin' club and we has lunch, I ain't never been to such a fancy restaurant, Mr. Chip he sure do know how to treat a lady.

So durin' lunch I tells him I's been modelin' ladies underthings for Barely Enough, that's the name of the brand, Barely Enough, but now I's been offered a chance to model ladies underthings for Victor's Little Secret and I ask Mr. Chip if I wuz allowed to do both. And Mr. Chip he says he'll look at the first contract, the one with Barely Enough, and then tell me if I can also model ladies underthings for Victor's Little Secret. Of course I didn't have the contract with me, I don't usually carry contracts around in my purse, so I says I can show it to him after lunch when we goes to my apartment. To celebrate my pi-tures bein' in *Playboy*.

So then I tells Mr. Chip about some stuff I learn't from my friend Honey. That's Honey Combe, she worked with me at Bottoms Up, Tops Down and Below the Belt. Then I shows Mr. Chip what Honey showed me, somebody wuz usin' my pi-tures in *Playboy* to promote some low-life strip clubs. And Mr. Chip, he says they can't do that without my permission and I says I didn't give no permission for my pi-tures to be used by them there strip clubs.

So next thing I knows Mr. Chip brings me back to that nice office on Fifth Avenue and Mr. Peters – that Mr. Peters (pointing) and the other Mr. Peters (pointing) – they tells me they gonna file a lawsuit to stop that there Greek fellow from usin' my pi-tures to promote his strip clubs. And so now we's in court again, but this time we's in court with Justice Chan. I don't see him in the courtroom, he must not be followin' my career like Justice Leghetti and Mr. . . . .

(Witness waves to another spectator)

The Witness: Oh, Justice Chan is here, that's who I wuz wavin' to this time. I think he and Justice Leghetti is friends. But I don't see his sidekick Mr. Lott with him, he musta' stayed in his office readin' that *Playboy* magazine Mr. Peters gave him at the trial. Now, where wuz I, I forgot what you wuz askin' me 'bout.

The Court: I wasn't asking you about anything. You've been talking nonstop, I can't get a word in edgewise.

The Witness: Edgewise? Where you tryin' to get words into?

The Court: It's just a figure of speech. Why don't . . . .

The Witness: A figure ah speech?

The Court: Never mind. Just tell us about your trial before Judge Chan and his sidekick Mr. Lott.

The Witness: Justice Chan. See, in New York State Court . . . .

The Court: Yes, I'm sorry, I misspoke. I'm just a judge but Mr. Leghetti and Mr. Chan are justices. But now, just tell us about your trial in front of Justice Chan. By the way, Mr. Lott is probably his clerk, not his sidekick.

The Witness: Okay. So's, we had us a trial before Justice Chan in that nice courthouse next door. Of course, it ain't as nice as this here federal courthouse, Mr. Peters says it's because the politicians won't provide e-nuff money to keep up the courthouse. Anyways, we has that there trial with Justice Chan and then Justice Chan says we wuz right, that Greek fellow can't use my pi-tures to promote his strip clubs, he has to pay me for it. And he did. We got lots of money from that there Greek fellow but I forget how much we got 'cause by then we wuz busy with this here case.

The Court: Okay, so let's talk about this case. I believe Mr. Peters said you were the one who discovered this Bunny Hop game?

The Witness: Well, yes and no. You see, when I's havin' that there lunch with Mr. Chip at that fancy restaurant – did I tell you it used to be a speakeasy? Mr. Chip, he told me all 'bout speakeasies and pro-bition and stuff. He's real smart. He didn't go to Yale like Mr. Peters but he gone to Dartmouth, they say it's for smart people too. Anyways, when we's havin' that lunch I tell Mr. Chip 'bout somethin' else Honey – that's my friend Honey Combe . . . .

The Court: Who worked with you at Bottoms Up, Tops Down and Below The Belt.

The Witness: How'd you knows that?

The Court: You told me. You's been tellin' me . . . . I'm sorry, I mean you've been telling me lots of things and that's one of the things I remember.

The Witness: Well, doggone. Now . . . . watt wuz I sayin', I seem to have lost my train of thought.

The Court: You were about to tell us something else that Honey Combe told you that you then told to Mr. Chip when you were having lunch at that speakeasy. It may or may not be relevant to anything going on here but you might as well tell us.

The Witness: Well, I don't guess it's a speakeasy no more, I think it was just a speakeasy durin' pro-bition. Well, anyways, I told Mr. Chip that Honey told me I was bein' used as an aviator in some video game 'bout trucker thefts. I didn't know nothin' 'bout bein' in some video game 'bout truckers. I don't even know if it wuz the truckers doin' the stealin' or if someone wuz stealin' the trucks. But Mr. Chip he was angry, he says they can't do that, he wuz gonna' talk to Mr. Peters 'bout it and they would do somethin' to make them pay. So you see, I didn't start any of this, I just keep findin' out that theys all usin' my pi-tures from *Playboy* without me knowin' nothin' 'bout it.

The Court: But this was another video game, not Bunny Hop?

The Witness: Of course. There weren't no truckers in Bunny Hop and there ain't no bunnies in that trucker thing. So now, Mr. Chip come to see me again – this wuz at my apartment, not that speakeasy place, and he tells me theys been in touch with the company that sells that trucker game and they says it wuz all a mistake. They says they wuz some teenager that saw my pi-tures in *Playboy* and decided to use 'em in that there trucker game without tellin' anyone. And so theys sent Mr. Peters a hu-nert and fifty thousand dollars as compasation. And Mr. Peters he says I's entitled to a hu-nert thousand of that and so Mr. Chip he shows up at my apartment one day and gives me a check for a hu-nert thousand dollars.

The Court: And that was the result of a lawsuit? That would be the third one.

The Witness: No M'am, there weren't no lawsuit there. That company, they says they made a mistake and wanted to make things right. As far as I's concerned, that hu-nert thousand sure made things right. Specially since I didn't even know things wuz wrong.

The Court: Okay, now it's this case, the Bunny Hop case, I'm concerned about. How did the case come about?

The Witness: Well, that day when Mr. Chip brings me that check for a hu-nert thousad dollars, we had us another celebration. And after we's done celebratin', Mr. Chip tells me I's bein' used as an aviator in another video game, this here Bunny Hop thing. I asked Mr. Chip how he knows that and he tells me he's been playin' the game and sees me in it. He tells me I's Bunny Number One and if the player scores with me he hits the jackpot. Mr. Chip tells me he always tries to hit the jackpot when he plays that game. And I tells him he don't have to hit the jackpot in that there game, he can hit it with me any time he wants.

The Court: Let's leave out your relationship with Mr. Chip. I mean Mr. Pierpont.

The Witness: Okay, but that's how I knows 'bout this here Bunny Hop thing and that's how I gots involved in this here lawsuit. As I said, this stuff just keeps happenin'. But now maybe everyone will stop tryin' to take a'vantage of me. They knows my lawyers will protect me. You don't think I wuz wrong to let my lawyers protect me, do you?

The Court: No, Miss Lowlace, I don't think you were wrong. You do seem to have been a tempting target for lots of unscrupulous companies. But I don't think you did anything wrong by allowing your friend Mr. Pierpont and his colleagues to protect your rights. I find that you are a good faith plaintiff in this action and that you are an appropriate representative of the class.

We'll take a fifteen minute break. Our court reporter needs to catch his breath, I'm sure this afternoon's been a challenge for him.

* * * *

The Court: Okay, let's resume. Mr. Peters, which of the other members of the class do you plan to call?

Mr. Peters: We'll call Miss Melony Harmony first. I'll ask Mr. Muffinsky to bring her in.

The Court: Very well. As with Miss Lowlace, I'll conduct the examination. To tell you the truth, I didn't so much conduct an examination of Miss Lowlace as wind her up and let her go. Perhaps I'll have better luck with Miss Harmony. Anyway, if there's anything you feel needs to be added, you can do so after I've finished.

(Witness is sworn in)

The Court: Good afternoon, Miss Harmony. I believe you are Bunny Number Two in the Bunny Hop game? I can see why you ranked so high.

The Witness: Thank you, Your Honor. But I'm afraid none of the rest of us girls quite measure up to Lydia. We all agree she deserved to be ranked Number One.

The Court: Speaking of Miss Lowlace, one thing I need to ask you is whether you or the other members of the class are satisfied with the settlement in light of the fact that Miss Lowlace is getting ten times more than the rest of you? The class representative always gets more than the rest of the class, but ten times more is a little on the high side.

The Witness: That is fine with all of us, Your Honor. Not only is Lydia the number one bunny in Bunny Hop, she's the one who uncovered the game, and the fact that all of us former Playmates are depicted in it.

The Court: Well, according to her testimony, it was her attorney, Mr. Pierpont, who discovered the game. I think she said he had bought the game and was playing it and saw her image.

The Witness: Okay, that could be true, but still it's Lydia who has the relationship with Mr. Pierpont. Some girls have all the luck. In any event, Lydia's relationship with Mr. Pierpont and his law firm is what led to the discovery of the game and our being used in the game, so we still owe everything to her.

The Court: So you're saying you have no objection to Miss Lowlace receiving ten times the amount of compensation you are receiving?

The Witness: No, I have no objection. Nor do any of the other eighteen girls. We discussed all this among ourselves and also with Mr. Peters and his brother.

The Court: Okay. Now what about the fact that none of you will receive any immediate financial recovery? In fact, you are actually starting out in debt to Electronic Arts.

The Witness: But with the ongoing license we'll quickly pay that off and start receiving monthly royalty checks. I discussed this with my father and he said it was an appropriate arrangement.

The Court: Your father? Is he a lawyer?

The Witness: No, Your Honor, he owns a Ford dealership in our town, just outside Seattle. He said our deferred compensation arrangement is just like the way his business works. He has a huge cash outlay in the summer when he pays for the new cars he'll be selling in the Fall. But as those cars are sold, he not only recoups his investment but begins earning a profit. I figure if that way of doing business is good enough for him it should be good enough for me.

The Court: Speaking of your father, what does he think about your being in this Bunny Hop game? And being a Playmate of the Month in *Playboy*?

The Witness: Oh, he's fine with that Your Honor. He said good looking young ladies are just like the cars he sells. They look great and run well for five or six years but then they begin to run down. He says I need to cash in now, while my looks and body are at their peak.

The Court: You have a very tolerant father.

The Witness: I certainly agree, Your Honor. My dad's the best.

The Court: So I take it you are perfectly happy with all the terms of the settlement agreement? And you believe it is fair to you and your fellow plaintiffs?

The Witness: I certainly do, Your Honor. Mr. Peters and his brother went through it with each of us and we appreciate everything they've achieved for us. And we're looking forward to our ongoing relationship with Erotic Arts. We believe it will prove to be quite lucrative.

The Court: Thank you Miss Harmony, that's all I have. Mr. Peters, do you wish to elicit anything further from this witness?

Mr. Peters: No Your Honor.

The Court: Okay, then please call your next witness. Who will it be?

Mr. Peters: It will be Bunny Number Three, Harmony Melony. Mr. Muffinsky, will you please show Miss Harmony out and bring Miss Melony in.

(Witness enters the Courtroom)

The Court: What? Miss Harmony, you just testified. We're done with you. I thought Mr. Peters was calling Miss Melony.

Mr. Peters: This is Miss Melony. She and Miss Harmony are twins. That's why they look alike.

The Court: Mr. Peters, I'm fully aware that twins frequently look alike. But they don't always dress exactly alike. And you never bothered to tell me Miss Harmony and Miss Melony are twins.

Mr. Peters: Your Honor, I wasn't trying to hide anything. I just didn't think it was all that important.

The Court: I think you were just having a little joke at my expense. Well, let's get on with it. Please swear in the witness.

(Witness is sworn in)

The Court: Miss Melony, as you may have noticed, this has caught me unawares.

The Witness: That's understandable, Your Honor.

The Court: Let me first get your names straight. Your name is Harmony Melony and your sister's name is Melony Harmony?

The Witness: That's correct Your Honor.

The Court: And you always dress alike? Always wear the same outfits?

The Witness: Yes we do. We take turns deciding what to wear each day.

The Court: And you always wear your hair the same way, so that you look exactly alike?

The Witness: That's correct. The only difference in our looks is that I have two dimples just above my backside but Melony only has one.

Mr. Rivers: Your Honor, I think we should examine the witness's dimples so that we can be certain the right one is testifying.

The Court: The Court appreciates your suggestion, Mr. Rivers, but I don't believe that will be necessary. If the witness says she's Miss Melony and the prior witness was Miss Harmony, the Court is prepared to accept that as true. Without the need for a physical inspection.

Now, let's get back to your names, which the Court finds baffling. Miss Melony, do you have any idea why your parents chose those names? It seems to me they will always lead to confusion. After all, your last name, Melony, could be a first name and your sister's last name, Harmony, could also be a first name. In fact, both are first names. But they're also last names.

In fact, I actually think of the first witness, your sister, as Melony. And I think of you as Harmony. But I have to address both of you by your last names. So your sister, who I think of as Melony, is actually Miss Harmony, while you, who I think of as Harmony, are actually Miss Melony. You see why it's confusing?

The Witness: Actually, Your Honor, our last name is Tuney. That's T-U-N-E-Y. So I'm legally Harmony Melony Tuney and my sister is Melony Harmony Tuney. I'm sure we used our full legal names when we filled out those certificates where we opted into the case. So, Your Honor, you could address me as Miss Tuney if you like.

The Court: But your sister would also be Miss Tuney. How could we have a transcript with two Miss Tuneys? Nobody would know which of you is speaking or which of you is being referred to.

The Witness: Okay, then you better stick with Miss Melony and Miss Harmony. I'm Miss Melony, even though you think of me as Harmony, and my sister is Miss Harmony, even though you think of her as Melony. That should solve the problem.

The Court: Perhaps it does. But I still don't understand why your parents chose those names for you.

The Witness: It was our mother's doing. She's a professional musician. In fact, she's the first chair cellist in the Seattle Symphony. She always wanted Melony and me to be musicians. I guess she thought giving us names like Melony and Harmony would help make it happen.

The Court: Were the two of you ever musicians?

The Witness: Oh yes. I play the cello and Melony plays the viola. We played in orchestras all through high school and college.

The Court: Why did you give it up? It must be a real disappointment to your mother.

The Witness: Oh, we haven't given it up. We still take private lessons once a week. But when we were in college, a friend got us jobs in a strip club and we started making lots of money. We actually made more than our mother was making playing in the symphony.

The Court: And your mother was okay with all this?

The Witness: Yes. Just so long as we didn't use our instruments as props. She really put her foot down when *Playboy* wanted to do a shot of me with my cello. And nothing on.

The Court: Okay, I think we'll move on. I was going to ask you the same questions I asked your sister, Miss Melony – sorry, I mean Miss Harmony, although I still think of her as Melony. But since you look exactly alike, except for the dimples, and you dress exactly alike, and you're both musicians, I suspect you also think alike. So, if Miss Harmony feels the settlement is fair and equitable you must also feel the same.

The Witness: That's correct, Your Honor. I feel the same about the settlement as Melony.

The Court: You see, there's the problem. I just referred to your sister as Miss Harmony and you just referred to her as Melony. This could be maddening for someone reading the transcript.

The Witness: That's okay, Your Honor, I don't think it matters which of us you think you're referring to. We basically view ourselves as interchangeable. Except for the fact that Melony plays the viola and I play the cello, we really are pretty much interchangeable. One time, though, that wasn't quite true as we played a mean trick on one of our music teachers. Mr. Stringer, my cello instructor, showed up for my weekly lesson and Melony showed up with my cello. She couldn't even hold it properly, much less play it. Poor Mr. Stringer, he was beside himself, he knew I was a good cello player.

Mr. Rivers: See Your Honor, this is exactly why we need to examine the witness's dimples. This witness could really be Melony pretending to be Harmony. And the sister we heard from earlier could really be Harmony pretending to be Melony. We need to get to the bottom of this, a visual exam is the only way.

The Witness: Melony and I would be happy to show you our dimples after court is over. Maybe we could do it at Mr. Peters' office uptown.

The Court: I'll leave that to you and the lawyers. I only need to make sure this witness – Harmony, also known as Miss Melony – is satisfied that the settlement is fair and equitable for herself and the other members of the class. What is your answer to that question, Miss Melony?

The Witness: Absolutely yes. It is fair and equitable and we hope you will approve it.

The Court: Yes, I plan to approve it. I'll be issuing a written opinion in a few days. Now Mr. Peters and Mr. Rivers, do either of you have anything more to bring to my attention? If not, we'll adjourn.

Oh, and Mr. Rivers, I'll leave it up to you to arrange a physical verification of the witness's identities if you feel it's necessary. But it's not being required by the Court. And anyway it doesn't really matter who's who, they both said the same thing about the settlement. As Miss Melony said, the two of them are interchangeable. We're adjourned.

Chapter 32

HAPPY COWS

On Wednesday of the week following the settlement hearing in the Bunny Hop case, Pap called everyone into his office for a meeting.

"Morning everyone" he began. "As you all know, we've had a nice string of wins over the past twelve months. And we even made some money on the cases. The Russkies. Corny Flakes. Lydia's strip club case and then Bunny Hop. It's been a pretty good twelve months."

"You didn't mention the Chimps case" said Pup. "We tried to tell you that case was a loser but no, you thought we could make a name for ourselves as a firm that champions animal rights. As I recall, the case didn't turn out so well."

"Pup, you're wrong. While we haven't yet won that case, we got tons of publicity. People all over the country have now heard of Peters and Peters, the firm that dared to file a groundbreaking lawsuit against the premier zoo in the country on behalf of imprisoned Chimps. That's worth a lot."

"They weren't imprisoned" said Pup. "They were living in one of the nicest, cleanest, caring zoos in the country. And by the way, what did you mean when you said 'we haven't won the case yet'? The case is over. We lost. The Appellate Division was amused by your argument but they ruled against us. Unanimously."

"Pup, surely you've heard of the New York Court of Appeals. It's the highest court in the state. Even Lydia knows about it, you explained it to her; it's the only New York court where the judges are called 'Judge' and not 'Justice'."

"Of course I've heard of it" said Pup irritably. "I argued two or three cases there when I was at Oliver and Cromwell. I hope you aren't thinking of trying to get them to hear an appeal in the Chimps case."

"That's exactly what I'm thinking. I've asked Brandon to do some research to see if we have a legitimate basis for asking them to allow an appeal. Don't forget, we received a favorable ruling from Justice Wright before the Appellate Division reversed her. A lower court decision in your favor is a huge factor in getting the Court of Appeals to take your case."

"I think we'd be wasting our time" said Pup petulantly. He knew he would lose this argument. He lost every argument with Pap.

"So let's see what Brandon turns up before we make a final decision" said Pap in his most reasonable voice. But he knew exactly what Brandon would turn up. And he knew that he would ask Pup and Melissa to prepare papers asking the Court of Appeals to hear the case.

"In the meantime, I have an idea that will allow us to build on our reputation as an animal rights firm. That's what I want to tell everyone about."

"Good Lord, not another animal rights case" Pup said to himself. Pap seemed to be obsessed with bringing cases on behalf of animals. They had enough difficulty dealing with the strange plaintiffs their cases attracted; having to also deal with animals as clients was not what they needed.

Melissa, who was always open to creative ideas, broke the silence. "Okay Pap, what's your idea?"

"Thanks for asking, Melissa. I'm sure you'll like the idea, even if my brother doesn't."

Pulling out a newspaper ad for Jen and Barry's Ice Cream, Pap pointed to the opening line of the ad and read it aloud:

"The ice cream made from milk and cream from happy cows."

"That claim is in every single ad that Jen and Barry's has run over the past six months. It's even on the ice cream container itself, which has a picture of a seemingly happy cow over the statement:

"Made from the Milk and Cream of Happy Cows."

"Do you have any idea how much ice cream Jen and Barry's has sold during this advertising campaign? Every single pint, quart and half-gallon of Jen and Barry's has been sold with the help of this claim."

"Why does this matter to anyone?" said Pup. "This is just a nonsensical advertising statement no one would take seriously."

"Are you kidding?" said Pap. "Who wants to ingest a dairy product from an unhappy cow? You want your girls drinking milk produced by unhappy cows?"

"I agree with Pap on this part" said Melissa. "We would have no trouble finding an animal lover who would say this claim is meaningful to him. Or her. Or someone transitioning from him to her. Or from her to him.

"Besides, Jen and Barry's Ice Cream is hugely popular in the Northeast. And the Northeast is the heart of animal rights country. People out in the Midwest or Texas probably don't care if their cows are happy. After all, they slaughter 'em for beef. But farms in the Northeast are largely dairy farms and you want happy cows on a dairy farm."

"Okay, but how do you know the claim is false?" said Pup. "How would we ever prove that the cows that produce milk and cream for Jen and Barry's Ice Cream are not happy?"

"That's where our expertise comes in" said Pap. "Dr. Doolittle, he's the guy we need. I'll bet he can talk with the cows and find out whether they're happy or not."

"Well, he did grow up on a farm" said Melissa. "He told us he grew up talking to all the animals on his family's farm, that's where he got his start as an animal communicator."

"There you go!" said Pap. "Melissa's always one step ahead of everyone. I think we should get Dr. Doolittle back in and talk with him about this claim. Maybe have him drive up to Vermont, that's where Jen and Barry's is located. I'm sure they have their own farm or buy from local farms there. So let's have Dr. Doolittle drive up to Vermont and look at some of the big dairy farms. Have him tell us if he thinks all those cows are happy. I'll bet they're not, especially in the winter."

"But ice cream's a summer thing" said Pup. "The cows are probably perfectly happy in the summer, when it's warm in Vermont. The claim would be true then."

"Pup, we're talking about Jen and Barry's. They don't just sell ice cream at an open-air stand on weekends in the summer. They sell it in grocery stores year round. So they have to make it year round. Including in the winter when the cows are cold and miserable."

"I'm still not sure this is a good use of our time" said Pup. "Look at all the time we put into the Chimps case. And for nothing."

"Pup, you've got to look at the big picture. Peters and Peters isn't a firm that brings only safe, traditional cases. We bring ground-breaking cases that blaze new legal trails. Why do you think we brought that Chimps case? Or the espionage case against the Russkies? These are cases that will make our reputation. And cause corporate America to tremble when we get them in our cross-hairs.

"Now, just think how many people will see our press conference when we announce a lawsuit against Jen and Barry's because its happy cows are actually quite unhappy. Especially in the winter, which lasts a long time in Vermont. It'll be great!"

"Yeah" said Pup. "Our press conferences are always great. But we don't get paid for doing press conferences. To get paid, we need to bring cases we can win."

"Pup" said Pap, "I'm confident you and Melissa can figure out a way for us to win the case. Use the Worry Room if you need to – but no funny stuff there, remember our firm policy."

"For heaven's sake, Pap, Melissa and I don't do funny stuff in the Worry Room. We only go there to worry."

"Right" said Pap. "But I think the two of you should put your heads together and figure out a way we can prosecute and win this Happy Cows case.

"Now, before you all go, I have a little something for Chip."

Reaching into his top desk drawer, Pap pulled out a large brown envelope and handed it to Chip.

"Chip, this is a little something to commemorate the role you played in bringing the Bunny Hop game to the firm's attention."

Opening the envelope, Chip broke into a wide smile as he pulled out a signed photograph of Melony and Harmony looking extremely seductive.

"Read us the inscription" said Pap.

"It says:

'Dear Chip. Lydia says you're the greatest. Come see us some time.' "

"I think they would like to spend some quality time with you" said Melissa.

"Maybe you could do a threesome with them" said Brandon.

"I'm not into kinky stuff like that" said Chip. "One at a time is enough for me."

"You mean, one at a time, three a day" said Brandon.

"Chip" said Pap, "we will eventually get this framed for you and have it mounted on the Wall of Fame in the Worry Room. But not until your mission has been accomplished. With both of them."

"But how will Chip know he completed his mission with both of them?" asked Melissa. "If he scores with the same one twice, that wouldn't count. Even if he thinks he scored with both."

"It's the dimples" said Brandon. "Chip, you've got to make sure you examine the dimples. Remember, Harmony has two but Melony only has one."

"Say, I've got an idea" said Pup. "When you're with Harmony, you should get her to teach you how to play the cello. It would add a little sophistication to your character."

"Listen" said Chip. "I know this all sounds like fun to you guys, but this is a real challenge for me. I'm not sure I can pull it off."

"You gotta be kidding" said Pap. "You've got two gorgeous ladies virtually begging you to bed them. Why is that suddenly a challenge?"

"Bedding them's the easy part" said Chip. "Finding a time to do so is the problem. I can't get away at night anymore. Francoise demands I be home by seven and she doesn't let me out of her sight the rest of the night."

"Just tell her you have to work late" said Brandon. "Everyone knows associates in law firms have to work late."

"That won't work any more. She finally figured out that's when I'm with Candy in the Worry Room. So, no more late nights for me."

"Pap" said Melissa, "here's a thought. This mission is kind of official firm business. Chip is our liaison to the Bunny World. First Lydia, now Melony and Harmony. Why don't you let him take two afternoons off – one for Melony and one for Harmony. He can report back that he's succeeded and that he's verified the dimples. And then we can get the picture framed and put it up on the Wall of Fame."

"Pup" said Pap, "what do you think abut that?"

"Well, I think we could allow him two afternoons off. But no more. If he wants to spend any more time with them, he needs to do it on his own time."

"What if I let Harmony teach me the cello?" asked Chip. "Couldn't I get an afternoon off each week to study the cello with her?"

"No" said Pap decisively. "Pup's right. You get two afternoons off and that's it. We're running a law firm here, not a dating service.

"Now, we've all go to get back to work. Pup and Melissa, please get going on the Happy Cows case. Brandon, you keep working on finding a way to get the Court of Appeals to take the Chimps case. And Chip, you have your mission.

"And I need to leave right now, I have a tee time at two-thirty in Greenwich. See you all tomorrow."

For sales, editorial information, subsidiary rights information
or a catalog, please write or phone or e-mail

IBOOKS
Manhanset House
Shelter Island Hts., New York 11965, US
Tel: 212-427-7139
www.BrickTowerPress.com
bricktower@aol.com
www.IngramContent.com

For sales in the UK and Europe please contact our distributor,
Gazelle Book Services
White Cross Mills
Lancaster, LA1 4XS, UK
Tel: (01524) 68765 Fax: (01524) 63232
email: jacky@gazellebooks.co.uk